A Longman Cultural Edition

DUBLINERS

James Joyce

Edited by

Sean Latham
University of Tulsa

Longman

Boston   Columbus   Indianapolis   New York   San Francisco   Upper Saddle River
Amsterdam   Cape Town   Dubai   London   Madrid   Milan   Munich   Paris   Montreal   Toronto
Delhi   Mexico City   Sao Paulo   Sydney   Hong Kong   Seoul   Singapore   Taipei   Tokyo

Senior Sponsoring Editor: Ginny Blanford
Assistant Editor: Rebecca Gilpin
Executive Marketing Manager: Joyce Nilsen
Production Manager: Fran Russello
Project Coordination, Text Design, and Electronic Page Makeup:
Cover Design Manager: Jayne Conte
Cover Designer:
Cover Illustration/Photo:
Printer and Binder: Courier Companies, Inc.

Library of Congress Cataloging-in-Publication Data
Joyce, James, 1882–1941.
  Dubliners / James Joyce ; edited by Sean Latham.—A Longman cultural ed.
    p. cm.
  Includes bibliographical references.
  ISBN-13: 978-0-205-53736-5
  ISBN-10: 0-205-53736-7
  1. Dublin (Ireland)—Fiction. I. Latham, Sean, 1971- II. Title.
  PR6019.O9D8 2010
  823'.912—dc22

                                                        2010000291

1 2 3 4 5 6 7 8 9 10—CRS—13 12 11 10

Longman
is an imprint of

www.pearsonhighered.com
ISBN-13: 978-0-205-53736-5
ISBN-10:   0-205-53736-7

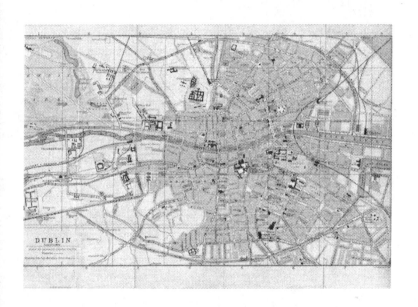

DUBLIN

Contents

Contexts   193

List of Illustrations

About Longman Cultural Editions

Inspired by the innovative *Longman Anthology of British Literature*, the Longman Cultural Editions are designed to illuminate the lively, ever variable intersections of literature, tradition, and culture. In each volume, a work or works of literary imagination gather new dimensions from materials that relate to informing traditions and debates, to contemporary conversations and controversies, and to later eras of reading and reaction. While the nature of the contexts vary from volume to volume, the reliable constants (in addition to handsome production and affordable pricing) are expert editing and helpful annotation throughout; a stimulating introduction; a table of dates to track composition, publication, and reception in relation to biographical, cultural, and historical events; illustrations guaranteed to spark conversation; and a guide for further browsing and study. Whether you are reading this volume along with the *Anthology*, or in a different or more specialized kind of course, or reading independently of any coursework, we hope you'll encounter much to stimulate your attention, curiosity, and pleasure.

Susan J. Wolfson
General Editor, Longman Cultural Editions
Professor of English, Princeton University

About this Edition

In 1904 James Joyce and Nora Barnacle made their way to the docks in Dublin and boarded a ship that carried them toward an itinerant yet ultimately brilliant life in Europe. Despite living in the bustling and cosmopolitan cities of Trieste, Zurich, and Paris, however, Joyce could never stop writing about the city and country he had left behind. Out of the fine details of an impoverished colonial city he once deemed a place "of failure, of rancor and of unhappiness," this quintessential modernist writer spun works of incredible daring, daunting complexity, and spectacular imagination. Joyce's work sustains this web by weaving the city's local idiosyncrasies into the symbolic networks of the European *Bildungsroman*, Homer's *Odyssey*, and the uncanny dreamwork. Decades before literary tourists trekked to Dublin every June 16th to retrace the real paths of imaginary characters, Joyce transformed Dublin from a real city into the imaginary capital of literary modernism.

For all this resonance, *Dubliners* remains the most Irish of all Joyce's works, the one most rooted in national debates about language, identity, culture, and history. Although a few stories were published while Joyce was resident in Ireland, most are the writing of an exile looking back on his home with a coldly critical eye. From childhood to the church, from courtship to mourning, these Dubliners reflect the desperation and hypocrisy rife in a colony still decimated by the Great Famine yet capable of raising "the cheer of the gratefully oppressed" (as one narrator puts it).

This Longman Cultural Edition illuminates the dense and complicated context of the Ireland that shaped the conception, creation, and initial circulation of *Dubliners*: the fall of Parnell, the aftermath of the Famine, the collapse of the countryside, and the brilliant yet often retrograde cultural movement known alternately as the Celtic Twilight and the Irish Revival—a nationalizing project to reclaim a distinctively Irish language, history, and identity. The section on the Irish Revival provides several of this movement's key documents, revealing the ways in which Joyce's modernism engaged and critiqued the culture of colonial artists.

The energizing turn to debate about cultural politics and art in turn-of-the-century Dublin coincided with the collapse of hopes for political independence after the fall of Charles Stewart Parnell in the wake of a divisive sexual scandal, and the subsequent failure of the Home Rule Bill in Parliament. Ireland, moreover, was still struggling with the aftermath of the Great Famine of the 1840s and the devastation of the countryside by the massive emigration that followed. The sections on Home Rule, emigration, and exile will give you a sense of this critical context, felt throughout the collection, and given its most evocative power in "The Dead."

While Revivalism, Famine, and politics all hang over the stories of *Dubliners*, the collection has a delicate intertextual structure as well. Across the volume, Joyce weaves together fragments of music, poetry, and popular narratives in ways that anticipate the grand accomplishments of his later works. The section on the individual stories gives a sample of these materials, from nineteenth-century light opera to popular boys' magazines. Some, such as the first version of "The Sisters" and the songs from Balfe's popular operetta, *The Bohemian Girl*, are well known; other items may surprise you: the passages from Jonah Barrington's *Personal Sketches*, for example, and the 1844 *Report of the Metropolitan Commissioners in Lunacy*.

Dubliners has a material history as important as its aesthetic innovations. Joyce's struggles with editors, publishers, lawyers, and courts are legendary; and the obscenity trial of *Ulysses* in the United States stands as a watershed in cultural history. *Dubliners* itself appeared in 1914 only after a nine-year struggle to see it into print. The Contexts section "Composition, Publication, Early Reviews" outlines the trying circumstances in which the tales were written, published, reviewed, and defended against charges of libel and obscenity.

The text in this Longman Edition is based on the 1916 American version published by B. W. Huebsch, which was created from sheets printed for the 1914 Grant Richards edition. I have silently corrected obvious typographical and printer's errors. Following Joyce's practice in subsequent works, my text indicates direct speech by a dash, indirect quotation by italics. Although *Dubliners* is now out of copyright, Joyce's letters are not, and so cannot be used to supply some corrections made to later revisions—for instance, the compound words that he preferred to originally hyphenated ones. I footnote a few textual variants (among hundreds) of particular importance. I am deeply indebted to those careful scholars and researchers who have published earlier annotated versions of *Dubliners*, and my own notes often draw heavily on their pioneering work—even as they seek to expand them. Don Gifford's *Joyce Annotated: Notes for Dubliners and A Portrait of the Artist as a Young Man* was invaluable, as were editions created by Margot Norris (Norton, 2006), Jeri Johnson (Oxford 2001), and Robert Scholes and A. Walton Litz (Penguin 1967). I'd also like to thank the series editor, Susan Wolfson, whose careful scholarship and rigorous attention to detail have strengthened this edition considerably. Finally, special thanks are due to the Aida Yared who made available the map of Dublin featured in this edition from her rich collections available online at www.joyceimages.com.

Sean Latham
Professor of English, University of Tulsa
Director, Modernist Journals Project
Editor, *James Joyce Quarterly*
September 2009

Introduction

At the turn of the twentieth century, Dublin was a city of political irresolution and cultural contradiction: A major European metropolis, it was also the deposed capital of a sometimes violently restive British colony. In its theaters, magazines, and literature a cultural revival was taking place, but this renaissance looked to the past rather than to the future, to the all-but-vanished language and folk culture of Ireland rather than to Western European modernity. Many of its leading figures—J. M. Synge, W. B. Yeats, and George Bernard Shaw among them—chose to live outside Ireland, adding to the generations who fled the Great Famine of 1845–52 and its aftermath. An 1895 tourist guide at once celebrated the vibrant life of this paradoxical city while nonetheless recommending that visitors take note of the dreary yet presumably picturesque Sunday morning funerals that "enliven the street" and provide the spectacle of hearses racing "up Sackville Street abreast" all trying to "arrive before the gates [to the cemetery] are shut."[1] One visitor noted, "there is but one step from magnificence to misery, from the splendid palace to the squalid hovel."[2] This was James Joyce's Dublin, a place he too fled in 1904 for a self-imposed exile in Trieste, Zurich, and Paris. His imagination, however, returned endlessly to its streets, pubs, and shops, transmuting this "semicolonial" city into an icon of modernity, a place through which millions of readers have now imaginatively passed.

Joyce restlessly walked Dublin's streets for a surprisingly short time before deciding on exile as the only possible means of escape from a place he considered the intellectual and aesthetic backwater of

[1] E. McDowell Cosgrave and Leonard R. Strangways, *The Illustrated Dictionary of Dublin: Being a Comprehensive Guide to the City and Its Neighborhood* (Dublin: Sealy, Bryers, and Walker, 1895, p. 10).

[2] James Johnson, cited in Joseph V. O'Brien, *Dear, Dirty Dublin: A City in Distress, 1899–1916* (U of California P, 1982, p. 9).

Europe. By age twenty-two, he had seen his once prosperous family slide into poverty. Nevertheless, equipped with perhaps the finest education available to a Catholic Irishman at the time, Joyce had decided to become an artist, setting for himself the immodest goal (as his young artist-hero Stephen Dedalus puts it) of "forg[ing] in the smithy of my soul the uncreated conscience of my race."[3] Such a project seemed impossible in Ireland, a place he believed had destroyed his own family as surely as it had undermined any possibility of its own independence from Britain. In June 1904, he met Nora Barnacle who, with great courage, agreed to leave with this penniless, unknown writer. Joyce eventually rose to fame and international influence with *A Portrait of the Artist as a Young Man*, *Ulysses*, and *Finnegans Wake*—three novels written abroad, yet magnetized by Dublin, a city he had to leave in order to forge it anew.

Joyce called the fifteen stories of *Dubliners* "a chapter of the moral history of my country."[4] Yet these sparse, often cryptic narratives are far more than archival documents of colonial Ireland's "paralysis" and "hemiplegia."[5] With an arresting, uncanny power, Joyce works his narratives to moments of sudden revelation, illuminating the deepest anxieties of his characters amidst their troubled modernity. We see this extraordinary effect in the opening story, "The Sisters," in which, like its child protagonist, we struggle to make sense of a priest's illness and death by filling in deliberate gaps marked on the pages by ellipses. "—I have my own theory about it" says one of the characters, "I think it was one of those ... peculiar cases ... But it's had to say ..." Joyce invites us to wonder what might be wrong with the partially paralyzed priest once found sitting in a church laughing to himself—and to ask why he held such a strange attraction for the young male narrator.

This is not a mystery story, however, and we are not meant to find a definitive answer. Instead, we enter an interpretive suspension that directs our attention ever more intently to the finest nuances of detail and description as this uncertainty itself yields its own distinctive mode of revelation. In the draft of Joyce's first attempt at a novel, *Stephen Hero*, he calls this new mode of knowledge an "epiphany" (a term he drew from his Catholic education): "a sudden spiritual manifestation, whether in the vulgarity of speech and gesture or in a memorable phrase of the mind itself."[6] Such moments are everywhere in

[3] *A Portrait of the Artist as a Young Man* (1914), chapter 5.

[4] *Letters of James Joyce* (May 5, 1906, II, p. 134).

[5] Ibid. (1904, I, p. 55).

[6] *Stephen Hero*, p. 211.

Dubliners, as Joyce charges mundane details with dense, ambiguous meaning. The laughing priest at the end of "The Sisters" is as opaque to us as the "darkened blind" at the beginning: an epiphanic revelation with its content unspecified. In a passage added to a late version of the story, the central character seizes on the odd word "gnomon," a term from classical geometry describing a figure from which a piece has been removed. This epitomizes the structure of all the stories: richly detailed and psychologically complex narratives that seem to be missing small yet crucial pieces of information. We thus constantly feel the eerie force of a never fully articulated revelation that remains locked in an unstable yet infinitely productive language. What initially appears to be a lack in the story—an absence of explanation or revelation—instead becomes an excess, a multiplication of meaning capable of eluding any attempt to impose an authoritative interpretation. Joyce, in short, insists that reading itself is work and that we must take a role ourselves in transmuting the random yet redolent experiences of this grubby urban modernity into something at least momentarily irradiated with wonder and meaning.

The stories themselves are elegantly structured and embedded within a larger arc that stretches from childhood through youth to maturity, public life, and eventually death. Complicated patterns and motifs constantly emerge, helping to bridge stories otherwise held together by nothing more than their interlinked descriptions of Dublin's lower middle class. The opening image of the boy contemplating the darkened window in "The Sisters," for example, is repeated and reworked time and again, his agonized uncertainty captured by the boy in "Araby" who looks out the window on his distant companions; by "Eveline" who "sat at the window watching the evening invade the avenue" as she reflects on her lover's uncertain promises; and finally by Gabriel Conroy in "The Dead" who ends the book by looking out a darkened window to greet the same deathly specter that so troubled the boy in "The Sisters." Similar patterns regularly emerge, whether in the popular songs woven into each of the stories or in the constant evocation of a ghostly yet not entirely insubstantial past that keeps intruding, often dangerously, on the present. "Other forms were near," Gabriel thinks in the final story as he senses their "wayward and flickering existence." So too we feel the ghostly hand of Joyce himself, giving deliberate shape to what often seem almost random moments of idiosyncratic experience. Thus some boys skipping a day at school, a young man having a drink with a successful friend, and a cynical political campaign all become linked, both to one another and to a larger vision of modernity oscillating in the gap between ellipsis and epiphany.

How surprising, then, to learn of the indifference, or even resistance and hostility that first met these captivating stories. First accepted for publication in 1905, they did not appear in print until nine years later when they were overshadowed by Europe's abrupt rush to war. Primed for something romantic with local urban color, editors, publishers, and printers were dismayed by tales that seemed confusing at best, libelous or even obscene at worst. Frustrated by an endless string of rejections and requests for revision, Joyce published an open letter (see "A Curious History" in the Contexts section "Composition, Publication, Early Reviews") in the press describing the "legal, social, and ceremonious" systems that effectively functioned to repress the brutal honesty and aesthetic innovation of a still nascent modernism. This would be only the first of Joyce's career-long legal and artistic fights against censorship, a battle more decisively joined following the ban on *Ulysses* and its eventual defeat in the landmark 1933 case, *The United States v. One Book Named Ulysses*. In these early stories, Joyce set himself on this combative trajectory and had little doubt about its potential importance, writing bombastically to a potential publisher that "I seriously believe ... you will retard the course of civilisation in Ireland by preventing the Irish people from having one good look at themselves in my nicely polished looking-glass."[7] A grandiose claim no doubt, but one that proved more prescient than even its hotheaded author might have dared imagine.

Dubliners is unstinting about the gritty details of urban life, a texture on which Joyce insisted even amidst the heyday of a movement in arts and letters, romantically dubbed "The Celtic Twilight," that looked nostalgically to the island's mythical past as a redoubt against a dreary and alienating present. W. B. Yeats was the most famous and influential voice of a movement you'll encounter in the Contexts section "The Irish Revival: Culture, Politics, and Identity," part of a large cultural debate about the future of a country that would, within a decade, be the first to escape the grip of the British empire. Joyce's characters are not patterned on ancient kings or mythical heroes; instead, they are unremarkable clerks, schoolboys, grifters, shopgirls, and drunks, all crippled by the interlocking powers of family, church, and state. These stories generally refuse the kind of sentimentality Joyce was willing to admit into *A Portrait of the Artist as a Young Man* and especially *Ulysses*. What they do

---

[7] *Letters of James Joyce* (May 20, 1906, I, p. 64).

share with these later high modernist narratives, however, is a refusal of firm closure or conclusion: a drunk (again) beats his child in "Counterparts"; two young men (again) manipulate a household servant in "Two Gallants"; cynical campaign workers (again) canvas neighborhoods for corrupt candidates in "Ivy Day in the Committee Room."

All these meager epiphanies register the consequences of Ireland's colonial situation, illuminated for you in the Contexts section. If Stephen Dedalus, a character carried over from *A Portrait of the Artist as a Young Man* to *Ulysses*, regards history as "a nightmare from which I am trying to awake,"[8] *Dubliners* marks Joyce's first determination to shake Ireland's "batlike souls" into consciousness.[9] The catastrophe of the Great Famine, the gradual extinction of the native language by the colonizer's English, and integration of the island into Britain's global empire inform these stories in ways large and small. This relatively narrow focus on a single island at the turn of the century thus becomes something more—indeed, a great deal more—than just a local study. After all, the agonies of exile, emigration, paralysis, and disempowerment are themselves part of a larger modernity we still share with Joyce. Characters like Eveline, Mr. Duffy, and Gabriel all struggle to develop an authentic language, only to discover that—like the Irish who have all but lost their native tongue—such moments of potentially liberating self-identity do not exist. Again and again the promise of some genuine sense of self recedes in these stories, their limited epiphanies offering only the gaps evident in "The Sisters," the "anguish and anger" of the failed heroic quest in "Araby," and the emotional cynicism of "Ivy Day in the Committee Room." These are all, of course, the symptoms of colonial rule: the consequence of a history that, at least in these stories, plunges only and ever into nightmare. Reading *Dubliners* opens us up to these uncanny encounters with a colonial history that is not yet past, haunted by the same "wayward and flickering" ghosts that stalk the book's final pages. The questions about selfhood, language, desire, failure, and freedom Joyce so deftly articulates through his characters still press upon us with often painful and familiar insistence, opening up troubled yet compelling connections between our confident twenty-first century selves and the shoddy lives of Joyce's imagined Dublin.

---

[8] Joyce, *Ulysses*, chapter 1.
[9] Joyce, *Portrait*, chapter 5.

Table of Dates

[JJ: James Joyce]

1882   February 2: James Augustine Joyce born to John and Mary (née Murray) Joyce in Rathgar, an affluent Dublin suburb.

1886   First Home Rule Bill ("Government of Ireland Bill") defeated in British House of Commons.

1888   JJ enters Clongowes Wood College, a prestigious Jesuit boarding school.

1890   Charles Stewart Parnell, known as "The Chief" and "The Uncrowned King of Ireland," ousted as leader of Irish Home Rule Party after a divorce case revealed his sexual affair with Katherine O'Shea. A rift emerges between Irish Nationalists and the Catholic Church.

1891   JJ withdraws from Clongowes Wood as the family finances decline; to avoid creditors, the family moves several times. Parnell dies and JJ writes "Et Tu, Healy," a poem about the politician's "betrayal" by Ireland.

1893   JJ briefly attends the free Christian Brothers School near his home in north Dublin; enrolls as a scholarship student at the prestigious Jesuit Belvedere College. Second Irish Home Rule Bill passes British Commons, but is vetoed by the House of Lords. Hopes for Irish independence dim. Yeats's *The Rose* and *The Celtic Twilight* published.

1898   JJ enrolls in University College, a Catholic school in the heart of Dublin; gains a command of Latin, French, Italian, German.

1900   JJ presents a paper, "Drama and Life," at the University; writes his first (now lost) play, *A Brilliant Career*; after his review of Ibsen's *When We Dead Awaken* appears in the prestigious *Fortnightly Review*, Ibsen writes to thank him, imagining the young Joyce a senior journalist.

1901   JJ publishes "The Day of the Rabblement," defending the Irish Literary Theatre against Irish "provincialism." It appears as a pamphlet, paired with a feminist essay by his friend, Francis Skeffington, entitled "A Forgotten Aspect of the University Question."

1902   JJ completes his B.A.; December: goes to Paris to study medicine; writes newspaper reviews.

1903   Attending few medical lectures, JJ spends most of his time at the St. Geneviève Library, filling up a series of notebooks. April: A telegram with news of his mother's cancer brings JJ back to Dublin, where he writes poetry, sketches, and reviews. August 3: Mother dies.

1904   June 16: JJ meets Nora Barnacle (who would become his companion and wife); this date will be the setting for *Ulysses*. A Dublin journal, *Dana*, publishes his first poem, but rejects a short essay, "Portrait of an Artist"; "The Sisters" and "Eveline" appear in the *Irish Homestead*. JJ teaches school in Dalkey. August: spends a few nights with Oliver St. John Gogarty and Samuel Chenevix Trench in the Martello Tower. October: JJ moves with Nora to Zurich then to Pola, planning to teach English.

1905   March: JJ and Nora move to Trieste (a wealthy and cosmopolitan port city for the Austrian-Hugarian empire) where JJ teaches at the Berlitz school. Summer: first child, Giorgio, is born; JJ's younger brother Stanislaus arrives, also to teach English. He becomes a crucial (if often resentful) source of financial support. JJ writes more stories and submits a collection, titled *Dubliners,* to Dublin publisher Grant Richards. Entangled in legal concerns about libel and obscenity, it will not be published until 1914.

1906   JJ and family move to Rome, where JJ works in a bank; returns to Trieste. JJ begins "The Dead" and a story titled "Ulysses."

1907   JJ's first book, *Chamber Music* (a collection of Symbolist-inspired poems) is published by the London-based Elkin Matthews. JJ publishes articles on Ireland in a Trieste paper, delivers some lectures, and begins revising *Stephen Hero* into *A Portrait of the Artist as a Young Man*. July: Lucia, second child, is born.

1909   JJ returns to Dublin twice, the second time to open the city's first cinema, The Volta, with the backing of investors from Trieste.

1910   JJ returns to Trieste, now caring for two sisters, Eva and Eileen. They help with childcare, but the family remains poor and largely dependent on Stanislaus's support. The Volta closes.

1911   JJ's letter about continuing difficulties with the publication of *Dubliners* appears in *Sinn Féin*.

1912   Nora and Lucia go to Ireland; JJ soon follows hoping to get *Dubliners* into print. As the family returns to Trieste, JJ privately prints his crude broadside, "Gas from a Burner," distributing it to the Dublin printers and publishers it derides.

1913   JJ begins friendship with Ezra Pound. Third Home Rule Bill defeated; political tensions rise in Ireland as armed groups supporting and opposing independence form.

1914   *Dubliners* published by Grant Richards, its reception blunted by the start of World War One. JJ finishes *Portrait*; with Ezra Pound's help, it is published serially in the *Egoist* (an avant-garde London periodical), with a preface by Pound recounting JJ's struggles with publishers. JJ begins *Exiles,* a play about marriage; composes an experimental work, "Giacomo Joyce" (published posthumously).

1915   As British subjects in Austria-Hungary, the family is at risk; Stanislaus is interned for the duration of the war; JJ and family move to neutral Switzerland and settle in Zurich.

1916   *A Portrait* published in New York. The Easter Rising in Dublin is violently put down, its leaders executed.

1917   *A Portrait* is published in England. JJ receives an anonymous gift of £200 from Harriet Shaw Weaver, a wealthy Englishwoman who will become a faithful patron. Summer: JJ endures the first of many eye operations, many of which will leave him nearly blind and in prolonged pain.

1918   Again encouraged by Pound, JJ sends the first three episodes of *Ulysses* to the *Little Review*, an avant-garde, New York periodical whose editors remove, without JJ's knowledge, some elements that may incur censorship. The novel appears serially through 1921.

1920   The war over, the family returns to Trieste, then moves to Paris. JJ meets famous artists and expatriates, forming close relationships with Adrienne Monnier, Valery Larbaud, and Sylvia Beach, owner of the bookshop Shakespeare & Co. September: Joyce learns that the *Little Review* has been suppressed for obscenity after publishing the "Nausicaa" episode of *Ulysses*.

1921   An obscenity trials ends the prospect of an American edition of *Ulysses*. Sylvia Beach decides to publish a limited edition of 1,000 copies by subscription, under the imprint of Shakespeare & Co; In the process JJ introduces significant changes.

1922   February 2 (JJ's birthday): *Ulysses* is published; widely reviewed, it is regarded as brilliant, difficult, and deeply scandalous. Irish Civil War begins; on a visit to Ireland, Nora and the children take cover when caught in a skirmish.

1923   JJ begins a "Work in Progress" (*Finnegans Wake*), a project that will take fifteen years to complete. Irish Civil War ends.

1924   *Work in Progress* begins to appear in *transatlantic review*. Even JJ's supporters (including Weaver and Pound) find it solipsistic and obscure.

1927　Further portions appear in *transition*, a Paris journal edited by Eugène and Maria Jolas. Shakespeare & Co. publishes *Pomes Penyeach*.

1929　French translations of *Ulysses* appear, as does the first book about the still-evolving *Wake*, titled *Our Examination Round His Factification for Incamination of Work in Progress*. Lucia begins to show the first signs of the mental illness that will consume JJ's energies and lead to her institutionalization. Samuel Roth begins publishing a pirated version of *Ulysses* in the United States.

1931　March: JJ and Nora travel to London to marry, a necessity to protect the family's rights of inheritance of JJ's real and intellectual property. Death of JJ's father.

1932　JJ's grandson, Giorgio's son, Stephen James Joyce is born. Lucia is hospitalized.

1933　In *The United States v. One Book Named Ulysses*, Judge John Woolsey lifts the U.S. ban.

1934　Random House publishes *Ulysses* in the United States.

1936　Bodley Head publishes first British edition of *Ulysses*.

1938　*Finnegans Wake* is completed.

1939　*Finnegans Wake* is published in the United States and Britain, to mixed, often uncomprehending reception. World War Two begins.

1940　As Germany invades France, JJ and Nora move to Zurich, leaving Lucia in a French sanitarium in Pornichet.

1941　January 13: after a botched operation for a perforated ulcer, Joyce dies; buried in Zurich.

Dubliners

The Sisters

THERE WAS no hope for him this time: it was the third stroke. Night after night I had passed the house (it was vacation time) and studied the lighted square of window: and night after night I had found it lighted in the same way, faintly and evenly. If he was dead, I thought, I would see the reflection of candles on the darkened blind for I knew that two candles must be set at the head of a corpse.[1] He had often said to me: *I am not long for this world*, and I had thought his words idle. Now I knew they were true. Every night as I gazed up at the window I said softly to myself the word *paralysis*. It had always sounded strangely in my ears, like the word *gnomon*[2] in the Euclid and the word *simony*[3] in the Catechism.[4] But now it sounded to me like the name of some maleficent and sinful being. It filled me with fear, and yet I longed to be nearer to it and to look upon its deadly work.

Old Cotter[5] was sitting at the fire, smoking, when I came downstairs to supper. While my aunt was ladling out my stirabout[6] he said, as if returning to some former remark of his:

—No, I wouldn't say he was exactly ... but there was something queer ... there was something uncanny about him. I'll tell you my opinion....

He began to puff at his pipe, no doubt arranging his opinion in his mind. Tiresome old fool! When we knew him first he used to be

---

[1] A tradition at Irish wakes (funeral celebrations).

[2] In Euclidian geometry, the part of a parallelogram that remains after removing a smaller parallelogram from one corner. The term also describes the shadow cast by a post on a sundial's face that blocks out a portion of the sun.

[3] Selling spiritual favors and preferments for profit, a sin.

[4] Summary of Catholic doctrine, used in education and learned by rote.

[5] English variant of "cottier" (Irish): "a peasant renting and cultivating a small holding" (*OED*).

[6] Cheap oatmeal porridge.

rather interesting, talking of faints and worms;[7] but I soon grew tired of him and his endless stories about the distillery.

—I have my own theory about it, he said. I think it was one of those ... peculiar cases.... But it's hard to say....

He began to puff again at his pipe without giving us his theory. My uncle saw me staring and said to me:

—Well, so your old friend is gone, you'll be sorry to hear.

—Who? said I.

—Father Flynn.

—Is he dead?

—Mr Cotter here has just told us. He was passing by the house.

I knew that I was under observation so I continued eating as if the news had not interested me. My uncle explained to old Cotter.

—The youngster and he were great friends. The old chap taught him a great deal, mind you; and they say he had a great wish for him.[8]

—God have mercy on his soul, said my aunt piously.

Old Cotter looked at me for a while. I felt that his little beady black eyes were examining me but I would not satisfy him by looking up from my plate. He returned to his pipe and finally spat rudely into the grate.

—I wouldn't like children of mine, he said, to have too much to say to a man like that.

—How do you mean, Mr Cotter? asked my aunt.

—What I mean is, said old Cotter, it's bad for children. My idea is: let a young lad run about and play with young lads of his own age and not be.... Am I right, Jack?

—That's my principle, too, said my uncle. Let him learn to box his corner.[9] That's what I'm always saying to that Rosicrucian[10] there: take exercise. Why, when I was a nipper every morning of my life I had a cold bath, winter and summer. And that's what stands to me now. Education is all very fine and large.... Mr Cotter might take a pick of that leg of mutton, he added to my aunt.

—No, no, not for me, said old Cotter.

My aunt brought the dish from the safe and laid it on the table.

---

[7] "Faints" are impurities in distillation; "worms" are the curving tubes that condense the alcoholic vapors.

[8] That the boy would enter the priesthood.

[9] Take care of himself.

[10] A member of a secret society supposedly founded by Christian Rosenkreuz in 1484 and devoted to the study of magical knowledge and the pursuit of eternal life.

—But why do you think it's not good for children, Mr Cotter? she asked.

It's bad for children, said old Cotter, because their minds are so impressionable. When children see things like that, you know, it has an effect....

I crammed my mouth with stirabout for fear I might give utterance to my anger. Tiresome old red-nosed imbecile!

It was late when I fell asleep. Though I was angry with old Cotter for alluding to me as a child, I puzzled my head to extract meaning from his unfinished sentences. In the dark of my room I imagined that I saw again the heavy grey face of the paralytic. I drew the blankets over my head and tried to think of Christmas. But the grey face still followed me. It murmured; and I understood that it desired to confess something. I felt my soul receding into some pleasant and vicious region; and there again I found it waiting for me. It began to confess to me in a murmuring voice and I wondered why it smiled continually and why the lips were so moist with spittle. But then I remembered that it had died of paralysis and I felt that I too was smiling feebly as if to absolve the simoniac[11] of his sin.

The next morning after breakfast I went down to look at the little house in Great Britain Street. It was an unassuming shop, registered under the vague name of *Drapery*.[12] The drapery consisted mainly of children's bootees and umbrellas; and on ordinary days a notice used to hang in the window, saying: *Umbrellas Re-covered*. No notice was visible now for the shutters were up. A crape bouquet was tied to the doorknocker with ribbon.[13] Two poor women and a telegram boy were reading the card pinned on the crape. I also approached and read:

July 1st, 1895

The Rev. James Flynn (formerly of S. Catherine's Church, Meath Street), aged sixty-five years.

R. I. P.[14]

---

[11] Simony is so serious a sin, however, that only the highest officers of the Catholic Church can absolve it.

[12] Shop selling cloth and textiles.

[13] Signifying a house in mourning.

[14] "*Requiescat in Pace*" (Latin): "Rest in Peace."

The reading of the card persuaded me that he was dead and I was disturbed to find myself at check. Had he not been dead I would have gone into the little dark room behind the shop to find him sitting in his arm-chair by the fire, nearly smothered in his great-coat. Perhaps my aunt would have given me a packet of High Toast[15] for him and this present would have roused him from his stupefied doze. It was always I who emptied the packet into his black snuff-box for his hands trembled too much to allow him to do this without spilling half the snuff about the floor. Even as he raised his large trembling hand to his nose little clouds of smoke[16] dribbled through his fingers over the front of his coat. It may have been these constant showers of snuff which gave his ancient priestly garments their green faded look for the red handkerchief, blackened, as it always was, with the snuff-stains of a week, with which he tried to brush away the fallen grains, was quite inefficacious.

I wished to go in and look at him but I had not the courage to knock. I walked away slowly along the sunny side of the street, reading all the theatrical advertisements in the shop-windows as I went. I found it strange that neither I nor the day seemed in a mourning mood and I felt even annoyed at discovering in myself a sensation of freedom as if I had been freed from something by his death. I wondered at this for, as my uncle had said the night before, he had taught me a great deal. He had studied in the Irish college[17] in Rome and he had taught me to pronounce Latin properly.[18] He had told me stories about the catacombs[19] and about Napoleon Bonaparte,[20] and he had explained to me the meaning of the different ceremonies of the Mass and of the different vestments worn by the priest. Sometimes he had amused himself by putting difficult questions to me, asking me what one should do in certain circumstances or whether such and such sins were mortal or venial or only imperfections.[21] His questions showed me how complex and mysterious were certain institutions of the Church

---

[15] A brand of snuff (pulverized tobacco inhaled through the nose).

[16] Tobacco.

[17] A Vatican seminary for training talented Irish priests.

[18] The Catholic mass was conducted in Latin.

[19] Extensive burial grounds beneath Rome where early Christians (at risk of persecution) secretly held Mass.

[20] After his invasion of Italy in 1798, this French general (and Emperor of France, 1804–15) closed the Irish College.

[21] The mortal sins cut one off from God and thus the salvation of one's soul. They can only be absolved through confession. Venial sins are less serious failings and only weaken the soul's state of grace.

which I had always regarded as the simplest acts. The duties of the priest towards the Eucharist[22] and towards the secrecy of the confessional[23] seemed so grave to me that I wondered how anybody had ever found in himself the courage to undertake them; and I was not surprised when he told me that the fathers of the Church had written books as thick as the *Post Office Directory* and as closely printed as the law notices in the newspaper, elucidating all these intricate questions. Often when I thought of this I could make no answer or only a very foolish and halting one upon which he used to smile and nod his head twice or thrice. Sometimes he used to put me through the responses of the Mass which he had made me learn by heart; and, as I pattered, he used to smile pensively and nod his head, now and then pushing huge pinches of snuff up each nostril alternately. When he smiled he used to uncover his big discoloured teeth and let his tongue lie upon his lower lip—a habit which had made me feel uneasy in the beginning of our acquaintance before I knew him well.

As I walked along in the sun I remembered old Cotter's words and tried to remember what had happened afterwards in the dream. I remembered that I had noticed long velvet curtains and a swinging lamp of antique fashion. I felt that I had been very far away, in some land where the customs were strange—in Persia, I thought.... But I could not remember the end of the dream.

In the evening my aunt took me with her to visit the house of mourning. It was after sunset; but the window-panes of the houses that looked to the west reflected the tawny gold of a great bank of clouds. Nannie received us in the hall; and, as it would have been unseemly to have shouted at her, my aunt shook hands with her for all. The old woman pointed upwards interrogatively and, on my aunt's nodding, proceeded to toil up the narrow staircase before us, her bowed head being scarcely above the level of the banister-rail. At the first landing she stopped and beckoned us forward encouragingly towards the open door of the dead-room. My aunt went in and the old woman, seeing that I hesitated to enter, began to beckon to me again repeatedly with her hand.

I went in on tiptoe. The room through the lace end of the blind was suffused with dusky golden light amid which the candles looked like pale thin flames. He had been coffined. Nannie gave the

---

[22] The central ritual of the Mass, when the priest miraculously transforms bread and wine into the body and blood of Christ.

[23] The small chamber for making confession: a sacrament that binds the priest to secrecy and permits him to absolve sin.

lead and we three knelt down at the foot of the bed. I pretended to pray but I could not gather my thoughts because the old woman's mutterings distracted me. I noticed how clumsily her skirt was hooked at the back and how the heels of her cloth boots were trodden down all to one side. The fancy came to me that the old priest was smiling as he lay there in his coffin.

But no. When we rose and went up to the head of the bed I saw that he was not smiling. There he lay, solemn and copious, vested as for the altar, his large hands loosely retaining a chalice.[24] His face was very truculent, grey and massive, with black cavernous nostrils and circled by a scanty white fur. There was a heavy odour in the room—the flowers.

We blessed ourselves[25] and came away. In the little room downstairs we found Eliza seated in his arm-chair in state. I groped my way towards my usual chair in the corner while Nannie went to the sideboard and brought out a decanter of sherry and some wine-glasses. She set these on the table and invited us to take a little glass of wine. Then, at her sister's bidding, she poured out the sherry into the glasses and passed them to us. She pressed me to take some cream crackers also, but I declined because I thought I would make too much noise eating them. She seemed to be somewhat disappointed at my refusal and went over quietly to the sofa where she sat down behind her sister. No one spoke: we all gazed at the empty fireplace.

My aunt waited until Eliza sighed and then said:

—Ah, well, he's gone to a better world.

Eliza sighed again and bowed her head in assent. My aunt fingered the stem of her wine-glass before sipping a little.

—Did he … peacefully? she asked.

—Oh, quite peacefully, ma'am, said Eliza. You couldn't tell when the breath went out of him. He had a beautiful death, God be praised.

—And everything …?

—Father O'Rourke was in with him a Tuesday and anointed him and prepared him and all.[26]

—He knew then?

---

[24] The cup for wine in the Eucharist.

[25] A Catholic ritual, touching the head, chest, and each shoulder to make the shape of a cross.

[26] Last rites, in which the priest anoints the body with oil and hears a final confession from a dying person.

—He was quite resigned.

—He looks quite resigned, said my aunt.

—That's what the woman we had in to wash him said. She said he just looked as if he was asleep, he looked that peaceful and resigned. No one would think he'd make such a beautiful corpse.

—Yes, indeed, said my aunt.

She sipped a little more from her glass and said:

—Well, Miss Flynn, at any rate it must be a great comfort for you to know that you did all you could for him. You were both very kind to him, I must say.

Eliza smoothed her dress over her knees.

—Ah, poor James! she said. God knows we done all we could, as poor as we were—we wouldn't see him want anything while he was in it.

Nannie had leaned her head against the sofa-pillow and seemed about to fall asleep.

—There's poor Nannie, said Eliza, looking at her, she's wore out. All the work we had, she and me, getting in the woman to wash him and then laying him out and then the coffin and then arranging about the Mass in the chapel. Only for Father O'Rourke I don't know what we'd have done at all. It was him brought us all them flowers and them two candlesticks out of the chapel and wrote out the notice for the *Freeman's General*[27] and took charge of all the papers for the cemetery and poor James's insurance.

—Wasn't that good of him? said my aunt.

Eliza closed her eyes and shook her head slowly.

—Ah, there's no friends like the old friends, she said, when all is said and done, no friends that a body can trust.

—Indeed, that's true, said my aunt. And I'm sure now that he's gone to his eternal reward he won't forget you and all your kindness to him.

—Ah, poor James! said Eliza. He was no great trouble to us. You wouldn't hear him in the house any more than now. Still, I know he's gone and all to that....

—It's when it's all over that you'll miss him, said my aunt.

—I know that, said Eliza. I won't be bringing him in his cup of beef-tea any more, nor you, ma'am, sending him his snuff. Ah, poor James!

---

[27] An ironic malapropism (see "rheumatic wheels" below). Eliza means the *Freeman's Journal*, a conservative daily newspaper.

She stopped, as if she were communing with the past and then said shrewdly:

—Mind you, I noticed there was something queer coming over him latterly. Whenever I'd bring in his soup to him there I'd find him with his breviary[28] fallen to the floor, lying back in the chair and his mouth open.

She laid a finger against her nose and frowned: then she continued:

—But still and all he kept on saying that before the summer was over he'd go out for a drive one fine day just to see the old house again where we were all born down in Irishtown[29] and take me and Nannie with him. If we could only get one of them new-fangled carriages that makes no noise that Father O'Rourke told him about—them with the rheumatic wheels[30] —for the day cheap, he said, at Johnny Rush's over the way there and drive out the three of us together of a Sunday evening. He had his mind set on that.... Poor James!

—The Lord have mercy on his soul! said my aunt.

Eliza took out her handkerchief and wiped her eyes with it. Then she put it back again in her pocket and gazed into the empty grate for some time without speaking.

—He was too scrupulous always, she said. The duties of the priesthood was too much for him. And then his life was, you might say, crossed.

—Yes, said my aunt. He was a disappointed man. You could see that.

A silence took possession of the little room and, under cover of it, I approached the table and tasted my sherry and then returned quietly to my chair in the corner. Eliza seemed to have fallen into a deep revery. We waited respectfully for her to break the silence: and after a long pause she said slowly:

—It was that chalice he broke.... That was what was the beginning of it. Of course, they say it was all right, that it contained nothing,[31] I mean. But still.... They say it was the boy's[32] fault. But poor James was so nervous, God be merciful to him!

---

[28] A book with the "Divine Office" for each day: a collection of psalms, prayers, and excerpts from scripture.

[29] Slum just south of Dublin.

[30] Another malapropism: "pneumatic wheels" (air-filled).

[31] That is, it was either empty or contained wine that had had not yet been transformed into the blood of Christ.

[32] The altar boy, a priest's assistant at Mass.

—And was that it? said my aunt. I heard something....

Eliza nodded.

—That affected his mind, she said. After that he began to mope by himself, talking to no one and wandering about by himself. So one night he was wanted for to go on a call and they couldn't find him anywhere. They looked high up and low down; and still they couldn't see a sight of him anywhere. So then the clerk suggested to try the chapel. So then they got the keys and opened the chapel and the clerk and Father O'Rourke and another priest that was there brought in a light for to look for him.... And what do you think but there he was, sitting up by himself in the dark in his confession-box, wide-awake and laughing-like softly to himself?

She stopped suddenly as if to listen. I too listened; but there was no sound in the house: and I knew that the old priest was lying still in his coffin as we had seen him, solemn and truculent in death, an idle chalice on his breast.

Eliza resumed:

—Wide-awake and laughing-like to himself.... So then, of course, when they saw that, that made them think that there was something gone wrong with him....

An Encounter

IT WAS Joe Dillon who introduced the Wild West to us. He had a little library made up of old numbers of *The Union Jack*, *Pluck* and *The Halfpenny Marvel*.[1] Every evening after school we met in his back garden and arranged Indian battles. He and his fat young brother Leo, the idler, held the loft of the stable while we tried to carry it by storm; or we fought a pitched battle on the grass. But, however well we fought, we never won siege or battle and all our bouts ended with Joe Dillon's war dance of victory. His parents went to eight-o'clock mass every morning in Gardiner Street and the peaceful odour of Mrs Dillon was prevalent in the hall of the house. But he played too fiercely for us who were younger and more timid. He looked like some kind of an Indian when he capered round the garden, an old tea-cosy[2] on his head, beating a tin with his fist and yelling:

—Ya! yaka, yaka, yaka![3]

Everyone was incredulous when it was reported that he had a vocation for the priesthood. Nevertheless it was true.

A spirit of unruliness diffused itself among us and, under its influence, differences of culture and constitution were waived. We banded ourselves together, some boldly, some in jest and some almost in fear: and of the number of these latter, the reluctant Indians who were afraid to seem studious or lacking in robustness, I was one. The adventures related in the literature of the Wild West were remote from my nature but, at least, they opened doors of escape. I liked better some American detective stories which were

[1] Popular, weekly British boys' magazines in the 1880s and 1890s, featuring sometimes violent stories of "plucky sailors, plucky soldiers, plucky firemen" as well as tales of American Indians and intrepid explorers. See p. xx for typical covers.

[2] Quilted bag put around a teapot to keep it warm.

[3] Imitation of a Native American war chant.

traversed from time to time by unkempt fierce and beautiful girls. Though there was nothing wrong in these stories and though their intention was sometimes literary they were circulated secretly at school. One day when Father Butler was hearing the four pages of Roman history clumsy Leo Dillon was discovered with a copy of *The Halfpenny Marvel.*

—This page or this page? This page? Now, Dillon, up! *Hardly had the day....* Go on! What day? *Hardly had the day dawned*[4].... Have you studied it? What have you there in your pocket?

Everyone's heart palpitated as Leo Dillon handed up the paper and everyone assumed an innocent face. Father Butler turned over the pages, frowning.

—What is this rubbish? he said. *The Apache Chief*! Is this what you read instead of studying your Roman history? Let me not find any more of this wretched stuff in this college.[5] The man who wrote it, I suppose, was some wretched scribbler who writes these things for a drink. I'm surprised at boys like you, educated, reading such stuff. I could understand it if you were ... National School[6] boys. Now, Dillon, I advise you strongly, get at your work or ...

This rebuke during the sober hours of school paled much of the glory of the Wild West for me and the confused puffy face of Leo Dillon awakened one of my consciences. But when the restraining influence of the school was at a distance I began to hunger again for wild sensations, for the escape which those chronicles of disorder alone seemed to offer me. The mimic warfare of the evening became at last as wearisome to me as the routine of school in the morning because I wanted real adventures to happen to myself. But real adventures, I reflected, do not happen to people who remain at home: they must be sought abroad.

The summer holidays were near at hand when I made up my mind to break out of the weariness of school-life for one day at least. With Leo Dillon and a boy named Mahony I planned a day's miching.[7] Each of us saved up sixpence. We were to meet at ten in the

---

[4] A common phrase in Julius Caesar's lively *Comentarii de Bello Gallico* (*Gallic Wars*); students had to rise and recite memorized portions of the text when called upon.

[5] Common term for elite private schools. Joyce attended the prestigious Jesuit Belvedere College from 1893 to 1898.

[6] Publicly funded schools that drew poorer students and focused on career training rather than academics.

[7] Archaism for deception; here, truancy.

morning on the Canal Bridge. Mahony's big sister was to write an excuse for him and Leo Dillon was to tell his brother to say he was sick. We arranged to go along the Wharf Road[8] until we came to the ships, then to cross in the ferryboat and walk out to see the Pigeon House.[9] Leo Dillon was afraid we might meet Father Butler or some-one out of the college; but Mahony asked, very sensibly, what would Father Butler be doing out at the Pigeon House. We were reassured: and I brought the first stage of the plot to an end by collecting sixpence from the other two, at the same time showing them my own sixpence. When we were making the last arrangements on the eve we were all vaguely excited. We shook hands, laughing, and Mahony said:

—Till tomorrow, mates!

That night I slept badly. In the morning I was first-comer to the bridge as I lived nearest. I hid my books in the long grass near the ashpit[10] at the end of the garden where nobody ever came and hurried along the canal bank. It was a mild sunny morning in the first week of June. I sat up on the coping[11] of the bridge admiring my frail canvas shoes which I had diligently pipeclayed[12] overnight and watching the docile horses pulling a tramload of business people up the hill. All the branches of the tall trees which lined the mall were gay with little light green leaves and the sunlight slanted through them on to the water. The granite stone of the bridge was beginning to be warm and I began to pat it with my hands in time to an air[13] in my head. I was very happy.

When I had been sitting there for five or ten minutes I saw Mahony's grey suit approaching. He came up the hill, smiling, and clambered up beside me on the bridge. While we were waiting he brought out the catapult[14] which bulged from his inner pocket and explained some improvements which he had made in it. I asked him why he had brought it and he told me he had brought it to have some gas[15] with the birds. Mahony used slang freely, and spoke of

---

[8] A circuitous route, along a sea wall north of the Liffey River.

[9] Power plant (and former fort) at the far end of a seawall extending into the harbor's breakwater.

[10] Refuse pile.

[11] Wall-top.

[12] Whitened, cleaned.

[13] A tune.

[14] Slingshot.

[15] Fun.

Father Butler as Bunsen Burner. We waited on for a quarter of an hour more but still there was no sign of Leo Dillon. Mahony, at last, jumped down and said:

—Come along. I knew Fatty'd funk it.[16]

—And his sixpence ...? I said.

—That's forfeit, said Mahony. And so much the better for us—a bob and a tanner instead of a bob.[17]

We walked along the North Strand Road till we came to the Vitriol Works[18] and then turned to the right along the Wharf Road. Mahony began to play the Indian as soon as we were out of public sight. He chased a crowd of ragged[19] girls, brandishing his unloaded catapult and, when two ragged boys began, out of chivalry, to fling stones at us, he proposed that we should charge them. I objected that the boys were too small and so we walked on, the ragged troop screaming after us: *Swaddlers! Swaddlers!*[20] thinking that we were Protestants because Mahony, who was dark-complexioned, wore the silver badge of a cricket club in his cap.[21] When we came to the Smoothing Iron[22] we arranged a siege; but it was a failure because you must have at least three. We revenged ourselves on Leo Dillon by saying what a funk he was and guessing how many he would get[23] at three o'clock from Mr Ryan.

We came then near the river. We spent a long time walking about the noisy streets flanked by high stone walls, watching the working of cranes and engines and often being shouted at for our immobility by the drivers of groaning carts. It was noon when we reached the quays and as all the labourers seemed to be eating their lunches, we bought two big currant buns and sat down to eat them on some metal piping beside the river. We pleased ourselves with the spectacle of Dublin's commerce—the barges signalled from far away by their curls of woolly smoke, the brown fishing fleet beyond Ringsend,[24] the big white sailing-vessel which was being discharged

---

[16] "Fat Leo Dillon" would lose his nerve.

[17] Slang for a shilling; a tanner is a sixpence.

[18] A landmark chemical factory that made corrosive materials.

[19] "Ragged" schools provide free education and social services for poor children.

[20] Slang for Protestants (specifically Methodists).

[21] Cricket is a British sport, scorned by Irish nationalists.

[22] A flat diving rock for swimmers in Dublin Bay.

[23] Disciplinary corporal punishment delivered with a stick on the open palms.

[24] Area on the Liffey's south bank opposite the boys.

on the opposite quay. Mahony said it would be right skit[25] to run away to sea on one of those big ships and even I, looking at the high masts, saw, or imagined, the geography which had been scantily dosed to me at school gradually taking substance under my eyes. School and home seemed to recede from us and their influences upon us seemed to wane.

We crossed the Liffey in the ferryboat, paying our toll to be transported in the company of two labourers and a little Jew[26] with a bag. We were serious to the point of solemnity, but once during the short voyage our eyes met and we laughed. When we landed we watched the discharging of the graceful three-master[27] which we had observed from the other quay. Some bystander said that she was a Norwegian vessel. I went to the stern and tried to decipher the legend upon it but, failing to do so, I came back and examined the foreign sailors to see had any of them green eyes for I had some confused notion....[28] The sailors' eyes were blue and grey and even black. The only sailor whose eyes could have been called green was a tall man who amused the crowd on the quay by calling out cheerfully every time the planks fell:

—All right! All right!

When we were tired of this sight we wandered slowly into Ringsend. The day had grown sultry, and in the windows of the grocers' shops musty biscuits lay bleaching. We bought some biscuits and chocolate which we ate sedulously as we wandered through the squalid streets where the families of the fishermen live. We could find no dairy and so we went into a huckster's shop[29] and bought a bottle of raspberry lemonade each. Refreshed by this, Mahony chased a cat down a lane, but the cat escaped into a wide field. We both felt rather tired and when we reached the field we made at once for a sloping bank over the ridge of which we could see the Dodder.[30]

It was too late and we were too tired to carry out our project of visiting the Pigeon House. We had to be home before four o'clock

---

[25] Exciting.

[26] Joyce would later make a Dublin Jew, Leopold Bloom, the hero of *Ulysses* (1922).

[27] A large, three-masted ship.

[28] Unclear, but legend stated that wily Odysseus had green eyes and a popular Irish street rhyme ran: "Green eyes and coppered hair / My mother wouldn't trust you." Green eyes might also connote homosexuality.

[29] For inexpensive goods.

[30] Tributary of the Liffey.

lest our adventure should be discovered. Mahony looked regretfully at his catapult and I had to suggest going home by train before he regained any cheerfulness. The sun went in behind some clouds and left us to our jaded thoughts and the crumbs of our provisions.

There was nobody but ourselves in the field. When we had lain on the bank for some time without speaking I saw a man approaching from the far end of the field. I watched him lazily as I chewed one of those green stems on which girls tell fortunes.[31] He came along by the bank slowly. He walked with one hand upon his hip and in the other hand he held a stick[32] with which he tapped the turf lightly. He was shabbily dressed in a suit of greenish-black and wore what we used to call a jerry hat with a high crown.[33] He seemed to be fairly old for his moustache was ashen-grey. When he passed at our feet he glanced up at us quickly and then continued his way. We followed him with our eyes and saw that when he had gone on for perhaps fifty paces he turned about and began to retrace his steps. He walked towards us very slowly, always tapping the ground with his stick, so slowly that I thought he was looking for something in the grass.

He stopped when he came level with us and bade us good-day. We answered him and he sat down beside us on the slope slowly and with great care. He began to talk of the weather, saying that it would be a very hot summer and adding that the seasons had changed greatly since he was a boy—a long time ago. He said that the happiest time of one's life was undoubtedly one's schoolboy days and that he would give anything to be young again. While he expressed these sentiments, which bored us a little, we kept silent. Then he began to talk of school and of books. He asked us whether we had read the poetry of Thomas Moore or the works of Sir Walter Scott and Lord Lytton.[34] I pretended that I had read every book he mentioned so that in the end he said:

—Ah, I can see you are a bookworm like myself. Now, he added, pointing to Mahony who was regarding us with open eyes, he is different; he goes in for games.

---

[31] Fortunes in love told by patterns on the torn stalk.

[32] A walking stick.

[33] A round felt hat.

[34] Thomas Moore (1779–1852) was a much loved Irish poet, singer, and songwriter; Sir Walter Scott (1771–1832) was a prolific Scots poet and extremely successful historical novelist; politician, poet, and novelist Edward Bulwer-Lytton (1803–73) was famed for his sensationalist novels.

He said he had all Sir Walter Scott's works and all Lord Lytton's works at home and never tired of reading them. Of course, he said, there were some of Lord Lytton's works which boys couldn't read. Mahony asked why couldn't boys read them—a question which agitated and pained me because I was afraid the man would think I was as stupid as Mahony. The man, however, only smiled. I saw that he had great gaps in his mouth between his yellow teeth. Then he asked us which of us had the most sweethearts. Mahony mentioned lightly that he had three totties.[35] The man asked me how many I had. I answered that I had none. He did not believe me and said he was sure I must have one. I was silent.

—Tell us, said Mahony pertly to the man, how many have you yourself?

The man smiled as before and said that when he was our age he had lots of sweethearts.

—Every boy, he said, has a little sweetheart.

His attitude on this point struck me as strangely liberal in a man of his age. In my heart I thought that what he said about boys and sweethearts was reasonable. But I disliked the words in his mouth and I wondered why he shivered once or twice as if he feared something or felt a sudden chill. As he proceeded I noticed that his accent was good.[36] He began to speak to us about girls, saying what nice soft hair they had and how soft their hands were and how all girls were not so good as they seemed to be if one only knew. There was nothing he liked, he said, so much as looking at a nice young girl, at her nice white hands and her beautiful soft hair. He gave me the impression that he was repeating something which he had learned by heart or that, magnetised by some words of his own speech, his mind was slowly circling round and round in the same orbit. At times he spoke as if he were simply alluding to some fact that everybody knew, and at times he lowered his voice and spoke mysteriously as if he were telling us something secret which he did not wish others to overhear. He repeated his phrases over and over again, varying them and surrounding them with his monotonous voice. I continued to gaze towards the foot of the slope, listening to him.

After a long while his monologue paused. He stood up slowly, saying that he had to leave us for a minute or so, a few minutes,

---

[35] Slang for girlfriend, but can also refer to a classy prostitute.

[36] An indication that he's well educated and of a better class social class than his shabby appearance suggests.

and, without changing the direction of my gaze, I saw him walking slowly away from us towards the near end of the field. We remained silent when he had gone. After a silence of a few minutes I heard Mahony exclaim:

—I say! Look what he's doing!

As I neither answered nor raised my eyes Mahony exclaimed again:

—I say…. He's a queer old josser![37]

—In case he asks us for our names, I said… let you be Murphy and I'll be Smith.

We said nothing further to each other. I was still considering whether I would go away or not when the man came back and sat down beside us again. Hardly had he sat down when Mahony, catching sight of the cat which had escaped him, sprang up and pursued her across the field. The man and I watched the chase. The cat escaped once more and Mahony began to throw stones at the wall she had escaladed.[38] Desisting from this, he began to wander about the far end of the field, aimlessly.

After an interval the man spoke to me. He said that my friend was a very rough boy and asked did he get whipped often at school. I was going to reply indignantly that we were not National School boys to be *whipped*,[39] as he called it; but I remained silent. He began to speak on the subject of chastising boys. His mind, as if magnetised again by his speech, seemed to circle slowly round and round its new centre. He said that when boys were that kind they ought to be whipped and well whipped. When a boy was rough and unruly there was nothing would do him any good but a good sound whipping. A slap on the hand or a box on the ear was no good: what he wanted was to get a nice warm whipping. I was surprised at this sentiment and involuntarily glanced up at his face. As I did so I met the gaze of a pair of bottle-green eyes peering at me from under a twitching forehead. I turned my eyes away again.

The man continued his monologue. He seemed to have forgotten his recent liberalism. He said that if ever he found a boy talking to girls or having a girl for a sweetheart he would whip him and whip him; and that would teach him not to be talking to girls. And if a boy had a girl for a sweetheart and told lies about it then he

---

[37] "A simpleton; a soft or silly fellow" (*OED*).

[38] Climbed, as on a staircase.

[39] Where discipline was more severe than in private schools.

would give him such a whipping as no boy ever got in this world. He said that there was nothing in this world he would like so well as that. He described to me how he would whip such a boy as if he were unfolding some elaborate mystery. He would love that, he said, better than anything in this world; and his voice, as he led me monotonously through the mystery, grew almost affectionate and seemed to plead with me that I should understand him.

I waited till his monologue paused again. Then I stood up abruptly. Lest I should betray my agitation I delayed a few moments pretending to fix my shoe properly and then, saying that I was obliged to go, I bade him good-day. I went up the slope calmly but my heart was beating quickly with fear that he would seize me by the ankles. When I reached the top of the slope I turned round and, without looking at him, called loudly across the field:

—Murphy!

My voice had an accent of forced bravery in it and I was ashamed of my paltry stratagem. I had to call the name again before Mahony saw me and hallooed in answer. How my heart beat as he came running across the field to me! He ran as if to bring me aid. And I was penitent;[40] for in my heart I had always despised him a little.

[40] As if atoning for a sin.

Araby[1]

North Richmond Street, being blind,[2] was a quiet street except at the hour when the Christian Brothers' School[3] set the boys free. An uninhabited house of two storeys stood at the blind end, detached from its neighbours in a square ground. The other houses of the street, conscious of decent lives within them, gazed at one another with brown imperturbable faces.

The former tenant of our house, a priest, had died in the back drawing-room.[4] Air, musty from having been long enclosed, hung in all the rooms, and the waste room behind the kitchen was littered with old useless papers. Among these I found a few paper-covered books, the pages of which were curled and damp: *The Abbot*, by Walter Scott, *The Devout Communicant* and *The Memoirs of Vidocq*.[5] I liked the last best because its leaves were yellow. The wild garden behind the house contained a central apple-tree and a few straggling bushes under one of which I found the late tenant's rusty bicycle-pump.[6] He had been a very charitable priest; in his will he had left all his money to institutions and the furniture of his house to his sister.

---

[1] Arabia, but tinged with Orientalist mysticism and sensualism. See p. xx. It is also the name of a fund-raising festival for Dublin's Jervis Street Hospital, May 14–19, 1894.

[2] A dead end. The Joyce family lived briefly on this street from 1895 to 1896.

[3] Catholic charity school.

[4] Contraction for "withdrawing"——originally where a household and its guests would withdraw after dinner, the term came to refer to a semi-formal room for hospitality.

[5] *The Abbot* (1820) is a historical romance by Walter Scott (see p.xx) relating the story of Mary Queen of Scotts (1542–87), the Catholic Queen of Scotland from 1542 to 1567 who was deposed and imprisoned by the Protestant nobility. Considered a threat to Protestant England because of her claim to the throne, she was beheaded by command of her cousin, Queen Elizabeth I. *The Devout Communicant* is a religious tract. The *Memoirs of Vidocq* (1829) is Eugène François Vidoq's (1775–1857) fictional account of his adventures as a thief and criminal; he eventually became the first chief of the French secret police.

[6] Tire pump.

When the short days of winter came dusk fell before we had well eaten our dinners. When we met in the street the houses had grown sombre. The space of sky above us was the colour of ever-changing violet and towards it the lamps of the street lifted their feeble lanterns. The cold air stung us and we played till our bodies glowed. Our shouts echoed in the silent street. The career[7] of our play brought us through the dark muddy lanes behind the houses where we ran the gantlet[8] of the rough tribes from the cottages,[9] to the back doors of the dark dripping gardens where odours arose from the ashpits,[10] to the dark odorous stables where a coachman smoothed and combed the horse or shook music from the buckled harness. When we returned to the street light from the kitchen windows had filled the areas.[11] If my uncle was seen turning the corner we hid in the shadow until we had seen him safely housed. Or if Mangan's sister came out on the doorstep to call her brother in to his tea[12] we watched her from our shadow peer up and down the street. We waited to see whether she would remain or go in and, if she remained, we left our shadow and walked up to Mangan's steps resignedly. She was waiting for us, her figure defined by the light from the half-opened door. Her brother always teased her before he obeyed and I stood by the railings looking at her. Her dress swung as she moved her body and the soft rope of her hair tossed from side to side.

Every morning I lay on the floor in the front parlour watching her door. The blind was pulled down to within an inch of the sash so that I could not be seen. When she came out on the doorstep my heart leaped. I ran to the hall, seized my books and followed her. I kept her brown figure always in my eye and, when we came near the point at which our ways diverged, I quickened my pace and passed her. This happened morning after morning. I had never spoken to her, except for a few casual words, and yet her name was like a summons to all my foolish blood.

[7] Course, momentum.

[8] Archaism for "gauntlet": a military punishment in which a convict runs between two rows of soldiers who beat him with stick and chords. For the boys, the term is partly mock-heroic and partly a register of real danger in this neighborhood.

[9] Low-rent houses just off Richmond Street.

[10] Refuse pile.

[11] A narrow space between ground-level railings and the front of the house that gives access to the basement.

[12] Late afternoon meal.

Her image accompanied me even in places the most hostile to romance.[13] On Saturday evenings when my aunt went marketing I had to go to carry some of the parcels. We walked through the flaring streets, jostled by drunken men and bargaining women, amid the curses of labourers, the shrill litanies of shop-boys who stood on guard by the barrels of pigs' cheeks, the nasal chanting of street-singers, who sang a *come-all-you* about O'Donovan Rossa,[14] or a ballad about the troubles in our native land. These noises converged in a single sensation of life for me: I imagined that I bore my chalice[15] safely through a throng of foes. Her name sprang to my lips at moments in strange prayers and praises which I myself did not understand. My eyes were often full of tears (I could not tell why) and at times a flood from my heart seemed to pour itself out into my bosom. I thought little of the future. I did not know whether I would ever speak to her or not or, if I spoke to her, how I could tell her of my confused adoration. But my body was like a harp and her words and gestures were like fingers running upon the wires.

One evening I went into the back drawing-room in which the priest had died. It was a dark rainy evening and there was no sound in the house. Through one of the broken panes I heard the rain impinge upon the earth, the fine incessant needles of water playing in the sodden beds. Some distant lamp or lighted window gleamed below me. I was thankful that I could see so little. All my senses seemed to desire to veil themselves and, feeling that I was about to slip from them, I pressed the palms of my hands together until they trembled, murmuring: *O love! O love!* many times.

At last she spoke to me. When she addressed the first words to me I was so confused that I did not know what to answer. She asked me was I going to *Araby*. I forget whether I answered yes or no. It would be a splendid bazaar, she said; she would love to go.

—And why can't you? I asked.

While she spoke she turned a silver bracelet round and round her wrist. She could not go, she said, because there would be a retreat

---

[13] An affair of the heart, but also a genre of heroism and magical adventure in which a knight's strength and virtue is tested.

[14] Irish nationalist and editor Jeremiah O'Donovan (1831–1915) twice imprisoned by the British for fomenting rebellion. Popular songs and street ballads sometimes begin with a call to the audience, as in "Come all you Irish gentlemen and listen to my song."

[15] Reference to stories about the quest for the Holy Grail—the cup Jesus used at the Last Supper and which later caught his blood at his crucifixion.

that week in her convent.[16] Her brother and two other boys were fighting for their caps and I was alone at the railings. She held one of the spikes, bowing her head towards me. The light from the lamp opposite our door caught the white curve of her neck, lit up her hair that rested there and, falling, lit up the hand upon the railing. It fell over one side of her dress and caught the white border of a petticoat, just visible as she stood at ease.

—It's well for you, she said.[17]

—If I go, I said, I will bring you something.

What innumerable follies laid waste my waking and sleeping thoughts after that evening! I wished to annihilate the tedious intervening days. I chafed against the work of school. At night in my bedroom and by day in the classroom her image came between me and the page I strove to read. The syllables of the word *Araby* were called to me through the silence in which my soul luxuriated and cast an Eastern enchantment over me. I asked for leave to go to the bazaar on Saturday night. My aunt was surprised and hoped it was not some Freemason[18] affair. I answered few questions in class. I watched my master's face pass from amiability to sternness; he hoped I was not beginning to idle. I could not call my wandering thoughts together. I had hardly any patience with the serious work of life which, now that it stood between me and my desire, seemed to me child's play, ugly monotonous child's play.

On Saturday morning I reminded my uncle that I wished to go to the bazaar in the evening. He was fussing at the hallstand, looking for the hat-brush, and answered me curtly:

—Yes, boy, I know.

As he was in the hall I could not go into the front parlour and lie at the window. I left the house in bad humour and walked slowly towards the school. The air was pitilessly raw and already my heart misgave me.

When I came home to dinner my uncle had not yet been home. Still it was early. I sat staring at the clock for some time and, when its ticking began to irritate me, I left the room. I mounted the staircase and gained the upper part of the house. The high cold empty gloomy rooms liberated me and I went from room to room singing. From

[16] Catholic girls' school run by nuns; a retreat is a period of withdrawal for reflection and prayer.

[17] A lightly sarcastic expression.

[18] The Masonic order, a secret fraternal society, was looked upon with some suspicion by Catholics.

the front window I saw my companions playing below in the street. Their cries reached me weakened and indistinct and, leaning my forehead against the cool glass, I looked over at the dark house where she lived. I may have stood there for an hour, seeing nothing but the brown-clad figure cast by my imagination, touched discreetly by the lamplight at the curved neck, at the hand upon the railings and at the border below the dress.

When I came downstairs again I found Mrs Mercer sitting at the fire. She was an old garrulous woman, a pawnbroker's widow, who collected used stamps[19] for some pious purpose. I had to endure the gossip of the tea-table. The meal was prolonged beyond an hour and still my uncle did not come. Mrs Mercer stood up to go: she was sorry she couldn't wait any longer, but it was after eight o'clock and she did not like to be out late, as the night air was bad for her. When she had gone I began to walk up and down the room, clenching my fists. My aunt said:

—I'm afraid you may put off your bazaar for this night of Our Lord.

At nine o'clock I heard my uncle's latchkey in the halldoor. I heard him talking to himself and heard the hallstand rocking when it had received the weight of his overcoat. I could interpret these signs. When he was midway through his dinner I asked him to give me the money to go to the bazaar. He had forgotten.

—The people are in bed and after their first sleep now, he said.

I did not smile. My aunt said to him energetically:

—Can't you give him the money and let him go? You've kept him late enough as it is.

My uncle said he was very sorry he had forgotten. He said he believed in the old saying: *All work and no play makes Jack a dull boy.* He asked me where I was going and when I had told him a second time he asked me did I know *The Arab's Farewell to his Steed.*[20] When I left the kitchen he was about to recite the opening lines of the piece to my aunt.

I held a florin[21] tightly in my hand as I strode down Buckingham Street towards the station. The sight of the streets thronged with buyers and glaring with gas recalled to me the purpose of my journey.

---

[19] These were saleable items, often collected for Catholic charities.

[20] A poem by the scandal-ridden political activist and author, Caroline Norton (1808–77) about an Arab who sells his prize horse only to change his mind at the last moment. See p. xx.

[21] Two-shilling coin—enough for tram fare, snacks, and trinkets.

I took my seat in a third-class carriage of a deserted train. After an intolerable delay the train moved out of the station slowly. It crept onward among ruinous houses and over the twinkling river. At Westland Row Station a crowd of people pressed to the carriage doors; but the porters moved them back, saying that it was a special train for the bazaar. I remained alone in the bare carriage. In a few minutes the train drew up beside an improvised wooden platform. I passed out on to the road and saw by the lighted dial of a clock that it was ten minutes to ten. In front of me was a large building which displayed the magical name.

I could not find any sixpenny entrance and, fearing that the bazaar would be closed, I passed in quickly through a turnstile, handing a shilling[22] to a weary-looking man. I found myself in a big hall girdled at half its height by a gallery. Nearly all the stalls were closed and the greater part of the hall was in darkness. I recognised a silence like that which pervades a church after a service. I walked into the centre of the bazaar timidly. A few people were gathered about the stalls which were still open. Before a curtain, over which the words *Café Chantant*[23] were written in coloured lamps, two men were counting money on a salver.[24] I listened to the fall of the coins.

Remembering with difficulty why I had come I went over to one of the stalls and examined porcelain vases and flowered tea-sets. At the door of the stall a young lady was talking and laughing with two young gentlemen. I remarked their English accents and listened vaguely to their conversation.

—O, I never said such a thing!

—O, but you did!

—O, but I didn't!

—Didn't she say that?

—Yes. I heard her.

—O, there's a … fib!

Observing me the young lady came over and asked me did I wish to buy anything. The tone of her voice was not encouraging; she seemed to have spoken to me out of a sense of duty. I looked humbly at the great jars that stood like eastern guards at either side of the dark entrance to the stall and murmured:

—No, thank you.

---

[22] Coin worth 12 pence—over half the money given to him.

[23] "Singing coffeehouse" (French), with musical and other popular entertainments.

[24] Metal tray.

The young lady changed the position of one of the vases and went back to the two young men. They began to talk of the same subject. Once or twice the young lady glanced at me over her shoulder.

I lingered before her stall, though I knew my stay was useless, to make my interest in her wares seem the more real. Then I turned away slowly and walked down the middle of the bazaar. I allowed the two pennies to fall against the sixpence in my pocket. I heard a voice call from one end of the gallery that the light was out. The upper part of the hall was now completely dark.

Gazing up into the darkness I saw myself as a creature driven and derided by vanity;[25] and my eyes burned with anguish and anger.

---

[25] Not just self-love but theologically a reference to the pointlessness of human effort in the world.

Eveline

She sat at the window watching the evening invade the avenue. Her head was leaned against the window curtains and in her nostrils was the odour of dusty cretonne.[1] She was tired.

Few people passed. The man out of the last house passed on his way home; she heard his footsteps clacking along the concrete pavement and afterwards crunching on the cinder path before the new red houses. One time there used to be a field there in which they used to play every evening with other people's children. Then a man from Belfast[2] bought the field and built houses in it—not like their little brown houses but bright brick houses with shining roofs. The children of the avenue used to play together in that field—the Devines, the Waters, the Dunns, little Keogh the cripple, she and her brothers and sisters. Ernest, however, never played: he was too grown up. Her father used often to hunt them in out of the field with his blackthorn stick;[3] but usually little Keogh used to keep nix[4] and call out when he saw her father coming. Still they seemed to have been rather happy then. Her father was not so bad then,; and besides, her mother was alive. That was a long time ago; she and her brothers and sisters were all grown up; her mother was dead. Tizzie Dunn was dead, too, and the Waters had gone back to England. Everything changes. Now she was going to go away like the others, to leave her home.

Home! She looked round the room, reviewing all its familiar objects which she had dusted once a week for so many years, wondering where on earth all the dust came from. Perhaps she would never see again those familiar objects from which she had never

[1] Heavy fabric, for curtains and upholstery.
[2] A major city in the North of Ireland with a large, wealthy Protestant population.
[3] Walking stick.
[4] Keep a lookout.

dreamed of being divided. And yet during all those years she had never found out the name of the priest whose yellowing photograph hung on the wall above the broken harmonium[5] beside the coloured print of the promises made to Blessed Margaret Mary Alacoque.[6] He had been a school friend of her father. Whenever he showed the photograph to a visitor her father used to pass it with a casual word:

—He is in Melbourne[7] now.

She had consented to go away, to leave her home. Was that wise? She tried to weigh each side of the question. In her home anyway she had shelter and food; she had those whom she had known all her life about her. Of course she had to work hard, both in the house and at business. What would they say of her in the Stores when they found out that she had run away with a fellow? Say she was a fool, perhaps; and her place would be filled up by advertisement. Miss Gavan would be glad. She had always had an edge on her, especially whenever there were people listening.

—Miss Hill, don't you see these ladies are waiting?

—Look lively, Miss Hill, please.

She would not cry many tears at leaving the Stores.

But in her new home, in a distant unknown country, it would not be like that. Then she would be married—she, Eveline. People would treat her with respect then. She would not be treated as her mother had been. Even now, though she was over nineteen, she sometimes felt herself in danger of her father's violence. She knew it was that that had given her the palpitations. When they were growing up he had never gone for her like he used to go for Harry and Ernest, because she was a girl; but latterly he had begun to threaten her and say what he would do to her only for her dead mother's sake. And now she had nobody to protect her. Ernest was dead and Harry, who was in the church decorating business, was nearly always down somewhere in the country. Besides, the invariable squabble for money on Saturday nights had begun to weary her unspeakably. She always gave her entire wages—seven shillings[8]—and Harry always sent up what he could but the trouble was to get any money from her father.

---

[5] Small reed organ.

[6] French nun Margaret Mary Alacoque (1647–90) helped establish the Devotion to the Sacred Heart of Jesus, receiving a vision of the twelve promises he made to the faithful (see p. xxx). The most relevant here: "I will establish peace in their homes." Beatified in 1864, she was canonized as a saint in 1920.

[7] This major city in colonial Australia was a destination for many Irish immigrants.

[8] A very low wage.

He said she used to squander the money, that she had no head, that he wasn't going to give her his hard-earned money to throw about the streets, and much more, for he was usually fairly bad on Saturday night. In the end he would give her the money and ask her had she any intention of buying Sunday's dinner. Then she had to rush out as quickly as she could and do her marketing, holding her black leather purse tightly in her hand as she elbowed her way through the crowds and returning home late under her load of provisions. She had hard work to keep the house together and to see that the two young children who had been left to her charge went to school regularly and got their meals regularly. It was hard work—a hard life—but now that she was about to leave it she did not find it a wholly undesirable life.

She was about to explore another life with Frank.[9] Frank was very kind, manly, open-hearted. She was to go away with him by the night-boat[10] to be his wife and to live with him in Buenos Ayres[11] where he had a home waiting for her. How well she remembered the first time she had seen him; he was lodging in a house on the main road where she used to visit. It seemed a few weeks ago. He was standing at the gate, his peaked cap pushed back on his head and his hair tumbled forward over a face of bronze. Then they had come to know each other. He used to meet her outside the Stores every evening and see her home. He took her to see *The Bohemian Girl*[12] and she felt elated as she sat in an unaccustomed part of the theatre with him.[13] He was awfully fond of music and sang a little. People knew that they were courting and, when he sang about the lass that loves a sailor,[14] she always felt pleasantly confused. He used to call her Poppens[15] out of fun. First of all it had

---

[9] The word "frank" means open and honest, but it's not clear if the pun is ironic or sincere.

[10] A steamer leaving Dublin every evening—likely for the international port of Liverpool in England. The phrase "to go to Buenos Aires" was also 19th-c. slang for working as a prostitute.

[11] This capital of Argentina was another destination for Irish immigrants. It means "good airs" in Spanish.

[12] A popular romantic operetta by Dublin musician Michael Balfe and Alfred Bunn, first performed in London in 1843, about an exiled nobleman and a young noblewoman who was kidnapped and raised by gypsies. See p. xxx.

[13] Expensive seats.

[14] Popular patriotic song by British composer Charles Dibdin (1745–1815) that includes the lines: "*the standing toast that pleased the most/Was the wind that blows,/The ship that goes,/And the lass that loves a sailor!*" See p. xxx.

[15] A term of endearment, from "poppet."

been an excitement for her to have a fellow and then she had begun to like him. He had tales of distant countries. He had started as a deck boy at a pound a month on a ship of the Allan Line[16] going out to Canada. He told her the names of the ships he had been on and the names of the different services. He had sailed through the Straits of Magellan[17] and he told her stories of the terrible Patagonians. He had fallen on his feet in Buenos Ayres, he said, and had come over to the old country just for a holiday. Of course, her father had found out the affair and had forbidden her to have anything to say to him.

—I know these sailor chaps, he said.

One day he had quarrelled with Frank and after that she had to meet her lover secretly.

The evening deepened in the avenue. The white of two letters in her lap grew indistinct. One was to Harry; the other was to her father. Ernest had been her favourite but she liked Harry too. Her father was becoming old lately, she noticed; he would miss her. Sometimes he could be very nice. Not long before, when she had been laid up for a day, he had read her out a ghost story and made toast for her at the fire. Another day, when their mother was alive, they had all gone for a picnic to the Hill of Howth.[18] She remembered her father putting on her mother's bonnet to make the children laugh.

Her time was running out but she continued to sit by the window, leaning her head against the window curtain, inhaling the odour of dusty cretonne. Down far in the avenue she could hear a street organ[19] playing. She knew the air.[20] Strange that it should come that very night to remind her of the promise to her mother, her promise to keep the home together as long as she could. She remembered the last night of her mother's illness; she was again in the close dark room at the other side of the hall and outside she heard a melancholy air of Italy. The organ-player had been ordered to go away and given sixpence. She remembered her father strutting back into the sickroom saying:

—Damned Italians! coming over here!

---

[16] A real steamship line that traveled to North and South America.

[17] Passage around the tip of South America (Patagonia), whose natives were described as primitive savages in Charles Darwin's *Voyage of the Beagle* (1839).

[18] A park-like, seaside bluff north of Dublin.

[19] A mechanical organ cranked by an operator who asks for money.

[20] Tune.

As she mused the pitiful vision of her mother's life laid its spell on the very quick of her being—that life of commonplace sacrifices closing in final craziness. She trembled as she heard again her mother's voice saying constantly with foolish insistence:

—Derevaun Seraun! Derevaun Seraun![21]

She stood up in a sudden impulse of terror. Escape! She must escape! Frank would save her. He would give her life, perhaps love, too. But she wanted to live. Why should she be unhappy? She had a right to happiness. Frank would take her in his arms, fold her in his arms. He would save her.

* * *

She stood among the swaying crowd in the station at the North Wall.[22] He held her hand and she knew that he was speaking to her, saying something about the passage over and over again. The station was full of soldiers with brown baggages. Through the wide doors of the sheds she caught a glimpse of the black mass of the boat, lying in beside the quay wall, with illumined portholes. She answered nothing. She felt her cheek pale and cold and, out of a maze of distress, she prayed to God to direct her, to show her what was her duty. The boat blew a long mournful whistle into the mist. If she went, tomorrow she would be on the sea with Frank, steaming towards Buenos Ayres. Their passage had been booked. Could she still draw back after all he had done for her? Her distress awoke a nausea in her body and she kept moving her lips in silent fervent prayer.

A bell clanged upon her heart. She felt him seize her hand:

—Come!

All the seas of the world tumbled about her heart. He was drawing her into them: he would drown her. She gripped with both hands at the iron railing.

—Come!

No! No! No! It was impossible. Her hands clutched the iron in frenzy. Amid the seas she sent a cry of anguish!

—Eveline! Evvy!

He rushed beyond the barrier and called to her to follow. He was shouted at to go on but he still called to her. She set her white face to him, passive, like a helpless animal. Her eyes gave him no sign of love or farewell or recognition.

[21] Apparently nonsense, though it sounds Gaelic. A famous textual crux, dozens of different interpretations have been offered by scholars.

[22] A large seawall and dock on Dublin Bay.

After the Race[1]

The cars came scudding in towards Dublin, running evenly like pellets in the groove of the Naas Road.[2] At the crest of the hill at Inchicore sightseers had gathered in clumps to watch the cars careering home-ward and through this channel of poverty and inaction the Continent[3] sped its wealth and industry. Now and again the clumps of people raised the cheer of the gratefully oppressed. Their sympathy, however, was for the blue cars—the cars of their friends, the French.[4]

The French, moreover, were virtual victors. Their team had fin-ished solidly; they had been placed second and third and the driver of the winning German car was reported a Belgian. Each blue car, there-fore, received a double measure of welcome as it topped the crest of the hill and each cheer of welcome was acknowledged with smiles and nods by those in the car. In one of these trimly built cars was a party of four young men whose spirits seemed to be at present well above the level of successful Gallicism:[5] in fact, these four young men were almost hilarious. They were Charles Ségouin, the owner of the car; André Rivière, a young electrician of Canadian birth; a huge Hungarian named Villona and a neatly groomed young man named Doyle. Ségouin was in good humour because he had unexpectedly received some orders in advance (he was about to start a motor estab-lishment in Paris) and Rivière was in good humour because he was to be appointed manager of the establishment; these two young men

[1] Refers to the July 2, 1903 Gordon-Bennett auto race, which pitted international teams of drivers against one another on a 370-mile course; but can also mean "a por-trait of the Irish people."

[2] This road courses from the southwest though the Dublin suburb of Inchicore and was part of the Gordon-Bennett race.

[3] Teams from Continental European countries.

[4] Catholic France often allied with Ireland against Protestant England.

[5] Gaul is the ancient name for France; the team is pleased with the Irish support.

(who were cousins) were also in good humour because of the success of the French cars. Villona was in good humour because he had had a very satisfactory luncheon; and besides he was an optimist by nature. The fourth member of the party, however, was too excited to be genuinely happy.

He was about twenty-six years of age, with a soft, light brown moustache and rather innocent-looking grey eyes. His father, who had begun life as an advanced Nationalist,[6] had modified his views early. He had made his money as a butcher in Kingstown[7] and by opening shops in Dublin and in the suburbs he had made his money many times over. He had also been fortunate enough to secure some of the police contracts[8] and in the end he had become rich enough to be alluded to in the Dublin newspapers as a merchant prince. He had sent his son to England to be educated in a big Catholic college and had afterwards sent him to Dublin University[9] to study law. Jimmy did not study very earnestly and took to bad courses for a while. He had money and he was popular; and he divided his time curiously between musical and motoring circles. Then he had been sent for a term to Cambridge[10] to see a little life. His father, remonstrative, but covertly proud of the excess, had paid his bills and brought him home. It was at Cambridge that he had met Ségouin. They were not much more than acquaintances as yet but Jimmy found great pleasure in the society of one who had seen so much of the world and was reputed to own some of the biggest hotels in France. Such a person (as his father agreed) was well worth knowing, even if he had not been the charming companion he was. Villona was entertaining also—a brilliant pianist—but, unfortunately, very poor.

The car ran on merrily with its cargo of hilarious youth. The two cousins sat on the front seat; Jimmy and his Hungarian friend sat behind. Decidedly Villona was in excellent spirits; he kept up a deep bass hum of melody for miles of the road. The Frenchmen flung their laughter and light words over their shoulders and often Jimmy had to strain forward to catch the quick phrase. This was not altogether pleasant for him, as he had nearly always to make a

---

[6] Supporter of Irish Home Rule and the Irish Parliamentary Party leader, Charles Stewart Parnell. See p. xxx.

[7] Large, relatively Unionist (pro-British; anti-Nationalist) town just southeast of Dublin.

[8] Government contracts to supply jails and police barracks.

[9] Trinity College, which primarily enrolled Anglo-Irish students.

[10] Prestigious English university where Jimmy might gain important social connections.

deft guess at the meaning and shout back a suitable answer in the face of a high wind. Besides Villona's humming would confuse anybody; the noise of the car, too.

Rapid motion through space elates one; so does notoriety; so does the possession of money. These were three good reasons for Jimmy's excitement. He had been seen by many of his friends that day in the company of these Continentals. At the control[11] Ségouin had presented him to one of the French competitors and, in answer to his confused murmur of compliment, the swarthy face of the driver had disclosed a line of shining white teeth. It was pleasant after that honour to return to the profane world of spectators amid nudges and significant looks. Then as to money—he really had a great sum under his control. Ségouin, perhaps, would not think it a great sum but Jimmy who, in spite of temporary errors, was at heart the inheritor of solid instincts knew well with what difficulty it had been got together. This knowledge had previously kept his bills within the limits of reasonable recklessness and, if he had been so conscious of the labour latent in money when there had been question merely of some freak[12] of the higher intelligence, how much more so now when he was about to stake the greater part of his substance! It was a serious thing for him.

Of course, the investment was a good one and Ségouin had managed to give the impression that it was by a favour of friendship the mite of Irish money was to be included in the capital of the concern. Jimmy had a respect for his father's shrewdness in business matters and in this case it had been his father who had first suggested the investment; money to be made in the motor business, pots of money. Moreover, Ségouin had the unmistakable air of wealth. Jimmy set out to translate into days' work that lordly car in which he sat. How smoothly it ran. In what style they had come careering along the country roads! The journey laid a magical finger on the genuine pulse of life and gallantly the machinery of human nerves strove to answer the bounding courses of the swift blue animal.

They drove down Dame Street.[13] The street was busy with unusual traffic, loud with the horns of motorists and the gongs of impatient tram-drivers. Near the Bank[14] Ségouin drew up and Jimmy

---

[11] A marker on the racecourse.

[12] Whim or caprice.

[13] A major boulevard in the south of Dublin.

[14] The Bank of Ireland building was the former home of the Irish Parliament before its dissolution by the 1800 Acts of Union.

and his friend alighted. A little knot of people collected on the footpath to pay homage to the snorting motor. The party was to dine together that evening in Ségouin's hotel and, meanwhile, Jimmy and his friend, who was staying with him, were to go home to dress. The car steered out slowly for Grafton Street[15] while the two young men pushed their way through the knot of gazers. They walked northward with a curious feeling of disappointment in the exercise, while the city hung its pale globes of light above them in a haze of summer evening.

In Jimmy's house this dinner had been pronounced an occasion. A certain pride mingled with his parents' trepidation, a certain eagerness, also, to play fast and loose for the names of great foreign cities have at least this virtue. Jimmy, too, looked very well when he was dressed and, as he stood in the hall giving a last equation to the bows of his dress tie, his father may have felt even commercially satisfied at having secured for his son qualities often unpurchasable. His father, therefore, was unusually friendly with Villona and his manner expressed a real respect for foreign accomplishments; but this subtlety of his host was probably lost upon the Hungarian, who was beginning to have a sharp desire for his dinner.

The dinner was excellent, exquisite. Ségouin, Jimmy decided, had a very refined taste. The party was increased by a young Englishman named Routh[16] whom Jimmy had seen with Ségouin at Cambridge. The young men supped in a snug room[17] lit by electric candle lamps. They talked volubly and with little reserve. Jimmy, whose imagination was kindling, conceived the lively youth of the Frenchmen twined elegantly upon the firm framework of the Englishman's manner. A graceful image of his, he thought, and a just one. He admired the dexterity with which their host directed the conversation. The five young men had various tastes and their tongues had been loosened. Villona, with immense respect, began to discover to the mildly surprised Englishman the beauties of the English madrigal,[18] deploring the loss of old instruments. Rivière, not wholly ingenuously, undertook to explain to Jimmy the triumph of the French mechanicians. The resonant voice of the Hungarian was about to prevail in ridicule of the spurious lutes of the romantic painters when Ségouin shepherded his party into politics.

---

[15] A central, fashionable thoroughfare.

[16] In Scots English, "routh" means "abundance or plenty" (*OED*).

[17] Private, usually curtained.

[18] A typically pastoral song based on complexly interwoven parts.

Here was congenial ground for all. Jimmy, under generous influences, felt the buried zeal of his father wake to life within him: he aroused the torpid Routh at last. The room grew doubly hot and Ségouin's task grew harder each moment: there was even danger of personal spite. The alert host at an opportunity lifted his glass to Humanity and, when the toast had been drunk, he threw open a window significantly.

That night the city wore the mask of a capital.[19] The five young men strolled along Stephen's Green[20] in a faint cloud of aromatic smoke. They talked loudly and gaily and their cloaks dangled from their shoulders. The people made way for them. At the corner of Grafton Street a short fat man was putting two handsome ladies on a car in charge of another fat man. The car drove off and the short fat man caught sight of the party.

—André.

—It's Farley!

A torrent of talk followed. Farley was an American. No one knew very well what the talk was about. Villona and Rivière were the noisiest, but all the men were excited. They got up on a car, squeezing themselves together amid much laughter. They drove by the crowd, blended now into soft colours, to a music of merry bells. They took the train at Westland Row and in a few seconds, as it seemed to Jimmy, they were walking out of Kingstown Station. The ticket-collector saluted Jimmy; he was an old man:

—Fine night, sir!

It was a serene summer night; the harbour lay like a darkened mirror at their feet. They proceeded towards it with linked arms, singing *Cadet Rousselle*[21] in chorus, stamping their feet at every:

—*Ho! Ho! Hohé, vraiment!*

They got into a rowboat at the slip and made out for the American's yacht. There was to be supper, music, cards. Villona said with conviction:

—It is beautiful!

There was a yacht piano in the cabin. Villona played a waltz for Farley and Rivière, Farley acting as cavalier and Rivière as lady. Then an impromptu square dance, the men devising original figures. What merriment! Jimmy took his part with a will; this was seeing life, at

---

[19] With the abolition of the Irish parliament, Dublin was no longer a capital city.

[20] A large and fashionable park.

[21] French marching song about an eccentric cadet, with this refrain: "Ho! Ho! Hohé, vraiment!/Cadet Rousselle est bon enfant" (... truly/Cadet Rousselle is a good kid).

least. Then Farley got out of breath and cried *Stop!* A man brought in a light supper, and the young men sat down to it for form's sake. They drank, however: it was Bohemian.[22] They drank[23] Ireland, England, France, Hungary, the United States of America. Jimmy made a speech, a long speech, Villona saying: *Hear! hear!* whenever there was a pause. There was a great clapping of hands when he sat down. It must have been a good speech. Farley clapped him on the back and laughed loudly. What jovial fellows! What good company they were!

Cards! cards! The table was cleared. Villona returned quietly to his piano and played voluntaries[24] for them. The other men played game after game, flinging themselves boldly into the adventure. They drank the health of the Queen of Hearts and of the Queen of Diamonds. Jimmy felt obscurely the lack of an audience: the wit was flashing. Play ran very high and paper[25] began to pass. Jimmy did not know exactly who was winning but he knew that he was losing. But it was his own fault for he frequently mistook his cards and the other men had to calculate his I.O.U.'s for him. They were devils of fellows but he wished they would stop: it was getting late. Someone gave the toast of the yacht *The Belle of Newport*[26] and then someone proposed one great game for a finish.

The piano had stopped; Villona must have gone up on deck. It was a terrible game. They stopped just before the end of it to drink for luck. Jimmy understood that the game lay between Routh and Ségouin. What excitement! Jimmy was excited too; he would lose, of course. How much had he written away? The men rose to their feet to play the last tricks, talking and gesticulating. Routh won. The cabin shook with the young men's cheering and the cards were bundled together. They began then to gather in what they had won. Farley and Jimmy were the heaviest losers.

He knew that he would regret in the morning but at present he was glad of the rest, glad of the dark stupor that would cover up his folly. He leaned his elbows on the table and rested his head between his hands, counting the beats of his temples. The cabin door opened and he saw the Hungarian standing in a shaft of grey light:

—Daybreak, gentlemen!

[22] Free-spirited.

[23] Toasted to.

[24] Improvisations.

[25] Debt markers, I.O.U.s.

[26] Newport, Rhode Island is a wealthy resort and fashionable yachting center.

Two Gallants[1]

THE GREY warm evening of August had descended upon the city and a mild warm air, a memory of summer, circulated in the streets. The streets, shuttered for the repose of Sunday, swarmed with a gaily coloured crowd. Like illumined pearls the lamps shone from the summits of their tall poles upon the living texture below which, changing shape and hue unceasingly, sent up into the warm grey evening air an unchanging unceasing murmur.

Two young men came down the hill of Rutland Square.[2] One of them was just bringing a long monologue to a close. The other, who walked on the verge of the path and was at times obliged to step on to the road, owing to his companion's rudeness, wore an amused listening face. He was squat and ruddy. A yachting cap was shoved far back from his forehead and the narrative to which he listened made constant waves of expression break forth over his face from the corners of his nose and eyes and mouth. Little jets of wheezing laughter followed one another out of his convulsed body. His eyes, twinkling with cunning enjoyment, glanced at every moment towards his companion's face. Once or twice he rearranged the light waterproof[3] which he had slung over one shoulder in toreador fashion.[4] His breeches, his white rubber shoes and his jauntily slung waterproof expressed youth. But his figure fell into rotundity at the waist, his hair was scant and grey and his face, when the waves of expression had passed over it, had a ravaged look.

---

[1] Archaism for a man of courtly manners, but in the 19th c. the word came to mean a lover, playboy, or flirt. Here it is used ironically to describe sexual aggression and brutality.

[2] Now Parnell Square, in central Dublin.

[3] Raincoat.

[4] Like a bullfighter's cape.

When he was quite sure that the narrative had ended he laughed noiselessly for fully half a minute. Then he said:

—Well! ... That takes the biscuit![5]

His voice seemed winnowed of vigour; and to enforce his words he added with humour:

—That takes the solitary, unique, and, if I may so call it, *recherché*[6] biscuit!

He became serious and silent when he had said this. His tongue was tired for he had been talking all the afternoon in a public-house[7] in Dorset Street.[8] Most people considered Lenehan a leech but, in spite of this reputation, his adroitness and eloquence had always prevented his friends from forming any general policy against him. He had a brave manner of coming up to a party of them in a bar and of holding himself nimbly at the borders of the company until he was included in a round.[9] He was a sporting vagrant armed with a vast stock of stories, limericks and riddles. He was insensitive to all kinds of discourtesy. No one knew how he achieved the stern task of living, but his name was vaguely associated with racing tissues.[10]

—And where did you pick her up, Corley? he asked.

Corley ran his tongue swiftly along his upper lip.

—One night, man, he said, I was going along Dame Street[11] and I spotted a fine tart[12] under Waterhouse's clock[13] and said good-night, you know. So we went for a walk round by the canal and she told me she was a slavey[14] in a house in Baggot Street.[15] I put my arm round her and squeezed her a bit that night. Then next Sunday, man, I met her by appointment. We went out to Donnybrook[16] and

---

[5] "That takes the cake."

[6] "Rare" (French).

[7] A pub or bar.

[8] Street in central Dublin connected vaguely with scandal.

[9] By custom, an individual buys drinks for the entire group, each member of which is then, in turn, expected to pay for the next "round" of drinks. Lenehan is thus cadging free drinks.

[10] Cheap news sheets about horse racing.

[11] Major thoroughfare south of the Liffey.

[12] Derogatory term for a woman; can refer to a prostitute.

[13] Waterhouse and Co. are jewelers.

[14] Domestic servant.

[15] Fashionable section of south Dublin.

[16] A rural village south of Dublin once famous for its raucous, often violent, annual fair.

I brought her into a field there. She told me she used to go with a dairyman.... It was fine, man. Cigarettes every night she'd bring me and paying the tram out and back. And one night she brought me two bloody fine cigars—O, the real cheese,[17] you know, that the old fellow used to smoke.... I was afraid, man, she'd get in the family way.[18] But she's up to the dodge.[19]

—Maybe she thinks you'll marry her, said Lenehan.

—I told her I was out of a job, said Corley. I told her I was in Pim's.[20] She doesn't know my name. I was too hairy[21] to tell her that. But she thinks I'm a bit of class,[22] you know.

Lenehan laughed again, noiselessly.

—Of all the good ones ever I heard, he said, that emphatically takes the biscuit.

Corley's stride acknowledged the compliment. The swing of his burly body made his friend execute a few light skips from the path to the roadway and back again. Corley was the son of an inspector of police[23] and he had inherited his father's frame and gait. He walked with his hands by his sides, holding himself erect and swaying his head from side to side. His head was large, globular and oily; it sweated in all weathers; and his large round hat, set upon it sideways, looked like a bulb which had grown out of another. He always stared straight before him as if he were on parade and, when he wished to gaze after someone in the street, it was necessary for him to move his body from the hips. At present he was about town.[24] Whenever any job was vacant a friend was always ready to give him the hard word.[25] He was often to be seen walking with policemen in plain clothes,[26] talking earnestly. He knew the inner side of all affairs and was fond of delivering final judgments. He spoke without listening to the speech of his companions. His conversation was mainly about himself: what he had said to such a

---

[17] Slang for "of high quality."

[18] Pregnant.

[19] Clever, cunning.

[20] Pim Brothers Ltd., a prosperous chain of furniture and interior decorating stores.

[21] Clever.

[22] Educated and cultured above the level of the working class.

[23] A position of some rank, closely connected to the colonial administration.

[24] Unemployed.

[25] Inside information.

[26] Secret police, often intent on suppressing Irish nationalist organizations.

person and what such a person had said to him and what he had said to settle the matter. When he reported these dialogues he aspirated the first letter of his name after the manner of Florentines.[27]

Lenehan offered his friend a cigarette. As the two young men walked on through the crowd Corley occasionally turned to smile at some of the passing girls but Lenehan's gaze was fixed on the large faint moon circled with a double halo. He watched earnestly the passing of the grey web of twilight across its face. At length he said:

—Well ... tell me, Corley, I suppose you'll be able to pull it off all right, eh?

Corley closed one eye expressively as an answer.

—Is she game for that? asked Lenehan dubiously. You can never know women.

—She's all right, said Corley. I know the way to get around her, man. She's a bit gone on me.

—You're what I call a gay Lothario,[28] said Lenehan. And the proper kind of a Lothario, too!

A shade of mockery relieved the servility of his manner. To save himself he had the habit of leaving his flattery open to the interpretation of raillery.[29] But Corley had not a subtle mind.

—There's nothing to touch a good slavey, he affirmed. Take my tip for it.

—By one who has tried them all, said Lenehan.

—First I used to go with girls, you know, said Corley, unbosoming; girls off the South Circular.[30] I used to take them out, man, on the tram somewhere and pay the tram or take them to a band or a play at the theatre or buy them chocolate and sweets or something that way. I used to spend money on them right enough, he added, in a convincing tone, as if he were conscious of being disbelieved.

But Lenehan could well believe it; he nodded gravely.

—I know that game, he said, and it's a mug's game.[31]

—And damn the thing I ever got out of it, said Corley.

---

[27] Affectedly pronouncing "c" as "h" ("Horley" or "Whorely").

[28] A libertine, from the name of a seducer in Nicholas Rowe's play, *The Fair Penitent* (1703), extremely popular in the 18th c.

[29] Teasing.

[30] South Circular Road. This road was a popular meeting place for poor singles.

[31] Pointless.

—Ditto here, said Lenehan.

—Only off of one of them, said Corley.

He moistened his upper lip by running his tongue along it. The recollection brightened his eyes. He too gazed at the pale disc of the moon, now nearly veiled, and seemed to meditate.

—She was ... a bit of all right, he said regretfully.

He was silent again. Then he added:

—She's on the turf[32] now. I saw her driving down Earl Street[33] one night with two fellows with her on a car.

—I suppose that's your doing, said Lenehan.

—There was others at her before me, said Corley philosophically.

This time Lenehan was inclined to disbelieve. He shook his head to and fro and smiled.

—You know you can't kid me, Corley, he said.

—Honest to God! said Corley. Didn't she tell me herself?

Lenehan made a tragic gesture.

—Base betrayer![34] he said.

As they passed along the railings of Trinity College,[35] Lenehan skipped out into the road and peered up at the clock.

—Twenty after, he said.

—Time enough, said Corley. She'll be there all right. I always let her wait a bit.

Lenehan laughed quietly.

—Ecod![36] Corley, you know how to take them, he said.

—I'm up to all their little tricks, Corley confessed.

—But tell me, said Lenehan again, are you sure you can bring it off all right? You know it's a ticklish job. They're damn close on that point. Eh? ... What?

His bright, small eyes searched his companion's face for reassurance. Corley swung his head to and fro as if to toss aside an insistent insect, and his brows gathered.

---

[32] A prostitute.

[33] A major street leading into Nighttown, Dublin's red-light district.

[34] In Sophocles's ancient Greek tragedy *Philoctetes* (5th c. BCE), the title character berates his son: "Thou worst of men! thou vile artificer / Of fraud most infamous! what hast thou done? / How have I been deceived? Dost thou not blush / To look on me, to behold me thus / Beneath thy feet imploring? Base betrayer! / To rob me of my bow, the means of life" (4. 795–800); translation by Cambridge professor of Greek, Thomas Francklin, 1834.

[35] The University, in the heart of the city, was surrounded by high iron fences.

[36] Egad!

—I'll pull it off, he said. Leave it to me, can't you?

Lenehan said no more. He did not wish to ruffle his friend's temper, to be sent to the devil and told that his advice was not wanted. A little tact was necessary. But Corley's brow was soon smooth again. His thoughts were running another way.

—She's a fine decent tart, he said, with appreciation; that's what she is.

They walked along Nassau Street and then turned into Kildare Street. Not far from the porch of the club a harpist stood in the roadway,[37] playing to a little ring of listeners. He plucked at the wires heedlessly, glancing quickly from time to time at the face of each new-comer and from time to time, wearily also, at the sky. His harp too, heedless that her coverings had fallen about her knees, seemed weary alike of the eyes of strangers and of her master's hands. One hand played in the bass the melody of *Silent, O Moyle*,[38] while the other hand careered in the treble after each group of notes. The notes of the air sounded deep and full.

The two young men walked up the street without speaking, the mournful music following them. When they reached Stephen's Green[39] they crossed the road. Here the noise of trams, the lights and the crowd released them from their silence.

—There she is! said Corley.

At the corner of Hume Street a young woman was standing. She wore a blue dress and a white sailor hat. She stood on the curbstone, swinging a sunshade in one hand. Lenehan grew lively.

—Let's have a squint at her, Corley, he said.

Corley glanced sideways at his friend and an unpleasant grin appeared on his face.

—Are you trying to get inside[40] me? he asked.

—Damn it! said Lenehan boldly, I don't want an introduction. All I want is to have a look at her. I'm not going to eat her.

—O ... A look at her? said Corley, more amiably. Well ... I'll tell you what. I'll go over and talk to her and you can pass by.

—Right! said Lenehan.

---

[37] They are passing the exclusive Kildare Street Club; the harp is a symbol of Ireland.

[38] Taken from the "Song of Fionnuala," a poem from Thomas Moore's *Irish Melodies*. (See p. xxx.) It tells the legend of a girl (the daughter of the sea-god, Lir) transformed into a swan and condemned to wander throughout Ireland until the spell is lifted by the arrival of Christianity. "Moyle" is a sea-channel.

[39] Large park surrounded by elegant homes.

[40] Get the advantage over (a horse-racing term).

Corley had already thrown one leg over the chains[41] when Lenehan called out:

—And after? Where will we meet?

—Half ten,[42] answered Corley, bringing over his other leg.

—Where?

—Corner of Merrion Street. We'll be coming back.

—Work it all right now, said Lenehan in farewell.

Corley did not answer. He sauntered across the road swaying his head from side to side. His bulk, his easy pace, and the solid sound of his boots had something of the conqueror in them. He approached the young woman and, without saluting, began at once to converse with her. She swung her umbrella more quickly and executed half turns on her heels. Once or twice when he spoke to her at close quarters she laughed and bent her head.

Lenehan observed them for a few minutes. Then he walked rapidly along beside the chains at some distance and crossed the road obliquely. As he approached Hume Street corner he found the air heavily scented and his eyes made a swift anxious scrutiny of the young woman's appearance. She had her Sunday finery on. Her blue serge skirt was held at the waist by a belt of black leather. The great silver buckle of her belt seemed to depress the centre of her body, catching the light stuff of her white blouse like a clip. She wore a short black jacket with mother-of-pearl buttons and a ragged black boa. The ends of her tulle collarette[43] had been carefully disordered and a big bunch of red flowers was pinned in her bosom stems upwards. Lenehan's eyes noted approvingly her stout short muscular body. Frank rude health glowed in her face, on her fat red cheeks and in her unabashed blue eyes. Her features were blunt. She had broad nostrils, a straggling mouth which lay open in a contented leer, and two projecting front teeth. As he passed Lenehan took off his cap and, after about ten seconds, Corley returned a salute to the air. This he did by raising his hand vaguely and pensively changing the angle of position of his hat.

Lenehan walked as far as the Shelbourne Hotel[44] where he halted and waited. After waiting for a little time he saw them coming towards him and, when they turned to the right, he followed

---

[41] Separating the street from the sidewalk.

[42] Half-past ten.

[43] High, decorative collar.

[44] Posh hotel facing Stephen's Green.

them, stepping lightly in his white shoes, down one side of Merrion Square. As he walked on slowly, timing his pace to theirs, he watched Corley's head which turned at every moment towards the young woman's face like a big ball revolving on a pivot. He kept the pair in view until he had seen them climbing the stairs of the Donnybrook tram;[45] then he turned about and went back the way he had come.

Now that he was alone his face looked older. His gaiety seemed to forsake him and, as he came by the railings of the Duke's Lawn,[46] he allowed his hand to run along them. The air which the harpist had played began to control his movements. His softly padded feet played the melody while his fingers swept a scale of variations idly along the railings after each group of notes.

He walked listlessly round Stephen's Green and then down Grafton Street. Though his eyes took note of many elements of the crowd through which he passed they did so morosely. He found trivial all that was meant to charm him and did not answer the glances which invited him to be bold. He knew that he would have to speak a great deal, to invent and to amuse, and his brain and throat were too dry for such a task. The problem of how he could pass the hours till he met Corley again troubled him a little. He could think of no way of passing them but to keep on walking. He turned to the left when he came to the corner of Rutland Square[47] and felt more at ease in the dark quiet street, the sombre look of which suited his mood. He paused at last before the window of a poor-looking shop over which the words *Refreshment Bar* were printed in white letters. On the glass of the window were two flying inscriptions: *Ginger Beer*[48] and *Ginger Ale*. A cut ham was exposed on a great blue dish while near it on a plate lay a segment of very light plum-pudding. He eyed this food earnestly for some time and then, after glancing warily up and down the street, went into the shop quickly.

He was hungry for, except some biscuits which he had asked two grudging curates[49] to bring him, he had eaten nothing since breakfast-time. He sat down at an uncovered wooden table opposite two work-girls and a mechanic. A slatternly[50] girl waited on him.

[45] See note 16.

[46] The lawn in front of Leinster House on affluent Merrion Square.

[47] Where this story began.

[48] Non-alcoholic soda.

[49] Technically a clergyman who assists a priest at mass; here it is slang for bartender.

[50] Untidy or slovenly.

—How much is a plate of peas? he asked.

—Three halfpence, sir, said the girl.

—Bring me a plate of peas, he said, and a bottle of ginger beer.

He spoke roughly in order to belie his air of gentility[51] for his entry had been followed by a pause of talk. His face was heated. To appear natural he pushed his cap back on his head and planted his elbows on the table. The mechanic and the two work-girls examined him point by point before resuming their conversation in a subdued voice. The girl brought him a plate of grocer's hot peas, seasoned with pepper and vinegar, a fork and his ginger beer. He ate his food greedily and found it so good that he made a note of the shop mentally. When he had eaten all the peas he sipped his ginger beer and sat for some time thinking of Corley's adventure. In his imagination he beheld the pair of lovers walking along some dark road; he heard Corley's voice in deep energetic gallantries and saw again the leer of the young woman's mouth. This vision made him feel keenly his own poverty of purse and spirit. He was tired of knocking about, of pulling the devil by the tail,[52] of shifts and intrigues. He would be thirty-one in November. Would he never get a good job? Would he never have a home of his own? He thought how pleasant it would be to have a warm fire to sit by and a good dinner to sit down to. He had walked the streets long enough with friends and with girls. He knew what those friends were worth: he knew the girls too. Experience had embittered his heart against the world. But all hope had not left him. He felt better after having eaten than he had felt before, less weary of his life, less vanquished in spirit. He might yet be able to settle down in some snug corner and live happily if he could only come across some good simple-minded girl with a little of the ready.[53]

He paid twopence halfpenny to the slatternly girl and went out of the shop to begin his wandering again. He went into Capel Street and walked along towards the City Hall. Then he turned into Dame Street.[54] At the corner of George's Street he met two friends of his and stopped to converse with them. He was glad that he could rest from all his walking. His friends asked him had he seen Corley and what

---

[51] He's trying to conceal his middle-class manners in this working-class café.

[52] Being broke.

[53] Money.

[54] He has again crossed to the south side of central Dublin and is slowly making his way back to Merrion Street.

was the latest. He replied that he had spent the day with Corley. His friends talked very little. They looked vacantly after some figures in the crowd and sometimes made a critical remark. One said that he had seen Mac an hour before in Westmoreland Street. At this Lenehan said that he had been with Mac the night before in Egan's.[55] The young man who had seen Mac in Westmoreland Street asked was it true that Mac had won a bit over a billiard match. Lenehan did not know: he said that Holohan had stood them drinks[56] in Egan's.

He left his friends at a quarter to ten and went up George's Street. He turned to the left at the City Markets and walked on into Grafton Street. The crowd of girls and young men had thinned and on his way up the street he heard many groups and couples bidding one another good-night. He went as far as the clock of the College of Surgeons:[57] it was on the stroke of ten. He set off briskly along the northern side of the Green hurrying for fear Corley should return too soon. When he reached the corner of Merrion Street he took his stand in the shadow of a lamp and brought out one of the cigarettes which he had reserved and lit it. He leaned against the lamp-post and kept his gaze fixed on the part from which he expected to see Corley and the young woman return.

His mind became active again. He wondered had Corley managed it successfully. He wondered if he had asked her yet or if he would leave it to the last. He suffered all the pangs and thrills of his friend's situation as well as those of his own. But the memory of Corley's slowly revolving head calmed him somewhat: he was sure Corley would pull it off all right. All at once the idea struck him that perhaps Corley had seen her home by another way and given him the slip. His eyes searched the street: there was no sign of them. Yet it was surely half-an-hour since he had seen the clock of the College of Surgeons. Would Corley do a thing like that? He lit his last cigarette and began to smoke it nervously. He strained his eyes as each tram stopped at the far corner of the square. They must have gone home by another way. The paper of his cigarette broke and he flung it into the road with a curse.

Suddenly he saw them coming towards him. He started with delight and, keeping close to his lamp-post tried to read the result in their walk. They were walking quickly, the young woman taking

---

[55] A pub named the Oval run by John J. Egan.

[56] Paid for drinks.

[57] He's come full circle after leaving Corley and is now back at Stephen's Green.

quick short steps, while Corley kept beside her with his long stride. They did not seem to be speaking. An intimation of the result pricked him like the point of a sharp instrument. He knew Corley would fail; he knew it was no go.

They turned down Baggot Street and he followed them at once, taking the other footpath. When they stopped he stopped too. They talked for a few moments and then the young woman went down the steps into the area[58] of a house. Corley remained standing at the edge of the path, a little distance from the front steps. Some minutes passed. Then the hall-door was opened slowly and cautiously. A woman came running down the front steps and coughed. Corley turned and went towards her. His broad figure hid hers from view for a few seconds and then she reappeared running up the steps. The door closed on her and Corley began to walk swiftly towards Stephen's Green.

Lenehan hurried on in the same direction. Some drops of light rain fell. He took them as a warning and, glancing back towards the house which the young woman had entered to see that he was not observed, he ran eagerly across the road. Anxiety and his swift run made him pant. He called out:

—Hallo, Corley!

—Corley turned his head to see who had called him, and then continued walking as before. Lenehan ran after him, settling the waterproof on his shoulders with one hand.

—Hallo, Corley! he cried again.

He came level with his friend and looked keenly in his face. He could see nothing there.

—Well? he said. Did it come off?

They had reached the corner of Ely Place.[59] Still without answering, Corley swerved to the left and went up the side street. His features were composed in stern calm. Lenehan kept up with his friend, breathing uneasily. He was baffled and a note of menace pierced through his voice.

—Can't you tell us? he said. Did you try her?

Corley halted at the first lamp and stared grimly before him. Then with a grave gesture he extended a hand towards the light and, smiling, opened it slowly to the gaze of his disciple. A small gold coin[60] shone in the palm.

[58] See "Araby," p. xx, n. 11.

[59] A quiet cul-de-sac off Baggot Street.

[60] A sovereign (worth 20 shillings or £1)—a very large sum for a servant.

The Boarding House

Mrs Mooney was a butcher's daughter. She was a woman who was quite able to keep things to herself: a determined woman. She had married her father's foreman and opened a butcher's shop near Spring Gardens.[1] But as soon as his father-in-law was dead Mr Mooney began to go to the devil. He drank, plundered the till, ran headlong into debt. It was no use making him take the pledge:[2] he was sure to break out again a few days after. By fighting his wife in the presence of customers and by buying bad meat he ruined his business. One night he went for his wife with the cleaver and she had to sleep in a neighbour's house.

After that they lived apart. She went to the priest and got a separation from him with care of the children.[3] She would give him neither money nor food nor house-room; and so he was obliged to enlist himself as a sheriff's man.[4] He was a shabby stooped little drunkard with a white face and a white moustache and white eyebrows, pencilled above his little eyes, which were pink-veined and raw; and all day long he sat in the bailiff's room, waiting to be put on a job. Mrs Mooney, who had taken what remained of her money out of the butcher business and set up a boarding house in Hardwicke Street, was a big imposing woman. Her house had a floating population made up of tourists from Liverpool and the Isle of Man and, occasionally, *artistes* from the music halls.[5] Its resident

---

[1] On the northeastern edge of the city.

[2] Public promise to stop drinking.

[3] Catholic doctrine basically prevented legal divorce, but a priest could provide this kind of formal separation; and it was customary for the father and not the mother to get custody of any children (one reason many women stayed in abusive marriages).

[4] A bailiff, who collected debts and served legal papers like eviction notices.

[5] Actors, singers, and entertainers—professions considered barely respectable and sometimes scandalous.

population was made up of clerks from the city. She governed the house cunningly and firmly, knew when to give credit, when to be stern and when to let things pass. All the resident young men[6] spoke of her as The Madam.[7]

Mrs Mooney's young men paid fifteen shillings a week for board and lodgings (beer or stout at dinner excluded). They shared in common tastes and occupations and for this reason they were very chummy with one another. They discussed with one another the chances of favourites and outsiders.[8] Jack Mooney, the Madam's son, who was clerk to a commission agent in Fleet Street,[9] had the reputation of being a hard case. He was fond of using soldiers' obscenities: usually he came home in the small hours. When he met his friends he had always a good one to tell them and he was always sure to be on to a good thing—that is to say, a likely horse or a likely *artiste*. He was also handy with the mits[10] and sang comic songs. On Sunday nights there would often be a reunion in Mrs Mooney's front drawing-room. The music-hall *artistes* would oblige; and Sheridan played waltzes and polkas and vamped[11] accompaniments. Polly Mooney, the Madam's daughter, would also sing. She sang:

> *I'm a ... naughty girl.*
> *You needn't sham:*
> *You know I am.*[12]

Polly was a slim girl of nineteen; she had light soft hair and a small full mouth. Her eyes, which were grey with a shade of green through them, had a habit of glancing upwards when she spoke with anyone, which made her look like a little perverse madonna. Mrs Mooney had first sent her daughter to be a typist in a corn-factor's office[13] but, as a disreputable sheriff's man used to come every other day to the office, asking to be allowed to say a word to

---

[6] The house is clearly for men only—a not uncommon restriction.

[7] While "Madam" is a term of respect, "The Madam" is typically the head of a brothel.

[8] Horse racing terms.

[9] A debt collector, working on commission.

[10] A good fighter or boxer.

[11] Improvised with flair.

[12] For this song, see p. xx.

[13] Grain-dealing business. Typing was a new, distinctly modern profession, replacing the work of scribes such as Farrington in "Counterparts."

his daughter, she had taken her daughter home again and set her to do housework. As Polly was very lively the intention was to give her the run of the young men. Besides, young men like to feel that there is a young woman not very far away. Polly, of course, flirted with the young men but Mrs Mooney, who was a shrewd judge, knew that the young men were only passing the time away: none of them meant business.[14] Things went on so for a long time and Mrs Mooney began to think of sending Polly back to typewriting when she noticed that something was going on between Polly and one of the young men. She watched the pair and kept her own counsel.

Polly knew that she was being watched, but still her mother's persistent silence could not be misunderstood. There had been no open complicity between mother and daughter, no open understanding but, though people in the house began to talk of the affair, still Mrs Mooney did not intervene. Polly began to grow a little strange in her manner and the young man was evidently perturbed. At last, when she judged it to be the right moment, Mrs Mooney intervened. She dealt with moral problems as a cleaver deals with meat: and in this case she had made up her mind.

It was a bright Sunday morning of early summer, promising heat, but with a fresh breeze blowing. All the windows of the boarding house were open and the lace curtains ballooned gently towards the street beneath the raised sashes. The belfry of George's Church[15] sent out constant peals and worshippers, singly or in groups, traversed the little circus[16] before the church, revealing their purpose by their self-contained demeanour no less than by the little volumes[17] in their gloved hands. Breakfast was over in the boarding house and the table of the breakfast-room was covered with plates on which lay yellow streaks of eggs with morsels of bacon-fat and bacon-rind. Mrs Mooney sat in the straw arm-chair and watched the servant Mary remove the breakfast things. She made Mary collect the crusts and pieces of broken bread to help to make Tuesday's bread-pudding.[18] When the table was cleared, the

---

[14] None were courting her for marriage.

[15] A Protestant church around the corner from the boarding house. St. George is the patron saint of England.

[16] Circular courtyard.

[17] Book of Common Prayer.

[18] A sign of Mrs. Mooney's economy, using the scraps to make dinner for her boarders later in the week. Bread pudding is a mixture of bread, milk, eggs, butter, sugar, and spices.

broken bread collected, the sugar and butter safe under lock and key, she began to reconstruct the interview which she had had the night before with Polly. Things were as she had suspected: she had been frank in her questions and Polly had been frank in her answers. Both had been somewhat awkward, of course. She had been made awkward by her not wishing to receive the news in too cavalier a fashion or to seem to have connived and Polly had been made awkward not merely because allusions of that kind always made her awkward but also because she did not wish it to be thought that in her wise innocence she had divined the intention behind her mother's tolerance.

Mrs Mooney glanced instinctively at the little gilt clock on the mantelpiece as soon as she had become aware through her revery that the bells of George's Church had stopped ringing. It was seventeen minutes past eleven: she would have lots of time to have the matter out with Mr Doran and then catch short twelve at Marlborough Street.[19] She was sure she would win. To begin with she had all the weight of social opinion on her side: she was an outraged mother. She had allowed him to live beneath her roof, assuming that he was a man of honour, and he had simply abused her hospitality. He was thirty-four or thirty-five years of age, so that youth could not be pleaded as his excuse; nor could ignorance be his excuse since he was a man who had seen something of the world. He had simply taken advantage of Polly's youth and inexperience: that was evident. The question was: What reparation[20] would he make?

There must be reparation made in such cases. It is all very well for the man: he can go his ways as if nothing had happened, having had his moment of pleasure, but the girl has to bear the brunt. Some mothers would be content to patch up such an affair for a sum of money; she had known cases of it. But she would not do so. For her only one reparation could make up for the loss of her daughter's honour: marriage.

She counted all her cards again before sending Mary up to Mr Doran's room to say that she wished to speak with him. She felt sure she would win. He was a serious young man, not rakish[21] or

---

[19] The short noon mass at the nearby Catholic Pro-Cathedral of the Immaculate Conception.

[20] The term carries a sense of both economic compensation for damage done and religious restoration (see n. 25 later). The term appears five times in the story, with subtly shifting meaning.

[21] Sexually aggressive.

loud-voiced like the others. If it had been Mr Sheridan or Mr Meade or Bantam Lyons her task would have been much harder. She did not think he would face publicity. All the lodgers in the house knew something of the affair; details had been invented by some. Besides, he had been employed for thirteen years in a great Catholic wine-merchant's office and publicity would mean for him, perhaps, the loss of his sit.[22] Whereas if he agreed all might be well. She knew he had a good screw for one thing and she suspected he had a bit of stuff put by.[23]

Nearly the half-hour! She stood up and surveyed herself in the pier-glass.[24] The decisive expression of her great florid face satisfied her and she thought of some mothers she knew who could not get their daughters off their hands.

Mr Doran was very anxious indeed this Sunday morning. He had made two attempts to shave but his hand had been so unsteady that he had been obliged to desist. Three days' reddish beard fringed his jaws and every two or three minutes a mist gathered on his glasses so that he had to take them off and polish them with his pocket-handkerchief. The recollection of his confession of the night before was a cause of acute pain to him; the priest had drawn out every ridiculous detail of the affair and in the end had so magnified his sin that he was almost thankful at being afforded a loophole of reparation.[25] The harm was done. What could he do now but marry her or run away? He could not brazen it out. The affair would be sure to be talked of and his employer would be certain to hear of it. Dublin is such a small city: everyone knows everyone else's business. He felt his heart leap warmly in his throat as he heard in his excited imagination old Mr Leonard calling out in his rasping voice: *Send Mr Doran here, please.*

All his long years of service gone for nothing! All his industry and diligence thrown away! As a young man he had sown his wild oats, of course; he had boasted of his free-thinking and denied the existence of God to his companions in public-houses. But that was all passed and done with ... nearly. He still bought a copy of *Reynolds's Newspaper*[26] every week but he attended to his religious

[22] Job.

[23] Money saved from his salary (screw).

[24] Large, wall-mounted mirror.

[25] After the ritual of confession, the priest orders penance in "reparation of the insult and injury offered to God by sin."

[26] London weekly featuring radical politics combined with scandal and sensationalism.

duties and for nine-tenths of the year lived a regular life. He had money enough to settle down on; it was not that. But the family would look down on her. First of all there was her disreputable father and then her mother's boarding house was beginning to get a certain fame. He had a notion that he was being had.[27] He could imagine his friends talking of the affair and laughing. She *was* a little vulgar; sometimes she said *I seen* and *If I had've known*. But what would grammar matter if he really loved her? He could not make up his mind whether to like her or despise her for what she had done. Of course, he had done it too. His instinct urged him to remain free, not to marry. Once you are married you are done for, it said.

While he was sitting helplessly on the side of the bed in shirt and trousers she tapped lightly at his door and entered. She told him all, that she had made a clean breast of it to her mother and that her mother would speak with him that morning. She cried and threw her arms round his neck, saying:

—O Bob! Bob! What am I to do? What am I to do at all?

She would put an end to herself, she said.

He comforted her feebly, telling her not to cry, that it would be all right, never fear. He felt against his shirt the agitation of her bosom.

It was not altogether his fault that it had happened. He remembered well, with the curious patient memory of the celibate, the first casual caresses her dress, her breath, her fingers had given him. Then late one night as he was undressing for bed she had tapped at his door, timidly. She wanted to relight her candle at his for hers had been blown out by a gust. It was her bath night. She wore a loose open combing-jacket[28] of printed flannel. Her white instep shone in the opening of her furry slippers and the blood glowed warmly behind her perfumed skin. From her hands and wrists too as she lit and steadied her candle a faint perfume arose.

On nights when he came in very late it was she who warmed up his dinner. He scarcely knew what he was eating feeling her beside him alone, at night, in the sleeping house. And her thoughtfulness! If the night was anyway cold or wet or windy there was sure to be a little tumbler of punch[29] ready for him. Perhaps they could be happy together....

---

[27] Tricked into marriage.

[28] Light robe.

[29] Warm, alcoholic drink.

They used to go upstairs together on tiptoe, each with a candle, and on the third landing exchange reluctant goodnights. They used to kiss. He remembered well her eyes, the touch of her hand and his delirium....

But delirium passes. He echoed her phrase, applying it to himself: *What am I to do?* The instinct of the celibate warned him to hold back. But the sin was there; even his sense of honour told him that reparation must be made for such a sin.

While he was sitting with her on the side of the bed Mary came to the door and said that the missus wanted to see him in the parlour. He stood up to put on his coat and waistcoat, more helpless than ever. When he was dressed he went over to her to comfort her. It would be all right, never fear. He left her crying on the bed and moaning softly: *O my God!*

Going down the stairs his glasses became so dimmed with moisture that he had to take them off and polish them. He longed to ascend through the roof and fly away to another country where he would never hear again of his trouble, and yet a force pushed him downstairs step by step. The implacable faces of his employer and of the Madam stared upon his discomfiture. On the last flight of stairs he passed Jack Mooney who was coming up from the pantry nursing two bottles of *Bass*.[30] They saluted coldly; and the lover's eyes rested for a second or two on a thick bulldog face and a pair of thick short arms. When he reached the foot of the staircase he glanced up and saw Jack regarding him from the door of the return-room.[31]

Suddenly he remembered the night when one of the music-hall *artistes*, a little blond Londoner, had made a rather free allusion to Polly. The reunion had been almost broken up on account of Jack's violence. Everyone tried to quiet him. The music-hall *artiste*, a little paler than usual, kept smiling and saying that there was no harm meant: but Jack kept shouting at him that if any fellow tried that sort of a game on with *his* sister he'd bloody well put his teeth down his throat, so he would.

∗ ∗ ∗

Polly sat for a little time on the side of the bed, crying. Then she dried her eyes and went over to the looking-glass. She dipped the end of the towel in the water-jug and refreshed her eyes with the cool water. She looked at herself in profile and readjusted a hairpin above

[30] A dark, English ale.
[31] A small annex for returning bottles to a vendor or getting them refilled (as with ale).

her ear. Then she went back to the bed again and sat at the foot. She regarded the pillows for a long time and the sight of them awakened in her mind secret amiable memories. She rested the nape of her neck against the cool iron bed-rail and fell into a reverie. There was no longer any perturbation visible on her face.

She waited on patiently, almost cheerfully, without alarm. Her memories gradually giving place to hopes and visions of the future. Her hopes and visions were so intricate that she no longer saw the white pillows on which her gaze was fixed or remembered that she was waiting for anything.

At last she heard her mother calling. She started to her feet and ran to the banisters.

—Polly! Polly!

—Yes, mamma?

—Come down, dear. Mr Doran wants to speak to you.

Then she remembered what she had been waiting for.

A Little Cloud[1]

EIGHT YEARS before he had seen his friend off at the North Wall[2] and wished him godspeed. Gallaher[3] had got on. You could tell that at once by his travelled air, his well-cut tweed suit, and fearless accent. Few fellows had talents like his and fewer still could remain unspoiled by such success. Gallaher's heart was in the right place and he had deserved to win. It was something to have a friend like that.

Little Chandler's thoughts ever since lunch-time had been of his meeting with Gallaher, of Gallaher's invitation and of the great city London where Gallaher lived. He was called Little Chandler[4] because, though he was but slightly under the average stature, he gave one the idea of being a little man. His hands were white and small, his frame was fragile, his voice was quiet and his manners were refined. He took the greatest care of his fair silken hair and moustache and used perfume discreetly on his handkerchief. The half-moons of his nails were perfect and when he smiled you caught a glimpse of a row of childish white teeth.

---

[1] Reference uncertain. Could be drawn from the King James Bible where Elijah's servant announces the end of a long drought inflicted by God: "Behold there ariseth a little cloud out of the sea, like a man's hand" (1 Kings 18:44). But could also be drawn from Guglielmo Ferrero's *L'Europe Giovane* (*Young Europe*, 1897), a book Joyce knew well, which describes the futility of human plans and activity: "What are the greatest conceptions of the human spirit before the infinite reality of life? A little cloud against the unbounded expanse of sky."

[2] Central Dublin dock (see "Eveline" p.xx n. 22).

[3] Ignatius Gallaher is one of many characters in *Dubliners* (including Bob Doran) mentioned in *Ulysses* (1922), also set in Dublin. In a subsection of ch. 7, "Aeolus," titled "The Great Gallaher," newspapermen praise his success as an enterprising reporter.

[4] A chandler is a candle-stick maker.

As he sat at his desk in the King's Inns[5] he thought what changes those eight years had brought. The friend whom he had known under a shabby and necessitous guise had become a brilliant figure on the London Press. He turned often from his tiresome writing to gaze out of the office window. The glow of a late autumn sunset covered the grass plots and walks. It cast a shower of kindly golden dust on the untidy nurses and decrepit old men who drowsed on the benches; it flickered upon all the moving figures—on the children who ran screaming along the gravel paths and on everyone who passed through the gardens. He watched the scene and thought of life; and (as always happened when he thought of life) he became sad. A gentle melancholy took possession of him. He felt how useless it was to struggle against fortune, this being the burden of wisdom which the ages had bequeathed to him.

He remembered the books of poetry upon his shelves at home. He had bought them in his bachelor days and many an evening, as he sat in the little room off the hall, he had been tempted to take one down from the bookshelf and read out something to his wife. But shyness had always held him back; and so the books had remained on their shelves. At times he repeated lines to himself and this consoled him.

When his hour had struck[6] he stood up and took leave of his desk and of his fellow-clerks punctiliously. He emerged from under the feudal arch of the King's Inns, a neat modest figure, and walked swiftly down Henrietta Street. The golden sunset was waning and the air had grown sharp. A horde of grimy children populated the street.[7] They stood or ran in the roadway or crawled up the steps before the gaping doors or squatted like mice upon the thresholds. Little Chandler gave them no thought. He picked his way deftly through all that minute vermin-like life and under the shadow of the gaunt spectral mansions in which the old nobility of Dublin had roystered.[8] No memory of the past touched him, for his mind was full of a present joy.

He had never been in Corless's[9] but he knew the value of the name. He knew that people went there after the theatre to eat

---

[5] A building north of the Liffey, housing legal offices.

[6] The end of the workday.

[7] A once distinguished area now dominated by slums.

[8] Archaism: caroused.

[9] Restaurant in the fashionable Burlington Hotel.

oysters and drink liqueurs; and he had heard that the waiters there spoke French and German. Walking swiftly by at night he had seen cabs drawn up before the door and richly dressed ladies, escorted by cavaliers,[10] alight and enter quickly. They wore noisy dresses and many wraps. Their faces were powdered and they caught up their dresses, when they touched earth, like alarmed Atalantas.[11] He had always passed without turning his head to look. It was his habit to walk swiftly in the street even by day and whenever he found himself in the city late at night he hurried on his way apprehensively and excitedly. Sometimes, however, he courted the causes of his fear. He chose the darkest and narrowest streets and, as he walked boldly forward, the silence that was spread about his footsteps troubled him, the wandering, silent figures troubled him; and at times a sound of low fugitive laughter made him tremble like a leaf.

He turned to the right towards Capel Street. Ignatius Gallaher on the London Press! Who would have thought it possible eight years before? Still, now that he reviewed the past, Little Chandler could remember many signs of future greatness in his friend. People used to say that Ignatius Gallaher was wild. Of course, he did mix with a rakish[12] set of fellows at that time, drank freely and borrowed money on all sides. In the end he had got mixed up in some shady affair, some money transaction: at least, that was one version of his flight. But nobody denied him talent. There was always a certain ... something in Ignatius Gallaher that impressed you in spite of yourself. Even when he was out at elbows[13] and at his wits' end for money he kept up a bold face. Little Chandler remembered (and the remembrance brought a slight flush of pride to his cheek) one of Ignatius Gallaher's sayings when he was in a tight corner:

—Half time, now, boys, he used to say light-heartedly. Where's my considering cap?

That was Ignatius Gallaher all out; and, damn it, you couldn't but admire him for it.

Little Chandler quickened his pace. For the first time in his life he felt himself superior to the people he passed. For the first time his soul revolted against the dull inelegance of Capel Street. There was

---

[10] Archaic term for fine gentlemen (16th c. term for knights).
[11] The fleet-footed huntress of Greek myth.
[12] See "The Boarding House," n. 21.
[13] Broke.

no doubt about it: if you wanted to succeed you had to go away. You could do nothing in Dublin. As he crossed Grattan Bridge[14] he looked down the river towards the lower quays and pitied the poor stunted houses. They seemed to him a band of tramps, huddled together along the riverbanks, their old coats covered with dust and soot, stupefied by the panorama of sunset and waiting for the first chill of night to bid them arise, shake themselves and begone. He wondered whether he could write a poem to express his idea. Perhaps Gallaher might be able to get it into some London paper for him. Could he write something original? He was not sure what idea he wished to express but the thought that a poetic moment had touched him took life within him like an infant hope. He stepped onward bravely.

Every step brought him nearer to London, farther from his own sober inartistic life. A light began to tremble on the horizon of his mind. He was not so old—thirty-two. His temperament might be said to be just at the point of maturity. There were so many different moods and impressions that he wished to express in verse. He felt them within him. He tried to weigh his soul to see if it was a poet's soul. Melancholy[15] was the dominant note of his temperament, he thought, but it was a melancholy tempered by recurrences of faith and resignation and simple joy. If he could give expression to it in a book of poems perhaps men would listen. He would never be popular: he saw that. He could not sway the crowd but he might appeal to a little circle of kindred minds. The English critics, perhaps, would recognise him as one of the Celtic school[16] by reason of the melancholy tone of his poems; besides that, he would put in allusions. He began to invent sentences and phrases from the notices which his book would get. *Mr Chandler has the gift of easy and graceful verse.... A wistful sadness pervades these poems.... The Celtic note.* It was a pity his name was not more Irish-looking.[17] Perhaps it would be better to insert his mother's name before

---

[14] Originally called Essex or Capel Street Bridge, this central thoroughfare was renamed in 1874 to honor Henry Grattan, a politician who fought for Irish independence.

[15] This stereotypically "poetic" emotion blends world-weariness, depression, and heightened aestheticism.

[16] Modern writers and poets (also called the Celtic Twilight and Irish Revivalists) who advanced new kinds of distinctly Irish writing that was often mystical, dreamy, and nostalgic for ancient Ireland. See pp. xxx–xxx.

[17] Thomas and Chandler are both distinctly English names, though Malone is Irish.

the surname: Thomas Malone Chandler, or better still: T. Malone Chandler. He would speak to Gallaher about it.

He pursued his revery so ardently that he passed his street and had to turn back. As he came near Corless's his former agitation began to overmaster him and he halted before the door in indecision. Finally he opened the door and entered.

The light and noise of the bar held him at the doorway for a few moments. He looked about him, but his sight was confused by the shining of many red and green wine-glasses. The bar seemed to him to be full of people and he felt that the people were observing him curiously. He glanced quickly to right and left (frowning slightly to make his errand appear serious), but when his sight cleared a little he saw that nobody had turned to look at him: and there, sure enough, was Ignatius Gallaher leaning with his back against the counter and his feet planted far apart.

—Hallo, Tommy,[18] old hero, here you are! What is it to be? What will you have? I'm taking whisky: better stuff than we get across the water. Soda? Lithia?[19] No mineral?[20] I'm the same. Spoils the flavour.... Here, *garçon*,[21] bring us two halves[22] of malt whisky, like a good fellow.... Well, and how have you been pulling along since I saw you last? Dear God, how old we're getting! Do you see any signs of aging in me—eh, what? A little grey and thin on the top—what?

Ignatius Gallaher took off his hat and displayed a large closely cropped head. His face was heavy, pale and clean-shaven. His eyes, which were of bluish slate colour, relieved his unhealthy pallor and shone out plainly above the vivid orange[23] tie he wore. Between these rival features the lips appeared very long and shapeless and colourless. He bent his head and felt with two sympathetic fingers the thin hair at the crown. Little Chandler shook his head as a denial. Ignatius Gallaher put on his hat again.

---

[18] Slang for a British soldier; see Rudyard Kipling's poem, "Tommy" (1892).

[19] Bottled spring water.

[20] Mineral water, for diluting whiskey.

[21] Waiter ("boy" in French).

[22] Half glasses.

[23] The color of Protestant Northern Ireland (and for the union of Ireland with Great Britain).

—It pulls you down, he said, press life. Always hurry and scurry, looking for copy[24] and sometimes not finding it: and then, always to have something new in your stuff. Damn proofs and printers, I say, for a few days. I'm deuced glad, I can tell you, to get back to the old country. Does a fellow good, a bit of a holiday. I feel a ton better since I landed again in dear dirty Dublin.... Here you are, Tommy. Water? Say when.

Little Chandler allowed his whisky to be very much diluted.

—You don't know what's good for you, my boy, said Ignatius Gallaher. I drink mine neat.[25]

—I drink very little as a rule, said Little Chandler modestly. An odd half-one or so when I meet any of the old crowd: that's all.

—Ah well, said Ignatius Gallaher, cheerfully, here's to us and to old times and old acquaintance.

They clinked glasses and drank the toast.

—I met some of the old gang today, said Ignatius Gallaher. O'Hara seems to be in a bad way. What's he doing?

—Nothing, said Little Chandler. He's gone to the dogs.

—But Hogan has a good sit, hasn't he?

—Yes; he's in the Land Commission.[26]

—I met him one night in London and he seemed to be very flush.[27]... Poor O'Hara! Boose, I suppose?

—Other things, too, said Little Chandler shortly.

Ignatius Gallaher laughed.

—Tommy, he said, I see you haven't changed an atom. You're the very same serious person that used to lecture me on Sunday mornings when I had a sore head and a fur on my tongue.[28] You'd want to knock about a bit in the world. Have you never been any-where even for a trip?

—I've been to the Isle of Man,[29] said Little Chandler.

Ignatius Gallaher laughed.

---

[24] Story material.

[25] Without ice, water, or soda (a man's drink).

[26] The good situation ("sit") is the Irish Land Commission Court, in charge of trans-ferring farms and pastures from large estates to small tenants; it was created after agitation over land rights at the end of the 19th c.

[27] Well off (though the Commission was famously corrupt).

[28] Colloquial symptoms of a hangover.

[29] Easily accessible resort between Ireland and England.

—The Isle of Man! he said. Go to London or Paris: Paris, for choice. That'd do you good.

—Have you seen Paris?

—I should think I have! I've knocked about there a little.

—And is it really so beautiful as they say? asked Little Chandler. He sipped a little of his drink while Ignatius Gallaher finished his boldly.

—Beautiful? said Ignatius Gallaher, pausing on the word and on the flavour of his drink. It's not so beautiful, you know. Of course, it is beautiful.... But it's the life of Paris; that's the thing. Ah, there's no city like Paris for gaiety, movement, excitement....

Little Chandler finished his whisky and, after some trouble, succeeded in catching the barman's eye. He ordered the same again.

—I've been to the Moulin Rouge,[30] Ignatius Gallaher continued when the barman had removed their glasses, and I've been to all the Bohemian cafés.[31] Hot stuff! Not for a pious chap like you, Tommy.

Little Chandler said nothing until the barman returned with two glasses:[32] then he touched his friend's glass lightly and reciprocated the former toast. He was beginning to feel somewhat disillusioned. Gallaher's accent and way of expressing himself did not please him. There was something vulgar in his friend which he had not observed before. But perhaps it was only the result of living in London amid the bustle and competition of the press. The old personal charm was still there under this new gaudy manner. And, after all, Gallaher had lived, he had seen the world. Little Chandler looked at his friend enviously.

—Everything in Paris is gay, said Ignatius Gallaher. They believe in enjoying life—and don't you think they're right? If you want to enjoy yourself properly you must go to Paris. And, mind you, they've a great feeling for the Irish there.[33] When they heard I was from Ireland they were ready to eat me, man.

Little Chandler took four or five sips from his glass.

—Tell me, he said, is it true that Paris is so ... immoral as they say?

---

[30] An infamous Parisian music hall that featured titillations like the cancan.

[31] Frequented by young artists and intellectuals.

[32] In the custom of alternating payment for each round of drinks (it's now Chandler's turn).

[33] The Catholic French and Irish were traditional political and even military allies against the British.

Ignatius Gallaher made a catholic gesture with his right arm.[34]

—Every place is immoral, he said. Of course you do find spicy bits in Paris. Go to one of the students' balls,[35] for instance. That's lively, if you like, when the *cocottes*[36] begin to let themselves loose. You know what they are, I suppose?

—I've heard of them, said Little Chandler.

Ignatius Gallaher drank off his whisky and shook his head.

—Ah, he said, you may say what you like. There's no woman like the Parisienne—for style, for go.

—Then it is an immoral city, said Little Chandler, with timid insistence—I mean, compared with London or Dublin?

—London! said Ignatius Gallaher. It's six of one and half-a-dozen of the other. You ask Hogan, my boy. I showed him a bit about London when he was over there. He'd open your eye.... I say, Tommy, don't make punch[37] of that whisky: liquor up.

—No, really....

—O, come on, another one won't do you any harm. What is it? The same again, I suppose?

—Well ... all right.

—*François*,[38] the same again.... Will you smoke, Tommy?

Ignatius Gallaher produced his cigar-case. The two friends lit their cigars and puffed at them in silence until their drinks were served.

—I'll tell you my opinion, said Ignatius Gallaher, emerging after some time from the clouds of smoke in which he had taken refuge, it's a rum world. Talk of immorality! I've heard of cases—what am I saying—I've known them: cases of ... immorality....

Ignatius Gallaher puffed thoughtfully at his cigar and then, in a calm historian's tone, he proceeded to sketch for his friend some pictures of the corruption which was rife abroad. He summarised the vices of many capitals and seemed inclined to award the palm to Berlin. Some things he could not vouch for (his friends had told him), but of others he had had personal experience. He spared neither rank nor caste. He revealed many of the secrets of religious

---

[34] A sweeping gesture, though punning on the Catholic sign of the cross.

[35] Wild nighttime parties in the "left bank" college district.

[36] Hens (prostitutes) in French.

[37] Punch is a highly diluted alcoholic drink often favored by women.

[38] Another snobbish term for the waiter.

houses on the Continent and described some of the practices which were fashionable in high society and ended by telling, with details, a story about an English duchess[39]—a story which he knew to be true. Little Chandler was astonished.

—Ah, well, said Ignatius Gallaher, here we are in old jog-along Dublin where nothing is known of such things.

—How dull you must find it, said Little Chandler, after all the other places you've seen!

—Well, said Ignatius Gallaher, it's a relaxation to come over here, you know. And, after all, it's the old country, as they say, isn't it? You can't help having a certain feeling for it. That's human nature.... But tell me something about yourself. Hogan told me you had ... tasted the joys of connubial bliss.[40] Two years ago, wasn't it?

Little Chandler blushed and smiled.

—Yes, he said. I was married last May twelve months.

—I hope it's not too late in the day to offer my best wishes, said Ignatius Gallaher. I didn't know your address or I'd have done so at the time.

He extended his hand, which Little Chandler took.

—Well, Tommy, he said, I wish you and yours every joy in life, old chap, and tons of money, and may you never die till I shoot you. And that's the wish of a sincere friend, an old friend. You know that?

—I know that, said Little Chandler.

—Any youngsters? said Ignatius Gallaher.

Little Chandler blushed again.

—We have one child, he said.

—Son or daughter?

—A little boy.

Ignatius Gallaher slapped his friend sonorously on the back.

—Bravo, he said, I wouldn't doubt you, Tommy.

Little Chandler smiled, looked confusedly at his glass and bit his lower lip with three childishly white front teeth.

—I hope you'll spend an evening with us, he said, before you go back. My wife will be delighted to meet you. We can have a little music and ...

---

[39] The sexual exploits of high-ranking clergy and aristocrats are a common feature of Victorian pornography.

[40] Marriage.

—Thanks awfully, old chap, said Ignatius Gallaher, I'm sorry we didn't meet earlier. But I must leave tomorrow night.

—To-night, perhaps ...?

—I'm awfully sorry, old man. You see I'm over here with another fellow, clever young chap he is too, and we arranged to go to a little card-party. Only for that ...

—O, in that case ...

—But who knows? said Ignatius Gallaher considerately. Next year I may take a little skip over here now that I've broken the ice. It's only a pleasure deferred.

—Very well, said Little Chandler, the next time you come we must have an evening together. That's agreed now, isn't it?

—Yes, that's agreed, said Ignatius Gallaher. Next year if I come, *parole d'honneur*.[41]

—And to clinch the bargain, said Little Chandler, we'll just have one more now.[42]

Ignatius Gallaher took out a large gold watch and looked at it.

—Is it to be the last? he said. Because you know, I have an a.p.[43]

—O, yes, positively, said Little Chandler.

—Very well, then, said Ignatius Gallaher, let us have another one as a *deoc an doruis*—[44]that's good vernacular for a small whisky, I believe.

Little Chandler ordered the drinks. The blush which had risen to his face a few moments before was establishing itself. A trifle made him blush at any time: and now he felt warm and excited. Three small whiskies had gone to his head and Gallaher's strong cigar had confused his mind, for he was a delicate and abstinent person. The adventure of meeting Gallaher after eight years, of finding himself with Gallaher in Corless's surrounded by lights and noise, of listening to Gallaher's stories and of sharing for a brief space Gallaher's vagrant and triumphant life, upset the equipoise of his sensitive nature. He felt acutely the contrast between his own life and his friend's and it seemed to him unjust. Gallaher was his inferior in birth and education. He was sure that he could do something better than his friend had ever done, or could ever do, something higher than mere tawdry journalism if he only got the chance.

---

[41] "Word of honor" in French.

[42] This completes the circuit of rounds Gallaher began.

[43] Appointment.

[44] "Drink at door," a farewell drink in Irish.

What was it that stood in his way? His unfortunate timidity! He wished to vindicate himself in some way, to assert his manhood. He saw behind Gallaher's refusal of his invitation. Gallaher was only patronising him by his friendliness just as he was patronising Ireland by his visit.

The barman brought their drinks. Little Chandler pushed one glass towards his friend and took up the other boldly.

—Who knows? he said, as they lifted their glasses. When you come next year I may have the pleasure of wishing long life and happiness to Mr and Mrs Ignatius Gallaher.

Ignatius Gallaher in the act of drinking closed one eye expressively over the rim of his glass. When he had drunk he smacked his lips decisively, set down his glass and said:

—No blooming fear of that, my boy. I'm going to have my fling first and see a bit of life and the world before I put my head in the sack—[45] if I ever do.

—Some day you will, said Little Chandler calmly.

Ignatius Gallaher turned his orange tie and slate-blue eyes full upon his friend.

—You think so? he said.

—You'll put your head in the sack, repeated Little Chandler stoutly, like everyone else if you can find the girl.

He had slightly emphasised his tone and he was aware that he had betrayed himself; but, though the colour had heightened in his cheek, he did not flinch from his friend's gaze. Ignatius Gallaher watched him for a few moments and then said:

—If ever it occurs, you may bet your bottom dollar there'll be no mooning and spooning about it. I mean to marry money. She'll have a good fat account at the bank or she won't do for me.

Little Chandler shook his head.

—Why, man alive, said Ignatius Gallaher, vehemently, do you know what it is? I've only to say the word and to-morrow I can have the woman and the cash. You don't believe it? Well, I know it. There are hundreds—what am I saying?—thousands of rich Germans and Jews, rotten with money, that'd only be too glad.... You wait a while my boy. See if I don't play my cards properly. When I go about a thing I mean business, I tell you. You just wait.

[45] Hangman's hood.

He tossed his glass to his mouth, finished his drink and laughed loudly. Then he looked thoughtfully before him and said in a calmer tone:

—But I'm in no hurry. They can wait. I don't fancy tying myself up to one woman, you know.

He imitated with his mouth the act of tasting and made a wry face.

—Must get a bit stale, I should think, he said.

* * *

Little Chandler sat in the room off the hall, holding a child in his arms. To save money they kept no servant[46] but Annie's young sister Monica came for an hour or so in the morning and an hour or so in the evening to help. But Monica had gone home long ago. It was a quarter to nine. Little Chandler had come home late for tea and, moreover, he had forgotten to bring Annie home the parcel of coffee from Bewley's.[47] Of course she was in a bad humour and gave him short answers. She said she would do without any tea but when it came near the time at which the shop at the corner closed she decided to go out herself for a quarter of a pound of tea and two pounds of sugar. She put the sleeping child deftly in his arms and said:

—Here. Don't waken him.

A little lamp with a white china shade stood upon the table and its light fell over a photograph which was enclosed in a frame of crumpled horn. It was Annie's photograph. Little Chandler looked at it, pausing at the thin tight lips. She wore the pale blue summer blouse which he had brought her home as a present one Saturday. It had cost him ten and elevenpence;[48] but what an agony of nervousness it had cost him! How he had suffered that day, waiting at the shop door until the shop was empty, standing at the counter and trying to appear at his ease while the girl piled ladies' blouses before him, paying at the desk and forgetting to take up the odd penny of his change, being called back by the cashier, and, finally, striving to hide his blushes as he left the shop by examining the parcel to see if it was securely tied. When he brought the blouse home Annie kissed him and said it was very pretty and stylish; but when she heard the price she threw the blouse on the table and said it was a regular swindle to charge ten and elevenpence for it. At first she wanted to

---

[46] Having a servant is an important sign of middle-class respectability.

[47] A chain of popular teashops; tea is a late-afternoon meal.

[48] 10 shillings, 11 pence—an extravagance for a clerk.

take it back but when she tried it on she was delighted with it, especially with the make of the sleeves, and kissed him and said he was very good to think of her.

Hm!...

He looked coldly into the eyes of the photograph and they answered coldly. Certainly they were pretty and the face itself was pretty. But he found something mean[49] in it. Why was it so unconscious and ladylike? The composure of the eyes irritated him. They repelled him and defied him: there was no passion in them, no rapture. He thought of what Gallaher had said about rich Jewesses. Those dark Oriental eyes, he thought, how full they are of passion, of voluptuous longing!... Why had he married the eyes in the photograph?

He caught himself up at the question and glanced nervously round the room. He found something mean in the pretty furniture which he had bought for his house on the hire system.[50] Annie had chosen it herself and it reminded him of her. It too was prim and pretty. A dull resentment against his life awoke within him. Could he not escape from his little house? Was it too late for him to try to live bravely like Gallaher? Could he go to London? There was the furniture still to be paid for. If he could only write a book and get it published, that might open the way for him.

A volume of Byron's[51] poems lay before him on the table. He opened it cautiously with his left hand lest he should waken the child and began to read the first poem in the book:

> *Hushed are the winds and still the evening gloom,*
> *Not e'en a Zephyr wanders through the grove,*
> *Whilst I return to view my Margaret's tomb*
> *And scatter flowers on the dust I love.*

He paused. He felt the rhythm of the verse about him in the room. How melancholy it was! Could he, too, write like that, express the melancholy of his soul in verse? There were so many

---

[49] Meaning here more crude or ordinary than cruel.

[50] On credit.

[51] In 1816, Lady Byron (1792-1860), married just over a year, suddenly and mysteriously left her husband, international celebrity poet Lord Byron (1788-1824), taking their infant daughter with her. Lord Byron signed a decree of separation and left England for Continental Europe, where he lived a life of political intrigue mixed with social scandal, even as he changed the course of English poetry; he never saw his wife or daughter again.

things he wanted to describe: his sensation of a few hours before on Grattan Bridge, for example. If he could get back again into that mood....

The child awoke and began to cry. He turned from the page and tried to hush it: but it would not be hushed. He began to rock it to and fro in his arms but its wailing cry grew keener. He rocked it faster while his eyes began to read the second stanza:

> *Within this narrow cell reclines her clay,*
> *That clay where once ...*[52]

It was useless. He couldn't read. He couldn't do anything. The wailing of the child pierced the drum of his ear. It was useless, useless! He was a prisoner for life. His arms trembled with anger and suddenly bending to the child's face he shouted:

—Stop!

The child stopped for an instant, had a spasm of fright and began to scream. He jumped up from his chair and walked hastily up and down the room with the child in his arms. It began to sob piteously, losing its breath for four or five seconds, and then bursting out anew. The thin walls of the room echoed the sound. He tried to soothe it but it sobbed more convulsively. He looked at the contracted and quivering face of the child and began to be alarmed. He counted seven sobs without a break between them and caught the child to his breast in fright. If it died!...

The door was burst open and a young woman ran in, panting.

—What is it? What is it? she cried.

The child, hearing its mother's voice, broke out into a paroxysm of sobbing.

—It's nothing, Annie ... it's nothing.... He began to cry ...

She flung her parcels on the floor and snatched the child from him.

—What have you done to him? she cried, glaring into his face.

---

[52] The first line of Byron's very early 1802 poem, "On the Death of a Young Lady, Cousin of the Author, and Very Dear to Him." It is not representative of the poet's mature work and suggests Chandler's lack of poetic taste. See Contexts section, p. xxx.

Little Chandler sustained for one moment the gaze of her eyes and his heart closed together as he met the hatred in them. He began to stammer:

—It's nothing.... He ... he began to cry.... I couldn't ... I didn't do anything.... What?

Giving no heed to him she began to walk up and down the room, clasping the child tightly in her arms and murmuring:

—My little man! My little mannie! Was 'ou frightened, love?... There now, love! There now! ... Lambabaun![53] Mamma's little lamb of the world!... There now!

Little Chandler felt his cheeks suffused with shame and he stood back out of the lamplight. He listened while the paroxysm of the child's sobbing grew less and less; and tears of remorse started to his eyes.

[53] Irish endearment, from *leanbhán*: pretty child.

Counterparts[1]

THE BELL rang furiously and, when Miss Parker went to the tube,[2] a furious voice called out in a piercing North of Ireland accent:[3]

—Send Farrington here!

Miss Parker returned to her machine,[4] saying to a man who was writing at a desk:

—Mr Alleyne wants you upstairs.

The man muttered *Blast him*! under his breath and pushed back his chair to stand up. When he stood up he was tall and of great bulk. He had a hanging face, dark wine-coloured, with fair eyebrows and moustache: his eyes bulged forward slightly and the whites of them were dirty. He lifted up the counter and, passing by the clients, went out of the office with a heavy step.

He went heavily upstairs until he came to the second landing, where a door bore a brass plate with the inscription *Mr Alleyne*. Here he halted, puffing with labour and vexation, and knocked. The shrill voice cried:

—Come in!

The man entered Mr Alleyne's room. Simultaneously Mr Alleyne, a little man wearing gold-rimmed glasses on a clean-shaven face, shot his head up over a pile of documents. The head itself was so pink and hairless it seemed like a large egg reposing on the papers. Mr Alleyne did not lose a moment:

—Farrington? What is the meaning of this? Why have I always to complain of you? May I ask you why you haven't made a copy of

---

[1] The pubs, pawnbroker, and law firm in this story were all real Dublin businesses, a fact that deterred publishers fearful of suits for libel. See p. xxx.

[2] Intercom.

[3] From the largely pro-Unionist, Protestant part of Ireland.

[4] Typewriter.

that contract[5] between Bodley and Kirwan? I told you it must be ready by four o'clock.

—But Mr Shelley said, sir—

—*Mr Shelley said, sir*.... Kindly attend to what I say and not to what *Mr Shelley says, sir*. You have always some excuse or another for shirking work. Let me tell you that if the contract is not copied before this evening I'll lay the matter before Mr Crosbie.... Do you hear me now?

—Yes, sir.

—Do you hear me now? ... Ay and another little matter! I might as well be talking to the wall as talking to you. Understand once for all that you get a half an hour for your lunch and not an hour and a half. How many courses do you want, I'd like to know.... Do you mind me now?

—Yes, sir.

Mr Alleyne bent his head again upon his pile of papers. The man stared fixedly at the polished skull which directed the affairs of Crosbie & Alleyne, gauging its fragility. A spasm of rage gripped his throat for a few moments and then passed, leaving after it a sharp sensation of thirst. The man recognised the sensation and felt that he must have a good night's drinking. The middle of the month was passed and, if he could get the copy done in time, Mr Alleyne might give him an order on the cashier.[6] He stood still, gazing fixedly at the head upon the pile of papers. Suddenly Mr Alleyne began to upset all the papers, searching for something. Then, as if he had been unaware of the man's presence till that moment, he shot up his head again, saying:

—Eh? Are you going to stand there all day? Upon my word, Farrington, you take things easy!

—I was waiting to see....

—Very good, you needn't wait to see. Go downstairs and do your work.

The man walked heavily towards the door and, as he went out of the room, he heard Mr Alleyne cry after him that if the contract was not copied by evening Mr Crosbie would hear of the matter.

He returned to his desk in the lower office and counted the sheets which remained to be copied. He took up his pen and dipped it in the ink but he continued to stare stupidly at the last words he

---

[5] At the time, legal documents had to be handwritten, not typed. Farrington's job is thus to copy this document in longhand.

[6] Advance on his salary.

had written: *In no case shall the said Bernard Bodley be....* The evening was falling and in a few minutes they would be lighting the gas:[7] then he could write. He felt that he must slake the thirst in his throat. He stood up from his desk and, lifting the counter as before, passed out of the office. As he was passing out the chief clerk looked at him inquiringly.

—It's all right, Mr Shelley, said the man, pointing with his finger to indicate the objective of his journey.[8]

The chief clerk glanced at the hat-rack, but, seeing the row complete, offered no remark.[9] As soon as he was on the landing the man pulled a shepherd's plaid cap[10] out of his pocket, put it on his head and ran quickly down the rickety stairs. From the street door he walked on furtively on the inner side of the path towards the corner and all at once dived into a doorway. He was now safe in the dark snug of O'Neill's shop, and filling up the little window that looked into the bar[11] with his inflamed face, the colour of dark wine or dark meat, he called out:

—Here, Pat, give us a g.p.,[12] like a good fellow.

The curate[13] brought him a glass of plain porter. The man drank it at a gulp and asked for a caraway seed.[14] He put his penny on the counter and, leaving the curate to grope for it in the gloom, retreated out of the snug as furtively as he had entered it.

Darkness, accompanied by a thick fog, was gaining upon the dusk of February and the lamps in Eustace Street had been lit. The man went up by the houses until he reached the door of the office, wondering whether he could finish his copy in time. On the stairs a moist pungent odour of perfumes saluted his nose: evidently Miss Delacour had come while he was out in O'Neill's. He crammed his cap back again into his pocket and re-entered the office, assuming an air of absent-mindedness.

---

[7] Gas-lit fixtures in the office.

[8] The bathroom.

[9] A man would presumably not go into the street without a hat, so the clerk assumes Farrington won't leave the building.

[10] A collapsible (and thus easily concealed) knit or felt hat.

[11] J.J. O'Neill's pub was at the corner of Essex and Dame streets; a snug is an enclosed and even curtained section of a pub served by the bar proper from a small window.

[12] Glass (or half-pint) of porter (beer).

[13] See "Two Gallants," n. 49.

[14] To freshen the breath.

—Mr Alleyne has been calling for you, said the chief clerk severely. Where were you?

The man glanced at the two clients who were standing at the counter as if to intimate that their presence prevented him from answering. As the clients were both male the chief clerk allowed himself a laugh.

—I know that game, he said. Five times in one day is a little bit. ... Well, you better look sharp and get a copy of our correspondence in the Delacour case for Mr Alleyne.

This address in the presence of the public, his run upstairs and the porter he had gulped down so hastily confused the man and, as he sat down at his desk to get what was required, he realised how hopeless was the task of finishing his copy of the contract before half past five. The dark damp night was coming and he longed to spend it in the bars, drinking with his friends amid the glare of gas and the clatter of glasses. He got out the Delacour correspondence and passed out of the office. He hoped Mr Alleyne would not discover that the last two letters were missing.

The moist pungent perfume lay all the way up to Mr Alleyne's room. Miss Delacour was a middle-aged woman of Jewish appearance. Mr Alleyne was said to be sweet on her or on her money. She came to the office often and stayed a long time when she came. She was sitting beside his desk now in an aroma of perfumes, smoothing the handle of her umbrella and nodding the great black feather in her hat. Mr Alleyne had swivelled his chair round to face her and thrown his right foot jauntily upon his left knee. The man put the correspondence on the desk and bowed respectfully but neither Mr Alleyne nor Miss Delacour took any notice of his bow. Mr Alleyne tapped a finger on the correspondence and then flicked it towards him as if to say: *That's all right: you can go.*

The man returned to the lower office and sat down again at his desk. He stared intently at the incomplete phrase: *In no case shall the said Bernard Bodley be...* and thought how strange it was that the last three words began with the same letter. The chief clerk began to hurry Miss Parker, saying she would never have the letters typed in time for post.[15] The man listened to the clicking of the machine for a few minutes and then set to work to finish his copy. But his head was not clear and his mind wandered away to the glare and rattle of the public-house. It was a night for hot punches.[16]

[15] Mail pickup.
[16] Alcoholic drinks made with whiskey and spices.

He struggled on with his copy, but when the clock struck five he had still fourteen pages to write. Blast it! He couldn't finish it in time. He longed to execrate aloud, to bring his fist down on something violently. He was so enraged that he wrote *Bernard Bernard* instead of *Bernard Bodley* and had to begin again on a clean sheet.[17]

He felt strong enough to clear out the whole office single-handed. His body ached to do something, to rush out and revel in violence. All the indignities of his life enraged him.... Could he ask the cashier privately for an advance? No, the cashier was no good, no damn good: he wouldn't give an advance.... He knew where he would meet the boys: Leonard and O'Halloran and Nosey Flynn. The barometer of his emotional nature was set for a spell of riot.

His imagination had so abstracted him that his name was called twice before he answered. Mr Alleyne and Miss Delacour were standing outside the counter and all the clerks had turned round in anticipation of something. The man got up from his desk. Mr Alleyne began a tirade of abuse, saying that two letters were missing. The man answered that he knew nothing about them, that he had made a faithful copy. The tirade continued: it was so bitter and violent that the man could hardly restrain his fist from descending upon the head of the manikin[18] before him:

—I know nothing about any other two letters, he said stupidly.

—*You—know—nothing*. Of course you know nothing, said Mr Alleyne. Tell me, he added, glancing first for approval to the lady beside him, do you take me for a fool? Do you think me an utter fool?

The man glanced from the lady's face to the little egg-shaped head and back again; and, almost before he was aware of it, his tongue had found a felicitous moment:

—I don't think, sir, he said, that that's a fair question to put to me.

There was a pause in the very breathing of the clerks. Everyone was astounded (the author of the witticism no less than his neighbours) and Miss Delacour, who was a stout amiable person, began to smile broadly. Mr Alleyne flushed to the hue of a wild rose and his mouth twitched with a dwarf's passion. He shook his fist in the man's face till it seemed to vibrate like the knob of some electric machine:

—You impertinent ruffian! You impertinent ruffian! I'll make short work of you! Wait till you see! You'll apologise to me for your

[17] The legal copy must be flawless and errors cannot be marked out or erased.

[18] Derogatory term for a dwarf or man of small stature.

impertinence or you'll quit the office instanter![19] You'll quit this, I'm telling you, or you'll apologise to me!

* * *

He stood in a doorway opposite the office watching to see if the cashier would come out alone. All the clerks passed out and finally the cashier came out with the chief clerk. It was no use trying to say a word to him when he was with the chief clerk. The man felt that his position was bad enough. He had been obliged to offer an abject apology to Mr Alleyne for his impertinence but he knew what a hornet's nest the office would be for him. He could remember the way in which Mr Alleyne had hounded little Peake out of the office in order to make room for his own nephew. He felt savage and thirsty and revengeful, annoyed with himself and with everyone else. Mr Alleyne would never give him an hour's rest; his life would be a hell to him. He had made a proper fool of himself this time. Could he not keep his tongue in his cheek? But they had never pulled together from the first, he and Mr Alleyne, ever since the day Mr Alleyne had overheard him mimicking his North of Ireland accent to amuse Higgins and Miss Parker: that had been the beginning of it. He might have tried Higgins for the money, but sure Higgins never had anything for himself. A man with two establishments to keep up,[20] of course he couldn't....

He felt his great body again aching for the comfort of the public-house. The fog had begun to chill him and he wondered could he touch Pat in O'Neill's. He could not touch him for more than a bob[21]—and a bob was no use. Yet he must get money somewhere or other: he had spent his last penny for the g.p. and soon it would be too late for getting money anywhere. Suddenly, as he was fingering his watch-chain, he thought of Terry Kelly's pawn-office[22] in Fleet Street. That was the dart![23] Why didn't he think of it sooner?

He went through the narrow alley of Temple Bar quickly, muttering to himself that they could all go to hell because he was going to have a good night of it. The clerk in Terry Kelly's said *A crown!*[24] but

---

[19] Immediately.

[20] In addition to his own family, Higgins supports a mistress and their children—often a consequence of the Catholic church's ban on divorce.

[21] Ask for a loan; a bob is a shilling.

[22] A pawnbroker gives cash for the consignment of collateral (such as a watch), to be redeemed with repayment plus interest. Failing this, the pawnbroker puts the consignment up for sale.

[23] Idea, scheme.

[24] A coin worth five shillings.

the consignor held out for six shillings; and in the end the six shillings was allowed him literally. He came out of the pawn-office joyfully, making a little cylinder of the coins between his thumb and fingers. In Westmoreland Street the footpaths were crowded with young men and women returning from business and ragged urchins ran here and there yelling out the names of the evening editions.[25] The man passed through the crowd, looking on the spectacle generally with proud satisfaction and staring masterfully at the office-girls. His head was full of the noises of tram-gongs and swishing trolleys and his nose already sniffed the curling fumes of punch. As he walked on he preconsidered the terms in which he would narrate the incident to the boys:[26]

—So, I just looked at him—coolly, you know, and looked at her. Then I looked back at him again—taking my time, you know. *I don't think that that's a fair question to put to me*, says I.

Nosey Flynn was sitting up in his usual corner of Davy Byrne's and, when he heard the story, he stood[27] Farrington a half-one, saying it was as smart a thing as ever he heard. Farrington stood a drink in his turn. After a while O'Halloran and Paddy Leonard came in and the story was repeated to them. O'Halloran stood tailors[28] of malt, hot, all round and told the story of the retort he had made to the chief clerk when he was in Callan's of Fownes's Street; but, as the retort was after the manner of the liberal shepherds in the eclogues,[29] he had to admit that it was not as clever as Farrington's retort. At this Farrington told the boys to polish off that and have another.

Just as they were naming their poisons[30] who should come in but Higgins! Of course he had to join in with the others. The men asked him to give his version of it, and he did so with great vivacity for the sight of five small[31] hot whiskies was very exhilarating. Everyone roared laughing when he showed the way in which Mr Alleyne shook his fist in Farrington's face. Then he imitated Farrington, saying, *And here was my nabs,*[32] *as cool as you please,*

---

[25] Newspapers.

[26] Drinking buddies.

[27] Bought.

[28] Three-ounce measures.

[29] In Shakespeare's *Hamlet* Queen Gertrude cites the sexually coarse names that "liberal shepherds" give to some flowers (*liberal* means *free-speaking*) (4.7). Roman poet Virgil's *Eclogues* are poems spoken by shepherds.

[30] Ordering another round of drinks.

[31] Two ounces, with a hot-water mixer.

[32] Colloquial Hiberno-English for boss.

while Farrington looked at the company out of his heavy dirty eyes, smiling and at times drawing forth stray drops of liquor from his moustache with the aid of his lower lip.

When that round was over there was a pause. O'Halloran had money but neither of the other two seemed to have any; so the whole party left the shop somewhat regretfully. At the corner of Duke Street Higgins and Nosey Flynn bevelled off to the left while the other three turned back towards the city. Rain was drizzling down on the cold streets and, when they reached the Ballast Office,[33] Farrington suggested the Scotch House. The bar was full of men and loud with the noise of tongues and glasses. The three men pushed past the whining match-sellers[34] at the door and formed a little party at the corner of the counter. They began to exchange stories. Leonard introduced them to a young fellow named Weathers who was performing at the Tivoli[35] as an acrobat and knockabout *artiste*. Farrington stood a drink all round. Weathers said he would take a small Irish and Apollinaris.[36] Farrington, who had definite notions of what was what, asked the boys would they have an Apollinaris too; but the boys told Tim to make theirs hot. The talk became theatrical. O'Halloran stood a round and then Farrington stood another round, Weathers protesting that the hospitality was too Irish. He promised to get them in behind the scenes and introduce them to some nice girls. O'Halloran said that he and Leonard would go, but that Farrington wouldn't go because he was a married man; and Farrington's heavy dirty eyes leered at the company in token that he understood he was being chaffed.[37] Weathers made them all have just one little tincture[38] at his expense and promised to meet them later on at Mulligan's in Poolbeg Street.

When the Scotch House closed they went round to Mulligan's. They went into the parlour at the back and O'Halloran ordered small hot specials all round. They were all beginning to feel mellow. Farrington was just standing another round when Weathers came back. Much to Farrington's relief he drank a glass of bitter[39] this time.

---

[33] Large administrative building on the Liffey.
[34] Beggars selling matches and small trinkets to avoid arrest for vagrancy.
[35] A nearby music hall.
[36] Irish whiskey with an expensive carbonated mineral water.
[37] Teased.
[38] Slang for drink.
[39] Beer.

Funds were getting low but they had enough to keep them going. Presently two young women with big hats and a young man in a check suit came in and sat at a table close by. Weathers saluted them and told the company that they were out of the Tivoli. Farrington's eyes wandered at every moment in the direction of one of the young women. There was something striking in her appearance. An immense scarf of peacock-blue muslin[40] was wound round her hat and knotted in a great bow under her chin; and she wore bright yellow gloves, reaching to the elbow. Farrington gazed admiringly at the plump arm which she moved very often and with much grace; and when, after a little time, she answered his gaze he admired still more her large dark brown eyes. The oblique staring expression in them fascinated him. She glanced at him once or twice and, when the party was leaving the room, she brushed against his chair and said *O, pardon!* in a London accent.[41] He watched her leave the room in the hope that she would look back at him, but he was disappointed. He cursed his want of money and cursed all the rounds he had stood, particularly all the whiskies and Apollinaris which he had stood to Weathers. If there was one thing that he hated it was a sponge. He was so angry that he lost count of the conversation of his friends.

When Paddy Leonard called him he found that they were talking about feats of strength. Weathers was showing his biceps muscle to the company and boasting so much that the other two had called on Farrington to uphold the national honour. Farrington pulled up his sleeve accordingly and showed his biceps muscle to the company. The two arms were examined and compared and finally it was agreed to have a trial of strength. The table was cleared and the two men rested their elbows on it, clasping hands. When Paddy Leonard said *Go!* each was to try to bring down the other's hand on to the table. Farrington looked very serious and determined.

The trial began. After about thirty seconds Weathers brought his opponent's hand slowly down on to the table. Farrington's dark wine-coloured face flushed darker still with anger and humiliation at having been defeated by such a stripling.[42]

---

[40] Light cotton.

[41] In the original 1910 manuscript, the sexual nature of this encounter is made explicit: "Farrington said he wouldn't mind having the far one and began to smile at her but when Weathers offered to introduce her he said 'No, he was only chaffing' because he knew he had not money enough. She continued to cast bold glances at him and changed the position of her legs often."

[42] An adolescent.

—You're not to put the weight of your body behind it. Play fair, he said.

—Who's not playing fair? said the other.

—Come on again. The two best out of three.

The trial began again. The veins stood out on Farrington's forehead, and the pallor of Weathers' complexion changed to peony. Their hands and arms trembled under the stress. After a long struggle Weathers again brought his opponent's hand slowly on to the table. There was a murmur of applause from the spectators. The curate, who was standing beside the table, nodded his red head towards the victor and said with stupid familiarity:

—Ah! that's the knack!

—What the hell do you know about it? said Farrington fiercely, turning on the man. What do you put in your gab[43] for?

—Sh, sh! said O'Halloran, observing the violent expression of Farrington's face. Pony up,[44] boys. We'll have just one little smahan[45] more and then we'll be off.

A very sullen-faced man stood at the corner of O'Connell Bridge waiting for the little Sandymount tram to take him home. He was full of smouldering anger and revengefulness. He felt humiliated and discontented; he did not even feel drunk; and he had only twopence in his pocket. He cursed everything. He had done for himself in the office, pawned his watch, spent all his money; and he had not even got drunk. He began to feel thirsty again and he longed to be back again in the hot reeking public-house. He had lost his reputation as a strong man, having been defeated twice by a mere boy. His heart swelled with fury and, when he thought of the woman in the big hat who had brushed against him and said *Pardon!* his fury nearly choked him.

His tram let him down at Shelbourne Road and he steered his great body along in the shadow of the wall of the barracks.[46] He loathed returning to his home. When he went in by the side-door he found the kitchen empty and the kitchen fire nearly out. He bawled upstairs:

—Ada! Ada!

---

[43] "Beak, nose, or snout" in Gaelic.

[44] Pay up ("pony" is also slang for a small whiskey).

[45] *Smeathán* means "taste" in Gaelic.

[46] Beggar's Bush Infantry Barracks quartered British troops.

His wife was a little sharp-faced woman who bullied her husband when he was sober and was bullied by him when he was drunk. They had five children. A little boy came running down the stairs.

—Who is that? said the man, peering through the darkness.

—Me, pa.

—Who are you? Charlie?

—No, pa. Tom.

—Where's your mother?

—She's out at the chapel.[47]

—That's right.... Did she think of leaving any dinner for me?

—Yes, pa. I—

—Light the lamp. What do you mean by having the place in darkness? Are the other children in bed?

The man sat down heavily on one of the chairs while the little boy lit the lamp. He began to mimic his son's flat accent, saying half to himself: *At the chapel. At the chapel, if you please!* When the lamp was lit he banged his fist on the table and shouted:

—What's for my dinner?

—I'm going ... to cook it, pa, said the little boy.

The man jumped up furiously and pointed to the fire.

—On that fire! You let the fire out! By God, I'll teach you to do that again!

He took a step to the door and seized the walking-stick which was standing behind it.

—I'll teach you to let the fire out! he said, rolling up his sleeve in order to give his arm free play.

The little boy cried *O, pa!* and ran whimpering round the table, but the man followed him and caught him by the coat. The little boy looked about him wildly but, seeing no way of escape, fell upon his knees.

—Now, you'll let the fire out the next time! said the man striking at him viciously with the stick. Take that, you little whelp!

The boy uttered a squeal of pain as the stick cut his thigh. He clasped his hands together in the air and his voice shook with fright.

—O, pa! he cried. Don't beat me, pa! And I'll ... I'll say a *Hail Mary*[48] for you.... I'll say a *Hail Mary* for you, pa, if you don't beat me.... I'll say a *Hail Mary*....

---

[47] Catholic midnight mass.

[48] Catholic prayer begging the Virgin Mary for intercession: "Hail Mary, full of grace, the Lord is with thee. Blessed art thou among women, and blessed is the fruit of thy womb, Jesus. Holy Mary, Mother of God, pray for us sinners now, and at the hour of death."

Clay[1]

THE MATRON had given her leave to go out as soon as the women's tea was over and Maria looked forward to her evening out. The kitchen was spick and span: the cook said you could see yourself in the big copper boilers. The fire was nice and bright and on one of the side-tables were four very big barmbracks.[2] These barmbracks seemed uncut; but if you went closer you would see that they had been cut into long thick even slices and were ready to be handed round at tea. Maria had cut them herself.

Maria was a very, very small person indeed but she had a very long nose and a very long chin. She talked a little through her nose, always soothingly: *Yes, my dear*, and *No, my dear*. She was always sent for when the women quarrelled over their tubs and always succeeded in making peace. One day the matron had said to her:

—Maria, you are a veritable peace-maker!

And the sub-matron and two of the Board ladies had heard the compliment. And Ginger Mooney was always saying what she wouldn't do to the dummy[3] who had charge of the irons[4] if it wasn't for Maria. Everyone was so fond of Maria.

The women would have their tea at six o'clock and she would be able to get away before seven. From Ballsbridge to the Pillar, twenty minutes; from the Pillar to Drumcondra, twenty minutes; and twenty

---

[1] Maria, the story's protagonist, works as a scullery maid in a "Magdalen laundry," an institution for the reform of prostitutes overseen by a Protestant board. The former prostitutes perform often grueling manual labor in exchange for room and board. Maria's position is not entirely clear: she is a Catholic and clearly not a former prostitute.

[2] Raisin-cakes or buns served on All-Hallow's Eve (October 31); small symbolic items are baked into them to tell the fortunes of those who get them.

[3] A lower servant in the laundry, likely one unable to speak.

[4] These heavy fabric pressers had to be fire-heated.

minutes to buy the things.[5] She would be there before eight. She took out her purse with the silver clasps and read again the words *A Present from Belfast*.[6] She was very fond of that purse because Joe had brought it to her five years before when he and Alphy had gone to Belfast on a Whit-Monday[7] trip. In the purse were two half-crowns and some coppers. She would have five shillings clear after paying tram fare. What a nice evening they would have, all the children singing! Only she hoped that Joe wouldn't come in drunk. He was so different when he took any drink.

Often he had wanted her to go and live with them; but she would have felt herself in the way (though Joe's wife was ever so nice with her) and she had become accustomed to the life of the laundry. Joe was a good fellow. She had nursed[8] him and Alphy too; and Joe used often say:

—Mamma is mamma but Maria is my proper mother.

After the break-up at home the boys had got her that position in the *Dublin by Lamplight* laundry, and she liked it. She used to have such a bad opinion of Protestants but now she thought they were very nice people, a little quiet and serious, but still very nice people to live with. Then she had her plants in the conservatory[9] and she liked looking after them. She had lovely ferns and wax-plants and, whenever anyone came to visit her, she always gave the visitor one or two slips[10] from her conservatory. There was one thing she didn't like and that was the tracts[11] on the walls; but the matron was such a nice person to deal with, so genteel.

When the cook told her everything was ready she went into the women's room and began to pull the big bell. In a few minutes the women began to come in by twos and threes, wiping their steaming hands in their petticoats and pulling down the sleeves of their

---

[5] In sequence: the village where the laundry is; the central station for suburban lines in the heart of Dublin; a village to the northeast. Nelson's Pillar honors British naval hero Admiral Horatio Nelson (1758-1805), who lost his life in the Battle of Trafalgar (1805), a signal victory over Napoleon. The nearly 135'-tall granite column and statue, completed in 1809, was a controversial symbol of British victory over Catholic Spain and formerly Catholic France.

[6] Major city in Protestant Northern Ireland.

[7] Holiday following Whitsunday, the 7th Sunday after Easter, when the Holy Spirit descended on the Apostles.

[8] Cared for as a child.

[9] Windowed room.

[10] Cuttings.

[11] Religious posters and pamphlets.

blouses over their red steaming arms. They settled down before their huge mugs which the cook and the dummy filled up with hot tea, already mixed with milk and sugar in huge tin cans. Maria superintended the distribution of the barmbrack and saw that every woman got her four slices. There was a great deal of laughing and joking during the meal. Lizzie Fleming said Maria was sure to get the ring[12] and, though Fleming had said that for so many Hallow Eves, Maria had to laugh and say she didn't want any ring or man either; and when she laughed her grey-green eyes sparkled with disappointed shyness and the tip of her nose nearly met the tip of her chin. Then Ginger Mooney lifted her mug of tea and proposed Maria's health while all the other women clattered with their mugs on the table, and said she was sorry she hadn't a sup of porter[13] to drink it in. And Maria laughed again till the tip of her nose nearly met the tip of her chin and till her minute body nearly shook itself asunder because she knew that Mooney meant well though, of course, she had the notions of a common[14] woman.

But wasn't Maria glad when the women had finished their tea and the cook and the dummy had begun to clear away the teathings! She went into her little bedroom and, remembering that the next morning was a mass morning,[15] changed the hand of the alarm from seven to six. Then she took off her working skirt and her house-boots and laid her best skirt out on the bed and her tiny dress-boots beside the foot of the bed. She changed her blouse too and, as she stood before the mirror, she thought of how she used to dress for mass on Sunday morning when she was a young girl; and she looked with quaint affection at the diminutive body which she had so often adorned. In spite of its years she found it a nice tidy little body.

When she got outside the streets were shining with rain and she was glad of her old brown raincloak. The tram was full and she had to sit on the little stool at the end of the car, facing all the people, with her toes barely touching the floor. She arranged in her mind all she was going to do and thought how much better it was to be independent and to have your own money in your pocket. She hoped

---

[12] Foretelling marriage.

[13] Glass of beer.

[14] Rural or working class; Maria is middle class and sensitive to such distinctions.

[15] All Saint's Day—Catholics would be expected to attend mass.

they would have a nice evening. She was sure they would but she could not help thinking what a pity it was Alphy and Joe were not speaking. They were always falling out now but when they were boys together they used to be the best of friends: but such was life.

She got out of her tram at the Pillar and ferreted her way quickly among the crowds. She went into Downes's cake-shop but the shop was so full of people that it was a long time before she could get herself attended to. She bought a dozen of mixed penny cakes, and at last came out of the shop laden with a big bag. Then she thought what else would she buy: she wanted to buy something really nice. They would be sure to have plenty of apples and nuts. It was hard to know what to buy and all she could think of was cake. She decided to buy some plumcake[16] but Downes's plumcake had not enough almond icing on top of it so she went over to a shop in Henry Street. Here she was a long time in suiting herself and the stylish young lady behind the counter, who was evidently a little annoyed by her, asked her was it wedding-cake she wanted to buy. That made Maria blush and smile at the young lady; but the young lady took it all very seriously and finally cut a thick slice of plum-cake, parcelled it up and said:

—Two-and-four, please.[17]

She thought she would have to stand in the Drumcondra tram because none of the young men seemed to notice her[18] but an elderly gentleman made room for her. He was a stout gentleman and he wore a brown hard hat; he had a square red face and a grey-ish moustache. Maria thought he was a colonel-looking gentleman and she reflected how much more polite he was than the young men who simply stared straight before them. The gentleman began to chat with her about Hallow Eve and the rainy weather. He sup-posed the bag was full of good things for the little ones and said it was only right that the youngsters should enjoy themselves while they were young. Maria agreed with him and favoured him with demure nods and hems. He was very nice with her, and when she was getting out at the Canal Bridge she thanked him and bowed, and he bowed to her and raised his hat and smiled agreeably, and while she was going up along the terrace, bending her tiny head

[16] Dense fruit and nut cake.

[17] This means Maria has spent over three shillings—most of the money she brought with her.

[18] Offer her a seat, a courtesy.

under the rain, she thought how easy it was to know a gentleman even when he has a drop taken.[19]

Everybody said: *O, here's Maria!* when she came to Joe's house. Joe was there, having come home from business, and all the children had their Sunday dresses on. There were two big girls in from next door and games were going on. Maria gave the bag of cakes to the eldest boy, Alphy, to divide and Mrs Donnelly said it was too good of her to bring such a big bag of cakes and made all the children say:

—Thanks, Maria.

But Maria said she had brought something special for papa and mamma, something they would be sure to like, and she began to look for her plumcake. She tried in Downes's bag and then in the pockets of her waterproof and then on the hallstand but nowhere could she find it. Then she asked all the children had any of them eaten it—by mistake, of course—but the children all said no and looked as if they did not like to eat cakes if they were to be accused of stealing. Everybody had a solution for the mystery and Mrs Donnelly said it was plain that Maria had left it behind her in the tram. Maria, remembering how confused the gentleman with the greyish moustache had made her, coloured with shame and vexation and disappointment. At the thought of the failure of her little surprise and of the two and fourpence she had thrown away for nothing she nearly cried outright.

But Joe said it didn't matter and made her sit down by the fire. He was very nice with her. He told her all that went on in his office, repeating for her a smart answer which he had made to the manager. Maria did not understand why Joe laughed so much over the answer he had made but she said that the manager must have been a very overbearing person to deal with. Joe said he wasn't so bad when you knew how to take him, that he was a decent sort so long as you didn't rub him the wrong way. Mrs Donnelly played the piano for the children and they danced and sang. Then the two next-door girls handed round the nuts. Nobody could find the nut-crackers and Joe was nearly getting cross over it and asked how did they expect Maria to crack nuts without a nutcracker. But Maria said she didn't like nuts and that they weren't to bother about her. Then Joe asked would she take a bottle of stout[20] and Mrs Donnelly

---

[19] Consumed alcohol.

[20] Strong, dark beer.

said there was port wine too in the house if she would prefer that. Maria said she would rather they didn't ask her to take anything: but Joe insisted.

So Maria let him have his way and they sat by the fire talking over old times and Maria thought she would put in a good word for Alphy. But Joe cried that God might strike him stone dead if ever he spoke a word to his brother again and Maria said she was sorry she had mentioned the matter. Mrs Donnelly told her husband it was a great shame for him to speak that way of his own flesh and blood but Joe said that Alphy was no brother of his and there was nearly being a row on the head of it. But Joe said he would not lose his temper on account of the night it was and asked his wife to open some more stout. The two next-door girls had arranged some Hallow Eve games and soon everything was merry again. Maria was delighted to see the children so merry and Joe and his wife in such good spirits. The next-door girls put some saucers[21] on the table and then led the children up to the table, blindfold. One got the prayer-book and the other three got the water; and when one of the next-door girls got the ring Mrs Donnelly shook her finger at the blushing girl as much as to say: O, *I know all about it!* They insisted then on blindfolding Maria and leading her up to the table to see what she would get; and, while they were putting on the bandage, Maria laughed and laughed again till the tip of her nose nearly met the tip of her chin.

They led her up to the table amid laughing and joking and she put her hand out in the air as she was told to do. She moved her hand about here and there in the air and descended on one of the saucers. She felt a soft wet substance with her fingers and was surprised that nobody spoke or took off her bandage. There was a pause for a few seconds; and then a great deal of scuffling and whispering. Somebody said something about the garden, and at last Mrs Donnelly said something very cross to one of the next-door girls and told her to throw it out at once: that was no play. Maria understood that it was wrong that time and so she had to do it over again: and this time she got the prayer-book.

After that Mrs Donnelly played Miss McCloud's Reel[22] for the children and Joe made Maria take a glass of wine. Soon they were

---

[21] In this game, saucers are filled with items that blindfolded players must choose to divine their futures: a prayer book (a life devoted to god), a ring (marriage), water (a trip), and clay (death)—though this last item was often politely omitted.

[22] Traditional dancing music.

all quite merry again and Mrs Donnelly said Maria would enter a convent before the year was out because she had got the prayer-book. Maria had never seen Joe so nice to her as he was that night, so full of pleasant talk and reminiscences. She said they were all very good to her.

At last the children grew tired and sleepy and Joe asked Maria would she not sing some little song before she went, one of the old songs. Mrs Donnelly said *Do, please, Maria!* and so Maria had to get up and stand beside the piano. Mrs Donnelly bade the children be quiet and listen to Maria's song. Then she played the prelude and said *Now, Maria!* and Maria, blushing very much, began to sing in a tiny quavering voice. She sang *I Dreamt that I Dwelt,* and when she came to the second verse she sang again:[23]

> *I dreamt that I dwelt in marble halls*
> *With vassals and serfs at my side*
> *And of all who assembled within those walls*
> *That I was the hope and the pride.*
>
> *I had riches too great to count, could boast*
> *Of a high ancestral name,*
> *But I also dreamt, which pleased me most,*
> *That you loved me still the same.*

But no one tried to show her her mistake; and when she had ended her song Joe was very much moved. He said that there was no time like the long ago and no music for him like poor old Balfe, whatever other people might say; and his eyes filled up so much with tears that he could not find what he was looking for and in the end he had to ask his wife to tell him where the corkscrew was.

[23] Maria repeats the song's first verse—a significant omission. For the verse she omits, see p. 000.

A Painful Case

MR JAMES DUFFY lived in Chapelizod[1] because he wished to live as far as possible from the city of which he was a citizen and because he found all the other suburbs of Dublin mean, modern and pretentious. He lived in an old sombre house and from his windows he could look into the disused distillery or upwards along the shallow river on which Dublin is built. The lofty walls of his uncarpeted room were free from pictures. He had himself bought every article of furniture in the room: a black iron bedstead, an iron washstand, four cane chairs, a clothes-rack, a coal-scuttle, a fender and irons and a square table on which lay a double desk.[2] A bookcase had been made in an alcove by means of shelves of white wood. The bed was clothed with white bed-clothes and a black and scarlet rug covered the foot. A little hand-mirror hung above the washstand and during the day a white-shaded lamp stood as the sole ornament of the mantelpiece. The books on the white wooden shelves were arranged from below upwards according to bulk. A complete Wordsworth[3] stood at one end of the lowest shelf and a copy of the *Maynooth Catechism*,[4] sewn into the cloth cover of a notebook, stood at one end of the top shelf. Writing materials were always on the desk. In the desk lay a manuscript translation of Hauptmann's *Michael Kramer*,[5] the stage directions of which were written in purple ink, and a little

---

[1] Western suburb, later featured prominently in *Finnegan's Wake*.

[2] Writing case; a scuttle is a coal container; the fender encloses the fireplace, and the irons hold the logs; a washstand holds a basin, pitcher, towels, etc.

[3] Romantic poet William Wordsworth (1770–1850).

[4] An 1882 book used for religious instruction; the suburb of Maynooth is home to a major seminary.

[5] Published in 1900, this play by German writer Gerhart Hauptmann (1862–1946) features an obsessive, demanding father whose self-obsession drives his talented son to suicide. Here it signifies, among other things, Duffy's cosmopolitanism.

sheaf of papers held together by a brass pin. In these sheets a sentence was inscribed from time to time and, in an ironical moment, the headline of an advertisement for Bile Beans[6] had been pasted on to the first sheet. On lifting the lid of the desk a faint fragrance escaped—the fragrance of new cedarwood pencils or of a bottle of gum[7] or of an overripe apple which might have been left there and forgotten.

Mr Duffy abhorred anything which betokened physical or mental disorder. A mediaeval doctor would have called him saturnine.[8] His face, which carried the entire tale of his years, was of the brown tint of Dublin streets. On his long and rather large head grew dry black hair and a tawny moustache did not quite cover an unamiable mouth. His cheekbones also gave his face a harsh character; but there was no harshness in the eyes which, looking at the world from under their tawny eyebrows, gave the impression of a man ever alert to greet a redeeming instinct in others but often disappointed. He lived at a little distance from his body, regarding his own acts with doubtful side-glances. He had an odd autobiographical habit which led him to compose in his mind from time to time a short sentence about himself containing a subject in the third person and a predicate in the past tense. He never gave alms to beggars and walked firmly, carrying a stout hazel.[9]

He had been for many years cashier of a private bank in Baggot Street. Every morning he came in from Chapelizod by tram. At midday he went to Dan Burke's[10] and took his lunch—a bottle of lager beer and a small trayful of arrowroot biscuits.[11] At four o'clock he was set free. He dined in an eating-house in George's Street where he felt himself safe from the society of Dublin's gilded youth and where there was a certain plain honesty in the bill of fare. His evenings were spent either before his landlady's piano or roaming about the outskirts of the city. His liking for Mozart's music brought him sometimes to an opera or a concert: these were the only dissipations of his life.

He had neither companions nor friends, church nor creed. He lived his spiritual life without any communion with others, visiting

---

[6] Widely advertised patent medicine for purging excess bile.

[7] Glue.

[8] Melancholy or sullen—thought to arise from an excess of bile.

[9] Walking-stick.

[10] Real pub on Baggot St.

[11] Cookies good for digestion.

his relatives at Christmas and escorting them to the cemetery when they died. He performed these two social duties for old dignity's sake but conceded nothing further to the conventions which regulate the civic life. He allowed himself to think that in certain circumstances he would rob his bank but, as these circumstances never arose, his life rolled out evenly—an adventureless tale.

One evening he found himself sitting beside two ladies in the Rotunda.[12] The house, thinly peopled and silent, gave distressing prophecy of failure. The lady who sat next him looked round at the deserted house once or twice and then said:

—What a pity there is such a poor house tonight! It's so hard on people to have to sing to empty benches.

He took the remark as an invitation to talk. He was surprised that she seemed so little awkward. While they talked he tried to fix her permanently in his memory. When he learned that the young girl beside her was her daughter he judged her to be a year or so younger than himself. Her face, which must have been handsome, had remained intelligent. It was an oval face with strongly marked features. The eyes were very dark blue and steady. Their gaze began with a defiant note but was confused by what seemed a deliberate swoon[13] of the pupil into the iris, revealing for an instant a temperament of great sensibility. The pupil reasserted itself quickly, this half-disclosed nature fell again under the reign of prudence, and her astrakhan[14] jacket, moulding a bosom of a certain fullness, struck the note of defiance more definitely.

He met her again a few weeks afterwards at a concert in Earlsfort Terrace[15] and seized the moments when her daughter's attention was diverted to become intimate. She alluded once or twice to her husband but her tone was not such as to make the allusion a warning. Her name was Mrs Sinico. Her husband's great-great-grandfather had come from Leghorn.[16] Her husband was captain of a mercantile boat plying between Dublin and Holland; and they had one child.

Meeting her a third time by accident he found courage to make an appointment. She came. This was the first of many meetings; they

---

[12] Fashionable concert hall in Rutland Square.

[13] Contraction.

[14] Fine lambskin.

[15] Exhibition hall near Stephen's Green.

[16] Italian seaport of Livorno.

met always in the evening and chose the most quiet quarters for their walks together. Mr Duffy, however, had a distaste for underhand ways and, finding that they were compelled to meet stealthily, he forced her to ask him to her house. Captain Sinico encouraged his visits, thinking that his daughter's hand was in question. He had dismissed his wife so sincerely from his gallery of pleasures that he did not suspect that anyone else would take an interest in her. As the husband was often away and the daughter out giving music lessons Mr Duffy had many opportunities of enjoying the lady's society. Neither he nor she had had any such adventure before and neither was conscious of any incongruity. Little by little he entangled his thoughts with hers. He lent her books, provided her with ideas, shared his intellectual life with her. She listened to all.

Sometimes in return for his theories she gave out some fact of her own life. With almost maternal solicitude she urged him to let his nature open to the full; she became his confessor.[17] He told her that for some time he had assisted at the meetings of an Irish Socialist Party[18] where he had felt himself a unique figure amidst a score of sober workmen in a garret lit by an inefficient oil-lamp. When the party had divided into three sections, each under its own leader and in its own garret, he had discontinued his attendances. The workmen's discussions, he said, were too timorous; the interest they took in the question of wages was inordinate. He felt that they were hard-featured realists and that they resented an exactitude which was the product of a leisure not within their reach. No social revolution, he told her, would be likely to strike Dublin for some centuries.

She asked him why did he not write out his thoughts. For what, he asked her, with careful scorn. To compete with phrasemongers, incapable of thinking consecutively for sixty seconds? To submit himself to the criticisms of an obtuse middle class which entrusted its morality to policemen and its fine arts to impresarios?[19]

He went often to her little cottage outside Dublin; often they spent their evenings alone. Little by little, as their thoughts entangled, they spoke of subjects less remote. Her companionship was like a warm soil about an exotic.[20] Many times she allowed the dark to fall

---

[17] Like other religious terms in the story (e.g., communion), here a profane adaptation of Catholic ritual.

[18] A minority party; socialism was more influential in European politics, advocating not only economic reform, but greater social and civic transformations.

[19] Promoters of popular entertainments.

[20] Hothouse plant.

upon them, refraining from lighting the lamp. The dark discreet room, their isolation, the music that still vibrated in their ears united them. This union exalted him, wore away the rough edges of his character, emotionalised his mental life. Sometimes he caught himself listening to the sound of his own voice. He thought that in her eyes he would ascend to an angelical stature; and, as he attached the fervent nature of his companion more and more closely to him, he heard the strange impersonal voice which he recognised as his own, insisting on the soul's incurable loneliness. We cannot give ourselves, it said: we are our own. The end of these discourses was that one night during which she had shown every sign of unusual excitement, Mrs Sinico caught up his hand passionately and pressed it to her cheek.

Mr Duffy was very much surprised. Her interpretation of his words disillusioned him. He did not visit her for a week; then he wrote to her asking her to meet him. As he did not wish their last interview to be troubled by the influence of their ruined confessional they meet in a little cakeshop near the Parkgate.[21] It was cold autumn weather but in spite of the cold they wandered up and down the roads of the Park for nearly three hours. They agreed to break off their intercourse:[22] every bond, he said, is a bond to sorrow. When they came out of the Park they walked in silence towards the tram; but here she began to tremble so violently that, fearing another collapse on her part, he bade her good-bye quickly and left her. A few days later he received a parcel containing his books and music.

Four years passed. Mr Duffy returned to his even way of life. His room still bore witness of the orderliness of his mind. Some new pieces of music encumbered the music-stand in the lower room and on his shelves stood two volumes by Nietzsche: *Thus Spake Zarathustra* and *The Gay Science*.[23] He wrote seldom in the sheaf of papers which lay in his desk. One of his sentences, written two months after his last interview with Mrs Sinico, read: Love between man and man is impossible because there must not be sexual intercourse and friendship between man and woman is impossible because there must be sexual intercourse. He kept away from concerts lest he should meet her. His father died; the junior partner of the bank retired. And still every

[21] The main entrance to Phoenix Park, west of central Dublin.

[22] Relationship (not connoting a sexual affair).

[23] Major works by radical German philosopher Friedrich Nietzsche (1844–1900) advocating personal, social, and political freedom from middle-class morality. *The Gay Science* claims "God is dead." See p. xxx.

morning he went into the city by tram and every evening walked home from the city after having dined moderately in George's Street and read the evening paper for dessert.

One evening as he was about to put a morsel of corned beef and cabbage into his mouth his hand stopped. His eyes fixed themselves on a paragraph in the evening paper which he had propped against the water-carafe. He replaced the morsel of food on his plate and read the paragraph attentively. Then he drank a glass of water, pushed his plate to one side, doubled the paper down before him between his elbows and read the paragraph over and over again. The cabbage began to deposit a cold white grease on his plate. The girl came over to him to ask was his dinner not properly cooked. He said it was very good and ate a few mouthfuls of it with difficulty. Then he paid his bill and went out.

He walked along quickly through the November twilight, his stout hazel stick striking the ground regularly, the fringe of the buff *Mail*[24] peeping out of a side-pocket of his tight reefer[25] overcoat. On the lonely road which leads from the Parkgate to Chapelizod he slackened his pace. His stick struck the ground less emphatically and his breath, issuing irregularly, almost with a sighing sound, condensed in the wintry air. When he reached his house he went up at once to his bedroom and, taking the paper from his pocket, read the paragraph again by the failing light of the window. He read it not aloud, but moving his lips as a priest does when he reads the prayers *In Secreto*.[26] This was the paragraph:

DEATH OF A LADY AT SYDNEY PARADE

A PAINFUL CASE

To-day at the City of Dublin Hospital[27] the Deputy Coroner (in the absence of Mr Leverett) held an inquest[28] on the body of Mrs Emily Sinico, aged forty-three years, who was killed at Sydney Parade Station[29] yesterday evening. The evidence showed that the deceased lady, while attempting to cross the line, was knocked down

---

[24] The resolutely pro-Unionist *Dublin Evening Mail* was printed on brown paper.

[25] Short, closely fitted.

[26] In a Latin mass, the celebrant recites some prayers quietly so they cannot be heard by the congregation.

[27] Charitable hospital in Baggot Street.

[28] Legal investigation into the cause of death.

[29] In the suburb of Merrion, south of Dublin.

by the engine of the ten o'clock slow train from Kingstown, thereby sustaining injuries of the head and right side which led to her death.

James Lennon, driver of the engine, stated that he had been in the employment of the railway company for fifteen years. On hearing the guard's whistle he set the train in motion and a second or two afterwards brought it to rest in response to loud cries. The train was going slowly.

P. Dunne, railway porter, stated that as the train was about to start he observed a woman attempting to cross the lines. He ran towards her and shouted, but, before he could reach her, she was caught by the buffer[30] of the engine and fell to the ground.

A juror—You saw the lady fall?

Witness—Yes.

Police Sergeant Croly deposed[31] that when he arrived he found the deceased lying on the platform apparently dead. He had the body taken to the waiting-room pending the arrival of the ambulance.

Constable 57E corroborated.

Dr Halpin, assistant house surgeon of the City of Dublin Hospital, stated that the deceased had two lower ribs fractured and had sustained severe contusions of the right shoulder. The right side of the head had been injured in the fall. The injuries were not sufficient to have caused death in a normal person. Death, in his opinion, had been probably due to shock and sudden failure of the heart's action.

Mr H. B. Patterson Finlay, on behalf of the railway company, expressed his deep regret at the accident. The company had always taken every precaution to prevent people crossing the lines except by the bridges, both by placing notices in every station and by the use of patent spring gates at level crossings. The deceased had been in the habit of crossing the lines late at night from platform to platform and, in view of certain other circumstances of the case, he did not think the railway officials were to blame.

Captain Sinico, of Leoville,[32] Sydney Parade, husband of the deceased, also gave evidence. He stated that the deceased was his wife. He was not in Dublin at the time of the accident as he had arrived only that morning from Rotterdam. They had been married for twenty-two years and had lived happily until about two years ago when his wife began to be rather intemperate in her habits.

---

[30] Guard or fender.

[31] Testified.

[32] The address of his shipping business in Holland.

Miss Mary Sinico said that of late her mother had been in the habit of going out at night to buy spirits. She, witness, had often tried to reason with her mother and had induced her to join a League.[33] She was not at home until an hour after the accident. The jury returned a verdict in accordance with the medical evidence and exonerated Lennon from all blame.

The Deputy Coroner said it was a most painful case, and expressed great sympathy with Captain Sinico and his daughter. He urged on the railway company to take strong measures to prevent the possibility of similar accidents in the future. No blame attached to anyone.

Mr Duffy raised his eyes from the paper and gazed out of his window on the cheerless evening landscape. The river lay quiet beside the empty distillery and from time to time a light appeared in some house on the Lucan road. What an end! The whole narrative of her death revolted him and it revolted him to think that he had ever spoken to her of what he held sacred. The threadbare phrases, the inane expressions of sympathy, the cautious words of a reporter won over to conceal the details of a commonplace vulgar death attacked his stomach. Not merely had she degraded herself; she had degraded him. He saw the squalid tract[34] of her vice, miserable and malodorous. His soul's companion! He thought of the hobbling wretches whom he had seen carrying cans and bottles to be filled by the barman. Just God, what an end! Evidently she had been unfit to live, without any strength of purpose, an easy prey to habits, one of the wrecks on which civilisation has been reared. But that she could have sunk so low! Was it possible he had deceived himself so utterly about her? He remembered her outburst of that night and interpreted it in a harsher sense than he had ever done. He had no difficulty now in approving of the course he had taken.

As the light failed and his memory began to wander he thought her hand touched his. The shock which had first attacked his stomach was now attacking his nerves. He put on his overcoat and hat quickly and went out. The cold air met him on the threshold; it crept into the sleeves of his coat. When he came to the public-house at Chapelizod Bridge he went in and ordered a hot punch.

The proprietor served him obsequiously but did not venture to talk. There were five or six workingmen in the shop discussing the

[33] Temperance leagues advocated prohibition and helped those who wanted to stop drinking; spirits is a term for strong alcohol.

[34] An odd word here referring either to a religious text or an expanse of land.

value of a gentleman's estate in County Kildare.[35] They drank at intervals from their huge pint tumblers and smoked, spitting often on the floor and sometimes dragging the sawdust over their spits with their heavy boots. Mr Duffy sat on his stool and gazed at them, without seeing or hearing them. After a while they went out and he called for another punch. He sat a long time over it. The shop was very quiet. The proprietor sprawled on the counter reading the *Herald*[36] and yawning. Now and again a tram was heard swishing along the lonely road outside.

As he sat there, living over his life with her and evoking alternately the two images in which he now conceived her, he realised that she was dead, that she had ceased to exist, that she had become a memory. He began to feel ill at ease. He asked himself what else could he have done. He could not have carried on a comedy of deception with her; he could not have lived with her openly. He had done what seemed to him best. How was he to blame? Now that she was gone he understood how lonely her life must have been, sitting night after night alone in that room. His life would be lonely too until he, too, died, ceased to exist, became a memory—if anyone remembered him.

It was after nine o'clock when he left the shop. The night was cold and gloomy. He entered the Park by the first gate and walked along under the gaunt trees. He walked through the bleak alleys where they had walked four years before. She seemed to be near him in the darkness. At moments he seemed to feel her voice touch his ear, her hand touch his. He stood still to listen. Why had he withheld life from her? Why had he sentenced her to death? He felt his moral nature falling to pieces.

When he gained the crest of the Magazine Hill[37] he halted and looked along the river towards Dublin, the lights of which burned redly[38] and hospitably in the cold night. He looked down the slope and, at the base, in the shadow of the wall of the Park, he saw some human figures lying. Those venal and furtive loves filled him with despair. He gnawed the rectitude of his life; he felt that he had been outcast from life's feast. One human being had seemed to love him

---

[35] Agricultural county just west of Dublin and near Chapelizod.

[36] The *Evening Herald*.

[37] Hill in Phoenix Park with commanding views; "Magazine" (armory) reflects its former military importance.

[38] The 1910 manuscript and proofs for the 1914 edition read "humanly" rather than "redly."

and he had denied her life and happiness: he had sentenced her to ignominy, a death of shame. He knew that the prostrate creatures down by the wall were watching him and wished him gone. No one wanted him; he was outcast from life's feast. He turned his eyes to the grey gleaming river, winding along towards Dublin. Beyond the river he saw a goods train winding out of Kingsbridge Station,[39] like a worm with a fiery head winding through the darkness, obstinately and laboriously. It passed slowly out of sight; but still he heard in his ears the laborious drone of the engine reiterating the syllables of her name.

He turned back the way he had come, the rhythm of the engine pounding in his ears. He began to doubt the reality of what memory told him. He halted under a tree and allowed the rhythm to die away. He could not feel her near him in the darkness nor her voice touch his ear. He waited for some minutes listening. He could hear nothing: the night was perfectly silent. He listened again: perfectly silent. He felt that he was alone.

[39] For trains running west and south.

Ivy Day in the Committee Room[1]

OLD JACK raked the cinders together with a piece of cardboard and spread them judiciously over the whitening dome of coals. When the dome was thinly covered his face lapsed into darkness but, as he set himself to fan the fire again, his crouching shadow ascended the opposite wall and his face slowly re-emerged into light. It was an old man's face, very bony and hairy. The moist blue eyes blinked at the fire and the moist mouth fell open at times, munching once or twice mechanically when it closed. When the cinders had caught he laid the piece of cardboard against the wall, sighed and said:

—That's better now, Mr O'Connor.

Mr O'Connor, a grey-haired young man, whose face was disfigured by many blotches and pimples, had just brought the tobacco for a cigarette into a shapely cylinder but when spoken to he undid his handiwork meditatively. Then he began to roll the tobacco again meditatively and after a moment's thought decided to lick the paper.

—Did Mr Tierney say when he'd be back? he asked in a husky falsetto.[2]

—He didn't say.

---

[1] On October 6, Irish nationalists wear sprigs of ivy to commemorate the death of Charles Stewart Parnell (1846–91), the Irish political leader who led the nation to the brink of political autonomy. It was in Committee Room 15 of the House of Parliament that Parnell delivered his final, highly emotional speech after resigning as leader of the Irish Parliamentary Party in December 1890, when his affair with Katharine ("Kitty") O'Shea came to light in a divorce trial. The event split Irish nationalist loyalties, pitting the stern moralists of the Catholic Church against more secular leaders—a breach that many, including young James Joyce and his father, regarded as treachery. See "Home Rule and Empire" (p. xxx).

[2] Artificial high-pitch.

Mr O'Connor put his cigarette into his mouth and began to search his pockets. He took out a pack of thin pasteboard cards.

—I'll get you a match, said the old man.

—Never mind, this'll do, said Mr O'Connor.

He selected one of the cards and read what was printed on it:

MUNICIPAL ELECTIONS[3]

ROYAL EXCHANGE WARD[4]

Mr Richard J. Tierney, P.L.G.,[5]
respectfully solicits the favour of your vote and influence at the coming election in the Royal Exchange Ward

---

Mr O'Connor had been engaged by Tierney's agent to canvass[6] one part of the ward but, as the weather was inclement and his boots let in the wet, he spent a great part of the day sitting by the fire in the Committee Room in Wicklow Street[7] with Jack, the old caretaker. They had been sitting thus since the short day had grown dark. It was the sixth of October, dismal and cold out of doors.

Mr O'Connor tore a strip off the card and, lighting it, lit his cigarette. As he did so the flame lit up a leaf of dark glossy ivy in the lapel of his coat. The old man watched him attentively and then, taking up the piece of cardboard again, began to fan the fire slowly while his companion smoked.

—Ah, yes, he said, continuing, it's hard to know what way to bring up children. Now who'd think he'd turn out like that! I sent him to the Christian Brothers[8] and I done what I could for him, and there he goes boosing[9] about. I tried to make him someway decent.

---

[3] For city council.

[4] Precinct that includes City Hall and Dublin Castle, the seat of British colonial power.

[5] Poor Law Guardian: elected welfare manager.

[6] Drum up votes and political support.

[7] Headquarters of the Nationalist Party, in the city center, just off Grafton Street.

[8] Conservative Catholic lay order operating schools for the poor (see "Araby," p. x n.3).

[9] Boozing.

He replaced the cardboard wearily.

—Only I'm an old man now I'd change his tune for him.[10] I'd take the stick to his back and beat him while I could stand over him—as I done many a time before. The mother, you know, she cocks[11] him up with this and that....

—That's what ruins children, said Mr O'Connor.

—To be sure it is, said the old man. And little thanks you get for it, only impudence. He takes th'upper hand of me whenever he sees I've a sup taken. What's the world coming to when sons speaks that way to their father?

—What age is he? said Mr O'Connor.

—Nineteen, said the old man.

—Why don't you put him to something?[12]

—Sure, amn't I never done at the drunken bowsy[13] ever since he left school? *I won't keep you*, I says. *You must get a job for yourself.* But, sure, it's worse whenever he gets a job; he drinks it all.

Mr O'Connor shook his head in sympathy, and the old man fell silent, gazing into the fire. Someone opened the door of the room and called out:

—Hello! Is this a Freemason's[14] meeting?

—Who's that? said the old man.

—What are you doing in the dark? asked a voice.

—Is that you, Hynes? asked Mr O'Connor.

—Yes. What are you doing in the dark? said Mr Hynes, advancing into the light of the fire.

He was a tall, slender young man with a light brown moustache. Imminent little drops of rain hung at the brim of his hat and the collar of his jacket-coat was turned up.

—Well, Mat, he said to Mr O'Connor, how goes it?

Mr O'Connor shook his head. The old man left the hearth and, after stumbling about the room returned with two candlesticks which he thrust one after the other into the fire and carried to the table. A denuded room came into view and the fire lost all its cheerful colour. The walls of the room were bare except for a copy of an

---

[10] In the initial drafts of the story, Joyce sought to produce a local dialect in the dialogue, so this sentence began: "On'y I'm an owl' man now I'd change." The final version was edited heavily to standardize the men's speech.

[11] Coddles and flatters him.

[12] Get him a job.

[13] Slang: lout.

[14] Secretive fraternal order (see "Araby," p. x n.19).

election address. In the middle of the room was a small table on which papers were heaped.

Mr Hynes leaned against the mantelpiece and asked:

—Has he paid you yet?[15]

—Not yet, said Mr O'Connor. I hope to God he'll not leave us in the lurch tonight.

Mr Hynes laughed.

—O, he'll pay you. Never fear, he said.

—I hope he'll look smart about it if he means business, said Mr O'Connor.

—What do you think, Jack? said Mr Hynes satirically to the old man.

The old man returned to his seat by the fire, saying:

—It isn't but he has it, anyway. Not like the other tinker.[16]

—What other tinker? said Mr Hynes.

—Colgan, said the old man scornfully.

—Is it because Colgan's a working-man you say that? What's the difference between a good honest bricklayer and a publican—eh? Hasn't the working-man as good a right to be in the Corporation[17] as anyone else—ay, and a better right than those shoneens[18] that are always hat in hand before any fellow with a handle[19] to his name? Isn't that so, Mat? said Mr Hynes, addressing Mr O'Connor.

—I think you're right, said Mr O'Connor.

—One man is a plain honest man with no hunker-sliding[20] about him. He goes in to represent the labour classes. This fellow you're working for only wants to get some job or other.

—Of course, the working-classes should be represented, said the old man.

—The working-man, said Mr Hynes, gets all kicks and no ha'pence.[21] But it's labour produces everything. The working-man is not looking for fat jobs for his sons and nephews and cousins. The working-man is not going to drag the honour of Dublin in the mud to please a German monarch.[22]

---

[15] For their work on the campaign.

[16] Derogatory term for beggar or gypsy.

[17] The city government.

[18] Contemptuous Gallic term for those who put on English airs for social and political advantage.

[19] Aristocratic-sounding title.

[20] Hypocrisy, dishonesty.

[21] Halfpence.

[22] German-descended King Edward VII of England.

—How's that? said the old man.

—Don't you know they want to present an address of welcome to Edward Rex[23] if he comes here next year? What do we want kowtowing to a foreign king?

—Our man won't vote for the address, said Mr O'Connor. He goes in on the Nationalist ticket.[24]

—Won't he? said Mr Hynes. Wait till you see whether he will or not. I know him. Is it Tricky Dicky Tierney?

—By God! perhaps you're right, Joe, said Mr O'Connor. Anyway, I wish he'd turn up with the spondulics.[25]

The three men fell silent. The old man began to rake more cinders together. Mr Hynes took off his hat, shook it and then turned down the collar of his coat, displaying, as he did so, an ivy leaf in the lapel.

—If this man was alive, he said, pointing to the leaf,[26] we'd have no talk of an address of welcome.

—That's true, said Mr O'Connor.

—Musha,[27] God be with them times! said the old man. There was some life in it then.

The room was silent again. Then a bustling little man with a snuffling nose and very cold ears pushed in the door. He walked over quickly to the fire, rubbing his hands as if he intended to produce a spark from them.

—No money, boys, he said.

—Sit down here, Mr Henchy, said the old man, offering him his chair.

—O, don't stir, Jack, don't stir, said Mr Henchy.

—He nodded curtly to Mr Hynes and sat down on the chair which the old man vacated.

—Did you serve[28] Aungier Street? he asked Mr O'Connor.

—Yes, said Mr O'Connor, beginning to search his pockets for memoranda.

—Did you call on Grimes?

—I did.

—Well? How does he stand?

---

[23] A formal welcome to the King of England acknowledging his dominion over Ireland. "Rex" is Latin for king.

[24] For Home Rule, opposing English rule.

[25] "Money" in American slang.

[26] Parnell. See n.1.

[27] Irish expression of surprise and frustration.

[28] Canvass.

—He wouldn't promise. He said: *I won't tell anyone what way I'm going to vote.* But I think he'll be all right.

—Why so?

—He asked me who the nominators[29] were, and I told him. I mentioned Father Burke's name. I think it'll be all right.

Mr Henchy began to snuffle and to rub his hands over the fire at a terrific speed. Then he said:

—For the love of God, Jack, bring us a bit of coal. There must be some left.

The old man went out of the room.

—It's no go, said Mr Henchy, shaking his head. I asked the little shoeboy, but he said: *Oh, now, Mr Henchy, when I see work going on properly I won't forget you, you may be sure.* Mean little tinker! 'Usha,[30] how could he be anything else?

—What did I tell you, Mat? said Mr Hynes. Tricky Dicky Tierney.

—O, he's as tricky as they make 'em, said Mr Henchy. He hasn't got those little pigs' eyes for nothing. Blast his soul! Couldn't he pay up like a man instead of: *O, now Mr Henchy, I must speak to Mr Fanning*[31]…. *I've spent a lot of money.* Mean little shoeboy of hell! I suppose he forgets the time his little old father kept the hand-me-down shop in Mary's Lane.

—But is that a fact? asked Mr O'Connor.

—God, yes, said Mr Henchy. Did you never hear that? And the men used to go in on Sunday morning before the houses[32] were open to buy a waistcoat or a trousers—moya![33] But Tricky Dicky's little old father always had a tricky little black bottle up in a corner.[34] Do you mind now? That's that. That's where he first saw the light.

The old man returned with a few lumps of coal which he placed here and there on the fire.

—That's a nice how-do-you-do, said Mr O'Connor. How does he expect us to work for him if he won't stump up?

—I can't help it, said Mr Henchy. I expect to find the bailiffs[35] in the hall when I go home.

[29] Prominent citizens supporting the candidate.

[30] Variant of *Musha.*

[31] Fictional sub-sheriff of Dublin: an office charged with the collection of debts and oversight of elections. See "Grace," p. xxx.

[32] Pubs.

[33] Irish expression of disbelief.

[34] Covertly sold liquor when the pubs were closed.

[35] Collection agents.

Mr Hynes laughed and, shoving himself away from the mantel-piece with the aid of his shoulders, made ready to leave.

—It'll be all right when King Eddie comes, he said. Well boys, I'm off for the present. See you later. 'Bye, 'bye.

He went out of the room slowly. Neither Mr Henchy nor the old man said anything, but, just as the door was closing, Mr O'Connor, who had been staring moodily into the fire, called out suddenly:

—'Bye, Joe.

Mr Henchy waited a few moments and then nodded in the direction of the door.

—Tell me, he said across the fire, what brings our friend in here? What does he want?

—'Usha, poor Joe! said Mr O'Connor, throwing the end of his cigarette into the fire, he's hard up like the rest of us.

Mr Henchy snuffled vigorously and spat so copiously that he nearly put out the fire which uttered a hissing protest.

—To tell you my private and candid opinion, he said, I think he's a man from the other camp. He's a spy of Colgan's if you ask me. *Just go round and try and find out how they're getting on. They won't suspect you.* Do you twig?[36]

—Ah, poor Joe is a decent skin, said Mr O'Connor.

—His father was a decent respectable man, Mr Henchy admitted. Poor old Larry Hynes! Many a good turn he did in his day! But I'm greatly afraid our friend is not nineteen carat.[37] Damn it, I can understand a fellow being hard up but what I can't understand is a fellow sponging. Couldn't he have some spark of manhood about him?

—He doesn't get a warm welcome from me when he comes, said the old man. Let him work for his own side and not come spying around here.

—I don't know, said Mr O'Connor dubiously, as he took out cigarette-papers and tobacco. I think Joe Hynes is a straight man. He's a clever chap, too, with the pen. Do you remember that thing he wrote...?

—Some of these hillsiders and fenians[38] are a bit too clever if you ask me, said Mr Henchy. Do you know what my private and

---

[36] Get my meaning.

[37] Dishonest (24-carat is pure gold).

[38] Irish Republican Brotherhood, a radical political organization that sought to overthrow British rule; "hillsiders" are people from the countryside, where nationalistist often engaged in guerilla tactics.

candid opinion is about some of those little jokers? I believe half of them are in the pay of the Castle.[39]

—There's no knowing, said the old man.

—O, but I know it for a fact, said Mr Henchy. They're Castle hacks.... I don't say Hynes.... No, damn it, I think he's a stroke above that.... But there's a certain little nobleman with a cock-eye—you know the patriot I'm alluding to?

Mr O'Connor nodded.

—There's a lineal descendant of Major Sirr[40] for you if you like! O, the heart's blood of a patriot! That's a fellow now that'd sell his country for fourpence—ay—and go down on his bended knees and thank the Almighty Christ he had a country to sell.

There was a knock at the door.

—Come in! said Mr Henchy.

A person resembling a poor clergyman or a poor actor appeared in the doorway. His black clothes were tightly buttoned on his short body and it was impossible to say whether he wore a clergyman's collar or a layman's, because the collar of his shabby frock-coat, the uncovered buttons of which reflected the candlelight, was turned up about his neck. He wore a round hat of hard black felt. His face, shining with raindrops, had the appearance of damp yellow cheese save where two rosy spots indicated the cheekbones. He opened his very long mouth suddenly to express disappointment and at the same time opened wide his very bright blue eyes to express pleasure and surprise.

—O, Father Keon! said Mr Henchy, jumping up from his chair. Is that you? Come in!

—O, no, no, no! said Father Keon quickly, pursing his lips as if he were addressing a child.

—Won't you come in and sit down?

—No, no, no! said Father Keon, speaking in a discreet indulgent velvety voice. Don't let me disturb you now! I'm just looking for Mr Fanning....

—He's round at the *Black Eagle*,[41] said Mr Henchy. But won't you come in and sit down a minute?

—No, no, thank you. It was just a little business matter, said Father Keon. Thank you, indeed.

[39] British government, headquartered at Dublin Castle.

[40] Term for a traitor: Dublin Chief of Police Henry Charles Sirr (1764–1841) aided the British against the rebellion of 1798 and continued to persecute the leaders of the Irish independence movement.

[41] Pub owned by Richard Tierney.

He retreated from the doorway and Mr Henchy, seizing one of the candlesticks, went to the door to light him downstairs.

—O, don't trouble, I beg!

—No, but the stairs is so dark.

—No, no, I can see.... Thank you, indeed.

—Are you right now?

—All right, thanks.... Thanks.

Mr Henchy returned with the candlestick and put it on the table. He sat down again at the fire. There was silence for a few moments.

—Tell me, John, said Mr O'Connor, lighting his cigarette with another pasteboard card.

—Hm?

—What is he exactly?[42]

—Ask me an easier one, said Mr Henchy.

—Fanning and himself seem to me very thick. They're often in Kavanagh's[43] together. Is he a priest at all?

—'Mmmyes, I believe so.... I think he's what you call black sheep.[44] We haven't many of them, thank God! but we have a few.... He's an unfortunate man of some kind....

—And how does he knock it out?[45] asked Mr O'Connor.

—That's another mystery.

—Is he attached to any chapel or church or institution or—

—No, said Mr Henchy, I think he's travelling on his own account.... God forgive me, he added, I thought he was the dozen of stout.[46]

—Is there any chance of a drink itself? asked Mr O'Connor.

—I'm dry too, said the old man.

—I asked that little shoeboy three times, said Mr Henchy, would he send up a dozen of stout. I asked him again now, but he was leaning on the counter in his shirt-sleeves having a deep goster[47] with Alderman Cowley.

—Why didn't you remind him? said Mr O'Connor.

[42] He's asking if Keon is really a priest or if he has been defrocked.

[43] A pub.

[44] Common idiom for a wayward family member; here it suggests he may be forbidden by the Church to perform any rituals.

[45] Earn a living.

[46] Delivery boy bringing beer (in payment for the men's work).

[47] Gabfest.

—Well, I couldn't go over while he was talking to Alderman Cowley. I just waited till I caught his eye, and said: *About that little matter I was speaking to you about.... That'll be all right, Mr H.*, he said. Yerra,[48] sure the little hop-o'-my-thumb[49] has forgotten all about it.

—There's some deal on in that quarter, said Mr O'Connor thoughtfully. I saw the three of them hard at it yesterday at Suffolk Street corner.

—I think I know the little game they're at, said Mr Henchy. You must owe the City Fathers money nowadays if you want to be made Lord Mayor. Then they'll make you Lord Mayor. By God! I'm thinking seriously of becoming a City Father myself. What do you think? Would I do for the job?

Mr O'Connor laughed.

—So far as owing money goes....

—Driving out of the Mansion House,[50] said Mr Henchy, in all my vermin,[51] with Jack here standing up behind me in a powdered wig—eh?

—And make me your private secretary, John.

—Yes. And I'll make Father Keon my private chaplain. We'll have a family party.

—Faith, Mr Henchy, said the old man, you'd keep up better style than some of them. I was talking one day to old Keegan, the porter.[52] *And how do you like your new master, Pat?* says I to him. *You haven't much entertaining now*, says I. *Entertaining!* says he. *He'd live on the smell of an oil-rag.*[53] And do you know what he told me? Now, I declare to God I didn't believe him.

—What? said Mr Henchy and Mr O'Connor.

—He told me: *What do you think of a Lord Mayor of Dublin sending out for a pound of chops for his dinner?*[54] *How's that for high living?* says he. *Wisha! wisha,*[55] says I. *A pound of chops*, says he, *coming into the Mansion House. Wisha!* says I, *what kind of people is going at all now?*

---

[48] "Sure" or "really" in Irish.

[49] Slang for small person.

[50] Residence of the Lord Mayor.

[51] Caustic pun on ermine, the lush fur trimming on official robes.

[52] Servant at the Mansion House.

[53] He's a miser.

[54] A modest meal.

[55] Irish expression of surprise.

At this point there was a knock at the door, and a boy put in his head.

—What is it? said the old man.

—From the *Black Eagle*, said the boy, walking in sideways and depositing a basket on the floor with a noise of shaken bottles.

The old man helped the boy to transfer the bottles from the basket to the table and counted the full tally. After the transfer the boy put his basket on his arm and asked:

—Any bottles?[56]

—What bottles? said the old man.

—Won't you let us drink them first? said Mr Henchy.

—I was told to ask for the bottles.[57]

—Come back to-morrow, said the old man.

—Here, boy! said Mr Henchy, will you run over to O'Farrell's and ask him to lend us a corkscrew—for Mr Henchy, say. Tell him we won't keep it a minute. Leave the basket there.

The boy went out and Mr Henchy began to rub his hands cheerfully, saying:

—Ah, well, he's not so bad after all. He's as good as his word, anyhow.

—There's no tumblers, said the old man.

—O, don't let that trouble you, Jack, said Mr Henchy. Many's the good man before now drank out of the bottle.

—Anyway, it's better than nothing, said Mr O'Connor.

—He's not a bad sort, said Mr Henchy, only Fanning has such a loan of[58] him. He means well, you know, in his own tinpot[59] way.

The boy came back with the corkscrew. The old man opened three bottles and was handing back the corkscrew when Mr Henchy said to the boy:

—Would ye like a drink, boy?

—If you please, sir, said the boy.

The old man opened another bottle grudgingly, and handed it to the boy.

—What age are you? he asked.

—Seventeen, said the boy.

As the old man said nothing further, the boy took the bottle, said: *Here's my best respects, sir*, to Mr Henchy, drank the contents,

---

[56] Empties, to return.

[57] A sign of Tierney's miserliness.

[58] Influence over.

[59] Cheap (better pots are ceramic).

put the bottle back on the table and wiped his mouth with his sleeve. Then he took up the corkscrew and went out of the door sideways, muttering some form of salutation.

—That's the way it begins, said the old man.

—The thin edge of the wedge, said Mr Henchy.

The old man distributed the three bottles which he had opened and the men drank from them simultaneously. After having drank each placed his bottle on the mantelpiece within hand's reach and drew in a long breath of satisfaction.

—Well, I did a good day's work to-day, said Mr Henchy, after a pause.

—That so, John?

—Yes. I got him one or two sure things in Dawson Street, Crofton and myself. Between ourselves, you know, Crofton (he's a decent chap, of course), but he's not worth a damn as a canvasser. He hasn't a word to throw to a dog. He stands and looks at the people while I do the talking.

Here two men entered the room. One of them was a very fat man whose blue serge[60] clothes seemed to be in danger of falling from his sloping figure. He had a big face which resembled a young ox's face in expression, staring blue eyes and a grizzled moustache. The other man, who was much younger and frailer, had a thin clean-shaven face. He wore a very high double collar and a wide-brimmed bowler hat.

—Hello, Crofton! said Mr Henchy to the fat man. Talk of the devil ...

—Where did the boose come from? asked the young man. Did the cow calve?[61]

—O, of course, Lyons spots the drink first thing! said Mr O'Connor, laughing.

—Is that the way you chaps canvass, said Mr Lyons, and Crofton and I out in the cold and rain looking for votes?

—Why, blast your soul, said Mr Henchy, I'd get more votes in five minutes than you two'd get in a week.

—Open two bottles of stout, Jack, said Mr O'Connor.

—How can I? said the old man, when there's no corkscrew?

—Wait now, wait now! said Mr Henchy, getting up quickly. Did you ever see this little trick?

---

[60] Durable wool fabric.

[61] A cow begins to produce milk after giving birth.

He took two bottles from the table and, carrying them to the fire, put them on the hob.[62] Then he sat down again by the fire and took another drink from his bottle. Mr Lyons sat on the edge of the table, pushed his hat towards the nape of his neck and began to swing his legs.

—Which is my bottle? he asked.

—This lad, said Mr Henchy.

Mr Crofton sat down on a box and looked fixedly at the other bottle on the hob. He was silent for two reasons. The first reason, sufficient in itself, was that he had nothing to say; the second reason was that he considered his companions beneath him. He had been a canvasser for Wilkins, the Conservative,[63] but when the Conservatives had withdrawn their man and, choosing the lesser of two evils, given their support to the Nationalist candidate, he had been engaged to work for Mr Tierney.

In a few minutes an apologetic *Pok!* was heard as the cork flew out of Mr Lyons' bottle. Mr Lyons jumped off the table, went to the fire, took his bottle and carried it back to the table.

—I was just telling them, Crofton, said Mr Henchy, that we got a good few votes to-day.

—Who did you get? asked Mr Lyons.

—Well, I got Parkes for one, and I got Atkinson for two, and I got Ward of Dawson Street. Fine old chap he is, too—regular old toff,[64] old Conservative! *But isn't your candidate a Nationalist?* said he. *He's a respectable man,* said I. *He's in favour of whatever will benefit this country. He's a big ratepayer,*[65] I said. *He has extensive house property in the city and three places of business and isn't it to his own advantage to keep down the rates? He's a prominent and respected citizen,* said I, *and a Poor Law Guardian, and he doesn't belong to any party, good, bad, or indifferent.* That's the way to talk to 'em.

—And what about the address to the King? said Mr Lyons, after drinking and smacking his lips.

—Listen to me, said Mr Henchy. What we want in this country, as I said to old Ward, is capital. The King's coming here will mean

---

[62] Flat metal portion of the grate surrounding the fireplace.

[63] Irish Conservative Party, which supported Home Rule. In this case, the Nationalist seems preferable to the working-class candidate, who would advocate for the redistribution of land and stricter labor laws.

[64] Stylish gent.

[65] Property tax payer.

an influx of money into this country. The citizens of Dublin will benefit by it. Look at all the factories down by the quays there, idle! Look at all the money there is in the country if we only worked the old industries, the mills, the shipbuilding yards and factories. It's capital we want.

—But look here, John, said Mr O'Connor. Why should we welcome the King of England? Didn't Parnell himself ...

—Parnell, said Mr Henchy, is dead. Now, here's the way I look at it. Here's this chap come to the throne after his old mother[66] keeping him out of it till the man was grey.[67] He's a man of the world, and he means well by us. He's a jolly fine decent fellow, if you ask me, and no damn nonsense about him. He just says to himself: *The old one never went to see these wild Irish.*[68] *By Christ, I'll go myself and see what they're like.* And are we going to insult the man when he comes over here on a friendly visit? Eh? Isn't that right, Crofton?

Mr Crofton nodded his head.

—But after all now, said Mr Lyons argumentatively, King Edward's life, you know, is not the very ...

—Let bygones be bygones, said Mr Henchy. I admire the man personally. He's just an ordinary knockabout like you and me. He's fond of his glass of grog and he's a bit of a rake, perhaps, and he's a good sportsman.Damn it, can't we Irish play fair?

—That's all very fine, said Mr Lyons. But look at the case of Parnell now.

—In the name of God, said Mr Henchy, where's the analogy between the two cases?

—What I mean, said Mr Lyons, is we have our ideals. Why, now, would we welcome a man like that? Do you think now after what he did Parnell was a fit man to lead us? And why, then, would we do it for Edward the Seventh?

—This is Parnell's anniversary, said Mr O'Connor, and don't let us stir up any bad blood. We all respect him now that he's dead and gone—even the Conservatives, he added, turning to Mr Crofton.

---

[66] This passage originally read "his bloody owl' mother," but Joyce agreed to delete the crude "bloody" to avoid the risk of libel and obscenity. For more on the changes to this story see "Composition, Publication, Early Reviews," p. xxx.

[67] Because Victoria lived until 1901, Edward did not become King until he was almost 60, and ruled for less than a decade. As Prince, he was known for his sexual appetite, which he indulged, safely, with married women (so that any pregnancy could be attributed elsewhere)—and so as "guilty" in Irish eyes as Parnell.

[68] Victoria actually visited four times, most recently in 1900.

Pok! The tardy cork flew out of Mr Crofton's bottle. Mr Crofton got up from his box and went to the fire. As he returned with his capture he said in a deep voice:

—Our side of the house respects him because he was a gentleman.[69]

—Right you are, Crofton! said Mr Henchy fiercely. He was the only man that could keep that bag of cats[70] in order. *Down, ye dogs! Lie down, ye curs!* That's the way he treated them. Come in, Joe! Come in! he called out, catching sight of Mr Hynes in the doorway.

Mr Hynes came in slowly.

—Open another bottle of stout, Jack, said Mr Henchy. O, I forgot there's no corkscrew! Here, show me one here and I'll put it at the fire.

The old man handed him another bottle and he placed it on the hob.

—Sit down, Joe, said Mr O'Connor, we're just talking about the Chief.[71]

—Ay, ay! said Mr Henchy.

Mr Hynes sat on the side of the table near Mr Lyons but said nothing.

—There's one of them, anyhow, said Mr Henchy, that didn't renege him. By God, I'll say for you, Joe! No, by God, you stuck to him like a man![72]

—O, Joe, said Mr O'Connor suddenly. Give us that thing you wrote—do you remember? Have you got it on you?

—O, ay! said Mr Henchy. Give us that. Did you ever hear that, Crofton? Listen to this now: splendid thing.

—Go on, said Mr O'Connor. Fire away, Joe.

Mr Hynes did not seem to remember at once the piece to which they were alluding, but, after reflecting a while, he said:

—O, that thing is it…. Sure, that's old now.

—Out with it, man! said Mr O'Connor.

—'Sh, 'sh, said Mr Henchy. Now, Joe!

---

[69] Parnell was a wealthy Protestant landowner, a class generally opposed to Home Rule.

[70] Slang for riotous group; here, the fractious Irish parliamentarians whom Parnell transformed into a potent voting block in the British House of Commons.

[71] Parnell's nickname.

[72] That is, he remained loyal to Parnell after the scandal emerged.

Mr Hynes hesitated a little longer. Then amid the silence he took off his hat, laid it on the table and stood up. He seemed to be rehearsing the piece in his mind. After a rather long pause he announced:

THE DEATH OF PARNELL

6th October, 1891

He cleared his throat once or twice and then began to recite:

He is dead. Our Uncrowned King[73] is dead.
O, Erin, ° mourn with grief and woe   *(Gaelic: Ireland)*
For he lies dead whom the fell gang
Of modern hypocrites laid low.

He lies slain by the coward hounds
He raised to glory from the mire;
And Erin's hopes and Erin's dreams
Perish upon her monarch's pyre. °   *(ceremonial fire)*

In palace, cabin or in cot °   *(cottage)*
The Irish heart where'er it be
Is bowed with woe—for he is gone
Who would have wrought her destiny.

He would have had his Erin famed,
The green flag gloriously unfurled,
Her statesmen, bards ° and warriors raised   *(poets)*
Before the nations of the World.

He dreamed (alas, 'twas but a dream!)
Of Liberty: but as he strove
To clutch that idol, treachery
Sundered him from the thing he loved.

Shame on the coward, caitiff hands   *(despicable)*
That smote their Lord or with a kiss
Betrayed him[74] to the rabble-rout
Of fawning priests—no friends of his.

May everlasting shame consume
The memory of those who tried
To befoul and smear the exalted name
Of one who spurned them in his pride.

---

[73] Title for Parnell coined by Timothy Michael Healy, who later turned against him.
[74] As Judas betrayed Jesus to the Romans.

He fell as fall the mighty ones,
Nobly undaunted to the last,
And death has now united him
With Erin's heroes of the past.

No sound of strife disturb his sleep!
Calmly he rests: no human pain
Or high ambition spurs him now
The peaks of glory to attain.

They had their way: they laid him low.
But Erin, list, ° his spirit may   (listen)
Rise, like the Phoenix from the flames,[75]
When breaks the dawning of the day,

The day that brings us Freedom's reign.
And on that day may Erin well
Pledge in the cup she lifts to Joy
One grief—the memory of Parnell.

Mr Hynes sat down again on the table. When he had finished his recitation there was a silence and then a burst of clapping: even Mr Lyons clapped. The applause continued for a little time. When it had ceased all the auditors drank from their bottles in silence.

Pok! The cork flew out of Mr Hynes' bottle, but Mr Hynes remained sitting flushed and bare-headed on the table. He did not seem to have heard the invitation.

—Good man, Joe! said Mr O'Connor, taking out his cigarette papers and pouch the better to hide his emotion.

—What do you think of that, Crofton? cried Mr Henchy. Isn't that fine? What?

Mr Crofton said that it was a very fine piece of writing.

---

[75] The mythological phoenix dies in flame and then rises from its own ashes.

A Mother

MR HOLOHAN, assistant secretary of the *Eire Abu*[1] Society, had been walking up and down Dublin for nearly a month, with his hands and pockets full of dirty pieces of paper, arranging about the series of concerts. He had a game leg and for this his friends called him Hoppy Holohan. He walked up and down constantly, stood by the hour at street corners arguing the point and made notes; but in the end it was Mrs Kearney who arranged everything.

Miss Devlin had become Mrs Kearney out of spite. She had been educated in a high-class convent[2] where she had learned French and music. As she was naturally pale and unbending in manner she made few friends at school. When she came to the age of marriage she was sent out to many houses, where her playing and ivory manners were much admired. She sat amid the chilly circle of her accomplishments, waiting for some suitor to brave it and offer her a brilliant life. But the young men whom she met were ordinary and she gave them no encouragement, trying to console her romantic desires by eating a great deal of Turkish Delight[3] in secret. However, when she drew near the limit[4] and her friends began to loosen their tongues about her she silenced them by marrying Mr Kearney, who was a bootmaker on Ormond Quay.[5]

He was much older than she. His conversation, which was serious, took place at intervals in his great brown beard. After the first year of married life, Mrs Kearney perceived that such a man would wear better than a romantic person, but she never put her own

---

[1] "Ireland Victorious!" (a fictional society) in Gaelic.

[2] Common schooling for Catholic girls.

[3] Sweet, chewy candy.

[4] The age of reasonable marriage—typically in one's late 20s—before being stigmatized as a spinster.

[5] Bootmaking was a respectable artisanal trade.

romantic ideas away. He was sober, thrifty and pious; he went to the altar every first Friday[6], sometimes with her, oftener by himself. But she never weakened in her religion and was a good wife to him. At some party in a strange house when she lifted her eyebrow ever so slightly he stood up to take his leave and, when his cough troubled him, she put the eider-down quilt over his feet and made a strong rum punch. For his part, he was a model father. By paying a small sum every week into a society, he ensured for both his daughters a dowry of one hundred pounds each when they came to the age of twenty-four.[7] He sent the elder daughter, Kathleen, to a good convent, where she learned French and music and afterward paid her fees at the Academy.[8] Every year in the month of July Mrs Kearney found occasion to say to some friend:

—My good man is packing us off to Skerries for a few weeks.

If it was not Skerries it was Howth or Greystones.[9]

When the Irish Revival[10] began to be appreciable Mrs Kearney determined to take advantage of her daughter's name[11] and brought an Irish teacher to the house. Kathleen and her sister sent Irish picture postcards to their friends and these friends sent back other Irish picture postcards. On special Sundays, when Mr Kearney went with his family to the pro-cathedral[12] a little crowd of people would assemble after mass at the corner of Cathedral Street. They were all friends of the Kearneys—musical friends or Nationalist friends; and, when they had played every little counter of gossip, they shook hands with one another all together, laughing at the crossing of so many hands and said good-bye to one another in

---

[6] To receive Communion. A sign of devotion in accordance with the promises of Blessed Margaret Mary Alacoque. See "Eveline," p.xxx n. 6.

[7] The weekly payments are interest-earning savings; a dowry (sum of money) increases a woman's attractiveness for marriage, since legally the money will become her husband's.

[8] The Royal Academy of Music.

[9] Skerries, Howth, and Greystones are all nearby seaside resort-villages.

[10] Cultural movement, involving by W. B. Yeats, Lady Gregory, J. M. Synge, and others, devoted to reviving Irish arts, language, folk stories, and myths. See "Revivalism," p. xxx.

[11] Kathleen ni Houlihan is a traditional symbolic figure for Ireland featured by Yeats in two important plays: *The Countess Cathleen* (1899) and *Cathleen ni Houlihan* (1902).

[12] St. Mary's on Marlborough Street, the center of Catholic worship in Dublin; a pro-cathedral is a church serving temporarily as the cathedral of a diocese—in this case because the Protestant Church of Ireland occupied the two main cathedrals in Dublin.

Irish. Soon the name of Miss Kathleen Kearney began to be heard often on people's lips. People said that she was very clever at music and a very nice girl and, moreover, that she was a believer in the language movement.[13] Mrs Kearney was well content at this. Therefore she was not surprised when one day Mr Holohan came to her and proposed that her daughter should be the accompanist at a series of four grand concerts which his Society was going to give in the Antient Concert Rooms.[14] She brought him into the drawing-room, made him sit down and brought out the decanter and the silver biscuit-barrel. She entered heart and soul into the details of the enterprise, advised and dissuaded; and finally a contract was drawn up by which Kathleen was to receive eight guineas for her services as accompanist at the four grand concerts.

As Mr Holohan was a novice in such delicate matters as the wording of bills[15] and the disposing of items for a programme, Mrs Kearney helped him. She had tact. She knew what *artistes* should go into capitals and what *artistes* should go into small type. She knew that the first tenor would not like to come on after Mr Meade's comic turn. To keep the audience continually diverted she slipped the doubtful items in between the old favourites. Mr Holohan called to see her every day to have her advice on some point. She was invariably friendly and advising—homely, in fact. She pushed the decanter towards him, saying:

—Now, help yourself, Mr Holohan!

And while he was helping himself she said:

—Don't be afraid! Don't be afraid of it!

Everything went on smoothly. Mrs Kearney bought some lovely blush-pink charmeuse in Brown Thomas's[16] to let into the front of Kathleen's dress. It cost a pretty penny; but there are occasions when a little expense is justifiable. She took a dozen of two-shilling tickets[17] for the final concert and sent them to those friends who could not be trusted to come otherwise. She forgot nothing and, thanks to her, everything that was to be done was done.

---

[13] To revive Irish. See "The Necessity for De-Anglicising Ireland," p. xxx.

[14] Notable venue where Joyce himself sang twice; Yeats's *The Countess Cathleen* (1899) and *Kathleen Ni Houlihan* (1902) had both been produced there.

[15] Advertisements.

[16] Fashionable shop on Grafton Street famed for laces and fine fabrics; charmeuse is a luxurious fabric.

[17] For good, if not the best, seats.

The concerts were to be on Wednesday, Thursday, Friday and Saturday. When Mrs Kearney arrived with her daughter at the Antient Concert Rooms on Wednesday night she did not like the look of things. A few young men, wearing bright blue badges in their coats, stood idle in the vestibule; none of them wore evening dress.[18] She passed by with her daughter and a quick glance through the open door of the hall showed her the cause of the stewards' idleness. At first she wondered had she mistaken the hour. No, it was twenty minutes to eight.

In the dressing-room behind the stage she was introduced to the secretary[19] of the Society, Mr Fitzpatrick. She smiled and shook his hand. He was a little man with a white vacant face. She noticed that he wore his soft brown hat carelessly on the side of his head and that his accent was flat.[20] He held a programme in his hand and, while he was talking to her, he chewed one end of it into a moist pulp. He seemed to bear disappointments lightly. Mr Holohan came into the dressing-room every few minutes with reports from the box-office. The *artistes* talked among themselves nervously, glanced from time to time at the mirror and rolled and unrolled their music. When it was nearly half-past eight, the few people in the hall began to express their desire to be entertained. Mr Fitzpatrick came in, smiled vacantly at the room, and said:

—Well now, ladies and gentlemen. I suppose we'd better open the ball.

Mrs Kearney rewarded his very flat final syllable with a quick stare of contempt and then said to her daughter encouragingly:

—Are you ready, dear?

When she had an opportunity, she called Mr Holohan aside and asked him to tell her what it meant. Mr Holohan did not know what it meant. He said that the committee had made a mistake in arranging for four concerts: four was too many.

—And the *artistes*! said Mrs Kearney. Of course they are doing their best, but really they are not good.

Mr Holohan admitted that the *artistes* were no good but the committee, he said, had decided to let the first three concerts go as they pleased and reserve all the talent for Saturday night. Mrs Kearney said nothing but, as the mediocre items followed one another on the

---

[18] Formal suits.

[19] Head officer.

[20] Not high class.

platform and the few people in the hall grew fewer and fewer, she began to regret that she had put herself to any expense for such a concert. There was something she didn't like in the look of things and Mr Fitzpatrick's vacant smile irritated her very much. However, she said nothing and waited to see how it would end. The concert expired shortly before ten and everyone went home quickly.

The concert on Thursday night was better attended but Mrs Kearney saw at once that the house was filled with paper.[21] The audience behaved indecorously as if the concert were an informal dress rehearsal. Mr Fitzpatrick seemed to enjoy himself; he was quite unconscious that Mrs Kearney was taking angry note of his conduct. He stood at the edge of the screen,[22] from time to time jutting out his head and exchanging a laugh with two friends in the corner of the balcony. In the course of the evening Mrs Kearney learned that the Friday concert was to be abandoned and that the committee was going to move heaven and earth to secure a bumper house on Saturday night. When she heard this she sought out Mr Holohan. She buttonholed him as he was limping out quickly with a glass of lemonade for a young lady and asked him was it true. Yes, it was true.

—But, of course, that doesn't alter the contract, she said. The contract was for four concerts.

Mr Holohan seemed to be in a hurry; he advised her to speak to Mr Fitzpatrick. Mrs Kearney was now beginning to be alarmed. She called Mr Fitzpatrick away from his screen and told him that her daughter had signed for four concerts and that, of course, according to the terms of the contract, she should receive the sum originally stipulated for whether the society gave the four concerts or not. Mr Fitzpatrick, who did not catch the point at issue very quickly, seemed unable to resolve the difficulty and said that he would bring the matter before the committee. Mrs Kearney's anger began to flutter in her cheek and she had all she could do to keep from asking:

—And who is the *cometty*[23] pray?

But she knew that it would not be ladylike to do that: so she was silent.

Little boys were sent out into the principal streets of Dublin early on Friday morning with bundles of handbills. Special puffs[24]

---

[21] Attended by people who had been given free tickets.

[22] Curtain at the side-stage.

[23] Mocking Mr Fitzpatrick's accent.

[24] Flattering pre-arranged reviews that serve as advertisements.

appeared in all the evening papers reminding the music loving public of the treat which was in store for it on the following evening. Mrs Kearney was somewhat reassured but she thought well to tell her husband part of her suspicions. He listened carefully and said that perhaps it would be better if he went with her on Saturday night. She agreed. She respected her husband in the same way as she respected the General Post Office, as something large, secure and fixed; and though she knew the small number of his talents she appreciated his abstract value as a male. She was glad that he had suggested coming with her. She thought her plans over.

The night of the grand concert came. Mrs Kearney, with her husband and daughter, arrived at the Antient Concert Rooms three-quarters of an hour before the time at which the concert was to begin. By ill luck it was a rainy evening. Mrs Kearney placed her daughter's clothes and music in charge of her husband and went all over the building looking for Mr Holohan or Mr Fitzpatrick. She could find neither. She asked the stewards was any member of the committee in the hall and, after a great deal of trouble, a steward brought out a little woman named Miss Beirne to whom Mrs Kearney explained that she wanted to see one of the secretaries. Miss Beirne expected them any minute and asked could she do anything. Mrs Kearney looked searchingly at the oldish face which was screwed into an expression of trustfulness and enthusiasm and answered:

—No, thank you!

The little woman hoped they would have a good house. She looked out at the rain until the melancholy of the wet street effaced all the trustfulness and enthusiasm from her twisted features. Then she gave a little sigh and said:

—Ah, well! We did our best, the dear knows.[25]

Mrs Kearney had to go back to the dressing-room.

The *artistes* were arriving. The bass and the second tenor had already come. The bass, Mr Duggan, was a slender young man with a scattered black moustache. He was the son of a hall porter in an office in the city and, as a boy, he had sung prolonged bass notes in the resounding hall. From this humble state he had raised himself until he had become a first-rate *artiste*. He had appeared in grand opera. One night, when an operatic *artiste* had fallen ill, he had undertaken the part of the king in the opera of *Maritana* at the

[25] "God knows."

Queen's Theatre.[26] He sang his music with great feeling and volume and was warmly welcomed by the gallery; but, unfortunately, he marred the good impression by wiping his nose in his gloved hand once or twice out of thoughtlessness. He was unassuming and spoke little. He said *yous*[27] so softly that it passed unnoticed and he never drank anything stronger than milk for his voice's sake. Mr Bell, the second tenor, was a fair-haired little man who competed every year for prizes at the Feis Ceoil. On his fourth trial he had been awarded a bronze medal.[28] He was extremely nervous and extremely jealous of other tenors and he covered his nervous jealousy with an ebullient friendliness. It was his humour to have people know what an ordeal a concert was to him. Therefore when he saw Mr Duggan he went over to him and asked:

—Are you in it too?

—Yes, said Mr Duggan.

Mr Bell laughed at his fellow-sufferer, held out his hand and said:

—Shake!

Mrs Kearney passed by these two young men and went to the edge of the screen to view the house. The seats were being filled up rapidly and a pleasant noise circulated in the auditorium. She came back and spoke to her husband privately. Their conversation was evidently about Kathleen for they both glanced at her often as she stood chatting to one of her Nationalist friends, Miss Healy, the contralto. An unknown solitary woman with a pale face walked through the room. The women followed with keen eyes the faded blue dress which was stretched upon a meagre body. Someone said that she was Madam Glynn, the soprano.

—I wonder where did they dig her up, said Kathleen to Miss Healy. I'm sure I never heard of her.

Miss Healy had to smile. Mr Holohan limped into the dressing-room at that moment and the two young ladies asked him who was the unknown woman. Mr Holohan said that she was Madam Glynn

---

[26] King Charles II is the hero who falls in love with street-singer Maritana in this popular operetta by William Wallace and Edward Fitzball, first performed in Dublin in 1846; Queen's is one of three principal Dublin theaters.

[27] Sign of lower-class diction.

[28] For third place; the Feis Ceoil is an annual Irish music competition often held in the Antient Concert Rooms. In 1904, Joyce himself won the bronze medal as a tenor in this competition.

from London. Madam Glynn took her stand in a corner of the room, holding a roll of music stiffly before her and from time to time changing the direction of her startled gaze. The shadow took her faded dress into shelter but fell revengefully into the little cup behind her collar-bone. The noise of the hall became more audible. The first tenor and the baritone arrived together. They were both well dressed, stout and complacent and they brought a breath of opulence among the company.

Mrs Kearney brought her daughter over to them, and talked to them amiably. She wanted to be on good terms with them but, while she strove to be polite, her eyes followed Mr Holohan in his limping and devious courses. As soon as she could she excused herself and went out after him.

—Mr Holohan, I want to speak to you for a moment, she said.

They went down to a discreet part of the corridor. Mrs Kearney asked him when was her daughter going to be paid. Mr Holohan said that Mr Fitzpatrick had charge of that. Mrs Kearney said that she didn't know anything about Mr Fitzpatrick. Her daughter had signed a contract for eight guineas and she would have to be paid. Mr Holohan said that it wasn't his business.

—Why isn't it your business? asked Mrs Kearney. Didn't you yourself bring her the contract? Anyway, if it's not your business it's my business and I mean to see to it.

—You'd better speak to Mr Fitzpatrick, said Mr Holohan distantly.

—I don't know anything about Mr Fitzpatrick, repeated Mrs Kearney. I have my contract, and I intend to see that it is carried out.

When she came back to the dressing-room her cheeks were slightly suffused. The room was lively. Two men in outdoor dress had taken possession of the fireplace and were chatting familiarly with Miss Healy and the baritone. They were the *Freeman*[29] man and Mr O'Madden Burke. The *Freeman* man had come in to say that he could not wait for the concert as he had to report the lecture which an American priest was giving in the Mansion House.[30] He said they were to leave the report for him at the *Freeman* office and he would see that it went in. He was a grey-haired man, with a plausible voice and careful manners. He held an extinguished cigar in his hand and the aroma of cigar smoke floated near him. He had

---

[29] The *Freeman's Journal*, a morning paper.
[30] Residence of the Lord Mayor.

not intended to stay a moment because concerts and *artistes* bored him considerably but he remained leaning against the mantelpiece. Miss Healy stood in front of him, talking and laughing. He was old enough to suspect one reason for her politeness but young enough in spirit to turn the moment to account. The warmth, fragrance and colour of her body appealed to his senses. He was pleasantly conscious that the bosom which he saw rise and fall slowly beneath him rose and fell at that moment for him, that the laughter and fragrance and wilful glances were his tribute. When he could stay no longer he took leave of her regretfully.

—O'Madden Burke will write the notice, he explained to Mr Holohan, and I'll see it in.

—Thank you very much, Mr Hendrick, said Mr Holohan. You'll see it in, I know. Now, won't you have a little something before you go?

—I don't mind, said Mr Hendrick.

The two men went along some tortuous passages and up a dark staircase and came to a secluded room where one of the stewards was uncorking bottles for a few gentlemen. One of these gentlemen was Mr O'Madden Burke, who had found out the room by instinct. He was a suave elderly man who balanced his imposing body, when at rest, upon a large silk umbrella. His magniloquent western name[31] was the moral umbrella upon which he balanced the fine problem of his finances. He was widely respected.

While Mr Holohan was entertaining the *Freeman* man Mrs Kearney was speaking so animatedly to her husband that he had to ask her to lower her voice. The conversation of the others in the dressing-room had become strained. Mr Bell, the first item, stood ready with his music but the accompanist made no sign. Evidently something was wrong. Mr Kearney looked straight before him, stroking his beard, while Mrs Kearney spoke into Kathleen's ear with subdued emphasis. From the hall came sounds of encouragement, clapping and stamping of feet. The first tenor and the baritone and Miss Healy stood together, waiting tranquilly, but Mr Bell's nerves were greatly agitated because he was afraid the audience would think that he had come late.

Mr Holohan and Mr O'Madden Burke came into the room. In a moment Mr Holohan perceived the hush. He went over to Mrs Kearney and spoke with her earnestly. While they were speaking the

[31] Distinctly Irish (rural, western Ireland was closely associated with the Revival).

noise in the hall grew louder. Mr Holohan became very red and excited. He spoke volubly, but Mrs Kearney said curtly at intervals:

—She won't go on. She must get her eight guineas.

Mr Holohan pointed desperately towards the hall where the audience was clapping and stamping. He appealed to Mr Kearney and to Kathleen. But Mr Kearney continued to stroke his beard and Kathleen looked down, moving the point of her new shoe: it was not her fault. Mrs Kearney repeated:

—She won't go on without her money.

After a swift struggle of tongues Mr Holohan hobbled out in haste. The room was silent. When the strain of the silence had become somewhat painful Miss Healy said to the baritone:

—Have you seen Mrs Pat Campbell[32] this week?

The baritone had not seen her but he had been told that she was very fine. The conversation went no further. The first tenor bent his head and began to count the links of the gold chain which was extended across his waist, smiling and humming random notes to observe the effect on the frontal sinus. From time to time everyone glanced at Mrs Kearney.

The noise in the auditorium had risen to a clamour when Mr Fitzpatrick burst into the room, followed by Mr Holohan who was panting. The clapping and stamping in the hall were punctuated by whistling. Mr Fitzpatrick held a few banknotes in his hand. He counted out four into Mrs Kearney's hand and said she would get the other half at the interval.[33] Mrs Kearney said:

—This is four shillings short.

But Kathleen gathered in her skirt and said *Now, Mr Bell*, to the first item, who was shaking like an aspen. The singer and the accompanist went out together. The noise in the hall died away. There was a pause of a few seconds: and then the piano was heard.

The first part of the concert was very successful except for Madam Glynn's item. The poor lady sang *Killarney*[34] in a bodiless gasping voice, with all the old-fashioned mannerisms of intonation and pronunciation which she believed lent elegance to her singing. She looked as if she had been resurrected from an old stage-wardrobe and the cheaper parts of the hall made fun of her high wailing notes. The first tenor and the contralto, however, brought

[32] Famous British actress, friend of Irishman George Bernard Shaw.

[33] Intermission.

[34] From the opera *Innisfallen* by M. W. Balfe, who also composed *The Bohemian Girl* (see "Eveline" and "Clay").

down the house. Kathleen played a selection of Irish airs which was generously applauded. The first part closed with a stirring patriotic recitation delivered by a young lady who arranged amateur theatricals. It was deservedly applauded; and, when it was ended, the men went out for the interval, content.

All this time the dressing-room was a hive of excitement. In one corner were Mr Holohan, Mr Fitzpatrick, Miss Beirne, two of the stewards, the baritone, the bass, and Mr O'Madden Burke. Mr O'Madden Burke said it was the most scandalous exhibition he had ever witnessed. Miss Kathleen Kearney's musical career was ended in Dublin after that, he said. The baritone was asked what did he think of Mrs Kearney's conduct. He did not like to say anything. He had been paid his money and wished to be at peace with men. However, he said that Mrs Kearney might have taken the *artistes* into consideration. The stewards and the secretaries debated hotly as to what should be done when the interval came.

—I agree with Miss Beirne, said Mr O'Madden Burke. Pay her nothing.

In another corner of the room were Mrs Kearney and her husband, Mr Bell, Miss Healy and the young lady who had to recite the patriotic piece. Mrs Kearney said that the committee had treated her scandalously. She had spared neither trouble nor expense and this was how she was repaid.

They thought they had only a girl to deal with and that therefore, they could ride roughshod over her. But she would show them their mistake. They wouldn't have dared to have treated her like that if she had been a man. But she would see that her daughter got her rights: she wouldn't be fooled. If they didn't pay her to the last farthing she would make Dublin ring. Of course she was sorry for the sake of the *artistes*. But what else could she do? She appealed to the second tenor who said he thought she had not been well treated. Then she appealed to Miss Healy. Miss Healy wanted to join the other group but she did not like to do so because she was a great friend of Kathleen's and the Kearneys had often invited her to their house.

As soon as the first part was ended Mr Fitzpatrick and Mr Holohan went over to Mrs Kearney and told her that the other four guineas would be paid after the committee meeting on the following Tuesday and that, in case her daughter did not play for the second part, the committee would consider the contract broken and would pay nothing.

—I haven't seen any committee, said Mrs Kearney angrily. My daughter has her contract. She will get four pounds eight into her hand or a foot she won't put on that platform.

—I'm surprised at you, Mrs Kearney, said Mr Holohan. I never thought you would treat us this way.

—And what way did you treat me? asked Mrs Kearney.

Her face was inundated with an angry colour and she looked as if she would attack someone with her hands.

—I'm asking for my rights, she said.

—You might have some sense of decency, said Mr Holohan.

—Might I, indeed? ... And when I ask when my daughter is going to be paid I can't get a civil answer.

She tossed her head and assumed a haughty voice:

—You must speak to the secretary. It's not my business. I'm a great fellow fol-the-diddle-I-do.

—I thought you were a lady, said Mr Holohan, walking away from her abruptly.

After that Mrs Kearney's conduct was condemned on all hands: everyone approved of what the committee had done. She stood at the door, haggard with rage, arguing with her husband and daughter, gesticulating with them. She waited until it was time for the second part to begin in the hope that the secretaries would approach her. But Miss Healy had kindly consented to play one or two accompaniments. Mrs Kearney had to stand aside to allow the baritone and his accompanist to pass up to the platform. She stood still for an instant like an angry stone image and, when the first notes of the song struck her ear, she caught up her daughter's cloak and said to her husband:

—Get a cab!

He went out at once. Mrs Kearney wrapped the cloak round her daughter and followed him. As she passed through the doorway she stopped and glared into Mr Holohan's face.

—I'm not done with you yet, she said.

—But I'm done with you, said Mr Holohan.

Kathleen followed her mother meekly. Mr Holohan began to pace up and down the room, in order to cool himself for he felt his skin on fire.

—That's a nice lady! he said. O, she's a nice lady!

—You did the proper thing, Holohan, said Mr O'Madden Burke, poised upon his umbrella in approval.

Grace[1]

TWO GENTLEMEN who were in the lavatory at the time tried to lift him
up: but he was quite helpless. He lay curled up at the foot of the stairs
down which he had fallen. They succeeded in turning him over. His
hat had rolled a few yards away and his clothes were smeared with
the filth and ooze of the floor on which he had lain, face downwards.
His eyes were closed and he breathed with a grunting noise. A thin
stream of blood trickled from the corner of his mouth.

These two gentlemen and one of the curates carried him up the
stairs and laid him down again on the floor of the bar. In two minutes
he was surrounded by a ring of men. The manager of the bar asked
everyone who he was and who was with him. No one knew who he
was but one of the curates said he had served the gentleman with a
small rum.

—Was he by himself? asked the manager.

—No, sir. There was two gentlemen with him.

—And where are they?

No one knew; a voice said:

—Give him air. He's fainted.

The ring of onlookers distended and closed again elastically. A
dark medal of blood had formed itself near the man's head on the
tessellated[2] floor. The manager, alarmed by the grey pallor of the
man's face, sent for a policeman.

His collar was unfastened and his necktie undone. He opened
his eyes for an instant, sighed and closed them again. One of the
gentlemen who had carried him upstairs held a dinged silk hat in his

---

[1] God's "grace" is forgiveness of penitent sinners; the word also connotes social style
and demeanor, as well as the "grace period" (without penalty) for owed payments.
The sermon at the end makes use of all these meanings.

[2] Tiled or mosaic.

hand. The manager asked repeatedly did no one know who the injured man was or where had his friends gone. The door of the bar opened and an immense constable entered. A crowd which had followed him down the laneway collected outside the door, struggling to look in through the glass panels.

The manager at once began to narrate what he knew. The constable, a young man with thick immobile features, listened. He moved his head slowly to right and left and from the manager to the person on the floor, as if he feared to be the victim of some delusion. Then he drew off his glove, produced a small book from his waist, licked the lead of his pencil and made ready to indite. He asked in a suspicious provincial accent:[3]

—Who is the man? What's his name and address?

A young man in a cycling-suit cleared his way through the ring of bystanders. He knelt down promptly beside the injured man and called for water. The constable knelt down also to help. The young man washed the blood from the injured man's mouth and then called for some brandy. The constable repeated the order in an authoritative voice until a curate came running with the glass. The brandy was forced down the man's throat. In a few seconds he opened his eyes and looked about him. He looked at the circle of faces and then, understanding, strove to rise to his feet.

—You're all right now? asked the young man in the cycling-suit.

—Sha, 's nothing, said the injured man, trying to stand up.

He was helped to his feet. The manager said something about a hospital and some of the bystanders gave advice. The battered silk hat was placed on the man's head. The constable asked:

—Where do you live?

The man, without answering, began to twirl the ends of his moustache. He made light of his accident. It was nothing, he said: only a little accident. He spoke very thickly.

—Where do you live? repeated the constable.

The man said they were to get a cab for him. While the point was being debated a tall agile gentleman of fair complexion, wearing a long yellow ulster,[4] came from the far end of the bar. Seeing the spectacle, he called out:

—Hallo, Tom, old man! What's the trouble?

—Sha, 's nothing, said the man.

---

[3] A rural accent. Policemen often came from the country, making the city and its ways somewhat foreign to them.

[4] Loose, belted overcoat.

The new-comer surveyed the deplorable figure before him and then turned to the constable saying:

—It's all right, constable. I'll see him home.

The constable touched his helmet and answered:

—All right, Mr Power!

—Come now, Tom, said Mr Power, taking his friend by the arm. No bones broken. What? Can you walk?

The young man in the cycling-suit took the man by the other arm and the crowd divided.

—How did you get yourself into this mess? asked Mr Power.

—The gentleman fell down the stairs, said the young man.

—I' 'ery 'uch o'liged to you, sir, said the injured man.

—Not at all.

—'ant we have a little...?

—Not now. Not now.

The three men left the bar and the crowd sifted through the doors into the laneway. The manager brought the constable to the stairs to inspect the scene of the accident. They agreed that the gentleman must have missed his footing. The customers returned to the counter and a curate set about removing the traces of blood from the floor.

When they came out into Grafton Street Mr Power whistled for an outsider.[5] The injured man said again as well as he could.

—I' 'ery 'uch o'liged to you, sir. I hope we'll 'eet again. 'y na'e is Kernan.

The shock and the incipient pain had partly sobered him.

—Don't mention it, said the young man.

They shook hands. Mr Kernan was hoisted on to the car and, while Mr Power was giving directions to the carman, he expressed his gratitude to the young man and regretted that they could not have a little drink together.

—Another time, said the young man.

The car drove off towards Westmoreland Street. As it passed the Ballast Office the clock showed half-past nine. A keen east wind hit them, blowing from the mouth of the river. Mr Kernan was huddled together with cold. His friend asked him to tell how the accident had happened.

—I' an't, 'an, he answered, 'y 'ongue is hurt.

—Show.

[5] Horse-drawn taxi.

The other leaned over the well of the car and peered into Mr Kernan's mouth but he could not see. He struck a match and, sheltering it in the shell of his hands, peered again into the mouth which Mr Kernan opened obediently. The swaying movement of the car brought the match to and from the opened mouth. The lower teeth and gums were covered with clotted blood and a minute piece of the tongue seemed to have been bitten off. The match was blown out.

—That's ugly, said Mr Power.

—Sha, 's nothing, said Mr Kernan, closing his mouth and pulling the collar of his filthy coat across his neck.

Mr Kernan was a commercial traveller[6] of the old school which believed in the dignity of its calling. He had never been seen in the city without a silk hat of some decency and a pair of gaiters. By grace of these two articles of clothing, he said, a man could always pass muster. He carried on the tradition of his Napoleon,[7] the great Blackwhite, whose memory he evoked at times by legend and mimicry. Modern business methods had spared him only so far as to allow him a little office in Crowe Street on the window blind of which was written the name of his firm with the address—London, E. C.[8] On the mantelpiece of this little office a little leaden battalion of canisters was drawn up and on the table before the window stood four or five china bowls which were usually half full of a black liquid. From these bowls Mr Kernan tasted tea. He took a mouthful, drew it up, saturated his palate with it and then spat it forth into the grate. Then he paused to judge.

Mr Power, a much younger man, was employed in the Royal Irish Constabulary Office in Dublin Castle.[9] The arc of his social rise intersected the arc of his friend's decline but Mr Kernan's decline was mitigated by the fact that certain of those friends who had known him at his highest point of success still esteemed him as a character. Mr Power was one of these friends. His inexplicable debts were a byword in his circle; he was a debonair young man.

The car halted before a small house on the Glasnevin road and Mr Kernan was helped into the house. His wife put him to bed while Mr Power sat downstairs in the kitchen asking the children where

---

[6] Traveling merchant.

[7] Here, role model.

[8] East Central postal district.

[9] The R.I.C. in Dublin is armed and under the control of the British government; headquartered in Dublin Castle it was also used for clandestine operations.

they went to school and what book[10] they were in. The children—two girls and a boy, conscious of their father's helplessness and of their mother's absence, began some horseplay with him. He was surprised at their manners and at their accents and his brow grew thoughtful. After a while Mrs Kernan entered the kitchen, exclaiming:

—Such a sight! O, he'll do for himself one day and that's the holy alls of it.[11] He's been drinking since Friday.

Mr Power was careful to explain to her that he was not responsible, that he had come on the scene by the merest accident. Mrs Kernan, remembering Mr Power's good offices during domestic quarrels as well as many small, but opportune loans, said:

—O, you needn't tell me that, Mr Power. I know you're a friend of his, not like some of the others he does be with. They're all right so long as he has money in his pocket to keep him out from his wife and family. Nice friends! Who was he with to-night, I'd like to know?

Mr Power shook his head but said nothing.

—I'm so sorry, she continued, that I've nothing in the house to offer you. But if you wait a minute I'll send round to Fogarty's at the corner.

Mr Power stood up.

—We were waiting for him to come home with the money. He never seems to think he has a home at all.

—O, now, Mrs Kernan, said Mr Power, we'll make him turn over a new leaf. I'll talk to Martin. He's the man. We'll come here one of these nights and talk it over.

She saw him to the door. The carman was stamping up and down the footpath and swinging his arms to warm himself.

—It's very kind of you to bring him home, she said.

—Not at all, said Mr Power.

He got up on the car. As it drove off he raised his hat to her gaily.

—We'll make a new man of him, he said. Good-night, Mrs Kernan.

＊ ＊ ＊

Mrs Kernan's puzzled eyes watched the car till it was out of sight. Then she withdrew them, went into the house and emptied her husband's pockets.

She was an active, practical woman of middle age. Not long before she had celebrated her silver wedding[12] and renewed her

---

[10] Grade.

[11] Irish expression meaning "That's a fact."

[12] Twenty-fifth anniversary (for which silver is a traditional gift).

intimacy with her husband by waltzing with him to Mr Power's accompaniment. In her days of courtship, Mr Kernan had seemed to her a not ungallant figure: and she still hurried to the chapel door whenever a wedding was reported and, seeing the bridal pair, recalled with vivid pleasure how she had passed out of the Star of the Sea Church in Sandymount, leaning on the arm of a jovial well-fed man who was dressed smartly in a frock-coat and lavender trousers and carried a silk hat gracefully balanced upon his other arm. After three weeks she had found a wife's life irksome and, later on, when she was beginning to find it unbearable, she had become a mother. The part of mother presented to her no insuperable[13] difficulties and for twenty-five years she had kept house shrewdly for her husband. Her two eldest sons were launched. One was in a draper's shop in Glasgow and the other was clerk to a tea-merchant in Belfast.[14] They were good sons, wrote regularly and sometimes sent home money. The other children were still at school.

Mr Kernan sent a letter to his office next day and remained in bed. She made beef-tea[15] for him and scolded him roundly. She accepted his frequent intemperance as part of the climate, healed him dutifully whenever he was sick and always tried to make him eat a breakfast. There were worse husbands. He had never been violent since the boys had grown up and she knew that he would walk to the end of Thomas Street[16] and back again to book even a small order.

Two nights after his friends came to see him. She brought them up to his bedroom, the air of which was impregnated with a personal odour, and gave them chairs at the fire. Mr Kernan's tongue, the occasional stinging pain of which had made him somewhat irritable during the day, became more polite. He sat propped up in the bed by pillows and the little colour in his puffy cheeks made them resemble warm cinders. He apologised to his guests for the disorder of the room but at the same time looked at them a little proudly, with a veteran's pride.

He was quite unconscious that he was the victim of a plot which his friends, Mr Cunningham, Mr M'Coy and Mr Power had disclosed to Mrs Kernan in the parlour. The idea had been Mr Power's but its

---

[13] Particularly difficult or insurmountable.

[14] Both locations suggest a connection to the Protestant world of Great Britain rather than Catholic Ireland.

[15] Broth.

[16] A street some distance from Mr Kernan's office.

development was entrusted to Mr Cunningham. Mr Kernan came of Protestant stock and, though he had been converted to the Catholic faith at the time of his marriage, he had not been in the pale[17] of the Church for twenty years. He was fond, moreover, of giving side-thrusts at Catholicism.

Mr Cunningham was the very man for such a case. He was an elder colleague of Mr Power. His own domestic life was not very happy. People had great sympathy with him for it was known that he had married an unpresentable woman who was an incurable drunkard. He had set up house for her six times; and each time she had pawned the furniture on him.

Everyone had respect for poor Martin Cunningham. He was a thoroughly sensible man, influential and intelligent. His blade of human knowledge, natural astuteness particularised by long association with cases in the police courts, had been tempered by brief immersions in the waters of general philosophy.[18] He was well informed. His friends bowed to his opinions and considered that his face was like Shakespeare's.

When the plot had been disclosed to her Mrs Kernan had said:

—I leave it all in your hands, Mr Cunningham.

After a quarter of a century of married life she had very few illusions left. Religion for her was a habit, and she suspected that a man of her husband's age would not change greatly before death. She was tempted to see a curious appropriateness in his accident and, but that she did not wish to seem bloody-minded, would have told the gentlemen that Mr Kernan's tongue would not suffer by being shortened. However, Mr Cunningham was a capable man; and religion was religion. The scheme might do good and, at least, it could do no harm. Her beliefs were not extravagant. She believed steadily in the Sacred Heart[19] as the most generally useful of all Catholic devotions and approved of the sacraments. Her faith was bounded by her kitchen but, if she was put to it, she could believe also in the banshee and in the Holy Ghost.[20]

The gentlemen began to talk of the accident. Mr Cunningham said that he had once known a similar case. A man of seventy had

---

[17] Influence, control, safety; "the Pale" is an old term for the British colonial area around Dublin ("beyond the pale" designates unprotected territory).

[18] Steel swords are hardened, or "tempered," by being plunged in cold water when hot.

[19] Sacred Heart of Jesus; see "Eveline," p.xxx n. 6.

[20] The banshee is a spirit from Irish folklore who wails at the approach of death; the Holy Ghost is the Spirit of God and Jesus in the Holy Trinity.

bitten off a piece of his tongue during an epileptic fit and the tongue had filled in again, so that no one could see a trace of the bite.

—Well, I'm not seventy, said the invalid.

—God forbid, said Mr Cunningham.

—It doesn't pain you now? asked Mr M'Coy.

Mr M'Coy had been at one time a tenor of some reputation. His wife, who had been a soprano, still taught young children to play the piano at low terms. His line of life had not been the shortest distance between two points and for short periods he had been driven to live by his wits. He had been a clerk in the Midland Railway, a canvasser for advertisements[21] for *The Irish Times* and for *The Freeman's Journal*, a town traveller for a coal firm on commission,[22] a private inquiry agent,[23] a clerk in the office of the Sub-Sheriff[24] and he had recently become secretary to the City Coroner. His new office made him professionally interested in Mr Kernan's case.

—Pain? Not much, answered Mr Kernan. But it's so sickening. I feel as if I wanted to retch off.

—That's the boose, said Mr Cunningham firmly.

—No, said Mr Kernan. I think I caught a cold on the car. There's something keeps coming into my throat, phlegm or—

—Mucus, said Mr M'Coy.

—It keeps coming like from down in my throat; sickening thing.

—Yes, yes, said Mr M'Coy, that's the thorax.

He looked at Mr Cunningham and Mr Power at the same time with an air of challenge. Mr Cunningham nodded his head rapidly and Mr Power said:

—Ah, well, all's well that ends well.

—I'm very much obliged to you, old man, said the invalid.

Mr Power waved his hand.

—Those other two fellows I was with—

—Who were you with? asked Mr Cunningham.

—A chap. I don't know his name. Damn it now, what's his name? Little chap with sandy hair....

—And who else?

—Harford.

—Hm, said Mr Cunningham.

---

[21] An agent who sells advertising space. Leopold Bloom, the central character of *Ulysses*, has this same occupation.

[22] That is, his pay was based on the amount of coal sold.

[23] A private detective.

[24] Enforcer of evictions and repossessions.

When Mr Cunningham made that remark, people were silent. It was known that the speaker had secret sources of information. In this case the monosyllable had a moral intention. Mr Harford sometimes formed one of a little detachment which left the city shortly after noon on Sunday with the purpose of arriving as soon as possible at some public-house on the outskirts of the city where its members duly qualified themselves as *bona-fide* travellers.[25] But his fellow-travellers had never consented to overlook his origin. He had begun life as an obscure financier by lending small sums of money to workmen at usurious[26] interest. Later on he had become the partner of a very fat short gentleman, Mr Goldberg, in the Liffey Loan Bank. Though he had never embraced more than the Jewish ethical code[27] his fellow-Catholics, whenever they had smarted in person or by proxy under his exactions, spoke of him bitterly as an Irish Jew and an illiterate and saw divine disapproval of usury made manifest through the person of his idiot son. At other times they remembered his good points.

—I wonder where did he go to, said Mr Kernan.

He wished the details of the incident to remain vague. He wished his friends to think there had been some mistake, that Mr Harford and he had missed each other. His friends, who knew quite well Mr Harford's manners in drinking, were silent. Mr Power said again:

—All's well that ends well.

Mr Kernan changed the subject at once.

—That was a decent young chap, that medical fellow, he said. Only for him—

—O, only for him, said Mr Power, it might have been a case of seven days[28] without the option of a fine.

—Yes, yes, said Mr Kernan, trying to remember. I remember now there was a policeman. Decent young fellow, he seemed. How did it happen at all?

—It happened that you were peloothered[29] Tom, said Mr Cunningham gravely.

[25] Travelers could be legally served alcohol on Sundays.

[26] Excessive.

[27] In this routine anti-Semitism, a Jewish banker's lending at interest is reviled since pawning was the preferred way to raise cash. Before the advent of modern banking, lending money at interest (called "usury") was considered immoral; Jews developed this business because they were shut out of most professions. Here Harford is being indirectly identified as a loan shark.

[28] Jail term for drunkenness.

[29] "Drunk" in Hiberno-English.

—True bill,[30] said Mr Kernan, equally gravely.

—I suppose you squared[31] the constable, Jack, said Mr M'Coy.

Mr Power did not relish the use of his Christian name.[32] He was not straight-laced but he could not forget that Mr M'Coy had recently made a crusade in search of valises and portmanteaus to enable Mrs M'Coy to fulfil imaginary engagements in the country. More than he resented the fact that he had been victimized he resented such low playing of the game.[33] He answered the question, therefore, as if Mr Kernan had asked it.

The narrative made Mr Kernan indignant. He was keenly conscious of his citizenship, wished to live with his city on terms mutually honourable and resented any affront put upon him by those whom he called country bumpkins.

—Is this what we pay rates for? he asked. To feed and clothe these ignorant bostoons[34] ... and they're nothing else.

Mr Cunningham laughed. He was a Castle official only during office hours.

—How could they be anything else, Tom? he said.

He assumed a thick, provincial accent and said in a tone of command:

—65,[35] catch your cabbage!

Everyone laughed. Mr M'Coy, who wanted to enter the conversation by any door, pretended that he had never heard the story. Mr Cunningham said:

—It is supposed—they say, you know—to take place in the depot[36] where they get these thundering big country fellows, omadhauns,[37] you know, to drill. The sergeant makes them stand in a row against the wall and hold up their plates.

He illustrated the story by grotesque gestures.

—At dinner, you know. Then he has a bloody big bowl of cabbage before him on the table and a bloody big spoon like a shovel.

---

[30] "True" in Hiberno-English (derived from a legal term for indictment).

[31] Came to terms with.

[32] First name—a presumptuous intimacy.

[33] The implication is that M'Coy pawned the suitcases (valises) he borrowed from friends.

[34] "Buffoons" in Irish.

[35] Constable's badge number.

[36] Barracks.

[37] "Fools" in Irish.

He takes up a wad of cabbage on the spoon and pegs it across the room and the poor devils have to try and catch it on their plates: *65, catch your cabbage.*

Everyone laughed again: but Mr Kernan was somewhat indignant still. He talked of writing a letter to the papers.

—These yahoos[38] coming up here, he said, think they can boss the people. I needn't tell you, Martin, what kind of men they are.

Mr Cunningham gave a qualified assent.

—It's like everything else in this world, he said. You get some bad ones and you get some good ones.

—O yes, you get some good ones, I admit, said Mr Kernan, satisfied.

—It's better to have nothing to say to them, said Mr M'Coy. That's my opinion!

Mrs Kernan entered the room and, placing a tray on the table, said:

—Help yourselves, gentlemen.

Mr Power stood up to officiate, offering her his chair. She declined it, saying she was ironing downstairs and, after having exchanged a nod with Mr Cunningham behind Mr Power's back, prepared to leave the room. Her husband called out to her:

—And have you nothing for me, duckie?

—O, you! The back of my hand to you! said Mrs Kernan tartly.

Her husband called after her:

—Nothing for poor little hubby!

He assumed such a comical face and voice that the distribution of the bottles of stout took place amid general merriment.

The gentlemen drank from their glasses, set the glasses again on the table and paused. Then Mr Cunningham turned towards Mr Power and said casually:

—On Thursday night, you said, Jack.

—Thursday, yes, said Mr Power.

—Righto! said Mr Cunningham promptly.

—We can meet in M'Auley's,[39] said Mr M'Coy. That'll be the most convenient place.

—But we mustn't be late, said Mr Power earnestly, because it is sure to be crammed to the doors.

—We can meet at half-seven, said Mr M'Coy.

[38] A term for inhuman beasts in human form coined by Irish writer Jonathan Swift in *Gulliver's Travels* (1726).

[39] Dublin pub.

—Righto! said Mr Cunningham.

—Half-seven at M'Auley's be it!

There was a short silence. Mr Kernan waited to see whether he would be taken into his friends' confidence. Then he asked:

—What's in the wind?

—O, it's nothing, said Mr Cunningham. It's only a little matter that we're arranging about for Thursday.

—The opera, is it? said Mr Kernan.

—No, no, said Mr Cunningham in an evasive tone, it's just a little ... spiritual matter.

—O, said Mr Kernan.

There was silence again. Then Mr Power said, point blank:

—To tell you the truth, Tom, we're going to make a retreat.[40]

—Yes, that's it, said Mr Cunningham, Jack and I and M'Coy here—we're all going to wash the pot.[41]

He uttered the metaphor with a certain homely energy and, encouraged by his own voice, proceeded:

—You see, we may as well all admit we're a nice collection of scoundrels, one and all. I say, one and all, he added with gruff charity and turning to Mr Power. Own up now!

—I own up, said Mr Power.

—And I own up, said Mr M'Coy.

—So we're going to wash the pot together, said Mr Cunningham.

A thought seemed to strike him. He turned suddenly to the invalid and said:

—Do you know what, Tom, has just occurred to me? You might join in and we'd have a four-handed reel.[42]

—Good idea, said Mr Power. The four of us together.

Mr Kernan was silent. The proposal conveyed very little meaning to his mind but, understanding that some spiritual agencies were about to concern themselves on his behalf, he thought he owed it to his dignity to show a stiff neck. He took no part in the conversation for a long while but listened, with an air of calm enmity, while his friends discussed the Jesuits.[43]

---

[40] Temporary withdrawal from the world for spiritual renewal.

[41] Crude term for cleansing the conscience.

[42] A full group for a dance.

[43] The Society of Jesus, a religious order founded in 1540 by St. Ignatius of Loyola, famed for their intelligence, sophistication, and cunning. Unlike other monastic orders, the Jesuits take a special oath of loyalty to the Pope.

—I haven't such a bad opinion of the Jesuits, he said, intervening at length. They're an educated order. I believe they mean well too.

—They're the grandest order in the Church, Tom, said Mr Cunningham, with enthusiasm. The General of the Jesuits stands next to the Pope.

—There's no mistake about it, said Mr M'Coy, if you want a thing well done and no flies about, you go to a Jesuit. They're the boyos have influence. I'll tell you a case in point....

—The Jesuits are a fine body of men, said Mr Power.

—It's a curious thing, said Mr Cunningham, about the Jesuit Order. Every other order of the Church had to be reformed[44] at some time or other but the Jesuit Order was never once reformed. It never fell away.

—Is that so? asked Mr M'Coy.

—That's a fact, said Mr Cunningham. That's history.

—Look at their church,[45] too, said Mr Power. Look at the congregation they have.

—The Jesuits cater for the upper classes, said Mr M'Coy.

—Of course, said Mr Power.

—Yes, said Mr Kernan. That's why I have a feeling for them. It's some of those secular priests, ignorant, bumptious—

—They're all good men, said Mr Cunningham, each in his own way. The Irish priesthood is honoured all the world over.

—O yes, said Mr Power.

—Not like some of the other priesthoods on the Continent, said Mr M'Coy, unworthy of the name.

—Perhaps you're right, said Mr Kernan, relenting.

—Of course I'm right, said Mr Cunningham. I haven't been in the world all this time and seen most sides of it without being a judge of character.

The gentlemen drank again, one following another's example. Mr Kernan seemed to be weighing something in his mind. He was impressed. He had a high opinion of Mr Cunningham as a judge of character and as a reader of faces. He asked for particulars.

—O, it's just a retreat, you know, said Mr Cunningham. Father Purdon[46] is giving it. It's for business men, you know.

---

[44] Purged of corruptions and heresies.

[45] The congregation of the Church of St. Francis Xavier, on Upper Gardiner Street, was fairly wealthy.

[46] A homophone for "pardon" and homonym for Purdon, a street in the red-light district.

—He won't be too hard on us, Tom, said Mr Power persuasively.

—Father Purdon? Father Purdon? said the invalid.

—O, you must know him, Tom, said Mr Cunningham stoutly. Fine, jolly fellow! —He's a man of the world like ourselves.

—Ah, ... yes. I think I know him. Rather red face; tall.

—That's the man.

—And tell me, Martin.... Is he a good preacher?

—Mmnno.... It's not exactly a sermon, you know. It's just kind of a friendly talk, you know, in a common-sense way.

Mr Kernan deliberated. Mr M'Coy said:

—Father Tom Burke,[47] that was the boy!

—O, Father Tom Burke, said Mr Cunningham, that was a born orator. Did you ever hear him, Tom?

—Did I ever hear him! said the invalid, nettled. Rather! I heard him....

—And yet they say he wasn't much of a theologian, said Mr Cunningham.

—Is that so? said Mr M'Coy.

—O, of course, nothing wrong, you know. Only sometimes, they say, he didn't preach what was quite orthodox.[48]

—Ah! ... he was a splendid man, said Mr M'Coy.

—I heard him once, Mr Kernan continued. I forget the subject of his discourse now. Crofton and I were in the back of the ... pit,[49] you know ... the—

—The body,[50] said Mr Cunningham.

—Yes, in the back near the door. I forget now what.... O yes, it was on the Pope, the late Pope. I remember it well. Upon my word it was magnificent, the style of the oratory. And his voice! God! hadn't he a voice! *The Prisoner of the Vatican*,[51] he called him. I remember Crofton saying to me when we came out—

—But he's an Orangeman,[52] Crofton, isn't he? said Mr Power.

---

[47] Thomas Nicholson Burke (1830–33), famed for his lively sermons and Nationalist politics.

[48] Within doctrine.

[49] Area of the theater for the main audience (Kernan is mistaking the architecture of the theater or dance-hall for that of a church).

[50] Where a congregation sits.

[51] In 1879 King of Italy Victor Emmanuel II stripped the Pope of civil and military power. Pope Pius (d. 1878) and Pope Leo XIII (d. 1903) were recent (late) pontiffs.

[52] A Protestant Irishman supporting British rule.

—'Course he is, said Mr Kernan, and a damned decent Orangeman too. We went into Butler's in Moore Street[53]—faith, I was genuinely moved, tell you the God's truth—and I remember well his very words. *Kernan*, he said, *we worship at different altars*, he said, *but our belief is the same*. Struck me as very well put.

—There's a good deal in that, said Mr Power. There used always be crowds of Protestants in the chapel when Father Tom was preaching.

—There's not much difference between us, said Mr M'Coy.

—We both believe in—

He hesitated for a moment.

—... in the Redeemer. Only they don't believe in the Pope and in the mother of God.[54]

—But, of course, said Mr Cunningham quietly and effectively, our religion is *the* religion, the old, original faith.[55]

—Not a doubt of it, said Mr Kernan warmly.

Mrs Kernan came to the door of the bedroom and announced:

—Here's a visitor for you!

—Who is it?

—Mr Fogarty.

—O, come in! come in!

A pale oval face came forward into the light. The arch of its fair trailing moustache was repeated in the fair eyebrows looped above pleasantly astonished eyes. Mr Fogarty was a modest grocer. He had failed in business in a licensed house in the city because his financial condition had constrained him to tie himself[56] to second-class distillers and brewers. He had opened a small shop on Glasnevin Road where, he flattered himself, his manners would ingratiate him with the housewives of the district. He bore himself with a certain grace, complimented little children and spoke with a neat enunciation. He was not without culture.

Mr Fogarty brought a gift with him, a half-pint of special whisky. He inquired politely for Mr Kernan, placed his gift on the table and sat down with the company on equal terms. Mr Kernan appreciated the gift all the more since he was aware that there was a

---

[53] Dublin pub.

[54] The infallibility of the Pope and the immaculate conception and divinity of the Virgin Mary.

[55] Protestant Christianity emerged in the early 16th c.

[56] Agreed to contracts that allowed him to sell only the products of specific brewers.

small account for groceries unsettled between him and Mr Fogarty. He said:

—I wouldn't doubt you, old man. Open that, Jack, will you?

Mr Power again officiated. Glasses were rinsed and five small measures of whisky were poured out. This new influence enlivened the conversation. Mr Fogarty, sitting on a small area of the chair, was specially interested.

—Pope Leo XIII, said Mr Cunningham, was one of the lights of the age.[57] His great idea, you know, was the union of the Latin and Greek Churches.[58] That was the aim of his life.

—I often heard he was one of the most intellectual men in Europe, said Mr Power. I mean apart from his being Pope.

—So he was, said Mr Cunningham, if not *the* most so. His motto, you know, as Pope, was *Lux upon Lux*—*Light upon Light*.

—No, no, said Mr Fogarty eagerly. I think you're wrong there. It was *Lux in Tenebris*, I think—*Light in Darkness*.

—O yes, said Mr M'Coy, *Tenebrae*.

—Allow me, said Mr Cunningham positively, it was *Lux upon Lux*. And Pius IX his predecessor's motto was *Crux upon Crux*— that is, *Cross upon Cross*—to show the difference between their two pontificates.

The inference was allowed. Mr Cunningham continued.

—Pope Leo, you know, was a great scholar and a poet.

—He had a strong face, said Mr Kernan.

—Yes, said Mr Cunningham. He wrote Latin poetry.

—Is that so? said Mr Fogarty.

Mr M'Coy tasted his whisky contentedly and shook his head with a double intention, saying:

—That's no joke, I can tell you.

—We didn't learn that, Tom, said Mr Power, following Mr M'Coy's example, when we went to the penny-a-week school.[59]

—There was many a good man went to the penny-a-week school with a sod of turf under his oxter,[60] said Mr Kernan sententiously. The old system was the best: plain honest education. None of your modern trumpery....

---

[57] Count Vincenzo Gioacchino Pecci (1810–1903; pope 1878–1903). Interested in philosophy and astronomy, he believed faith and science could be reconciled.

[58] Roman Catholic and Greek Orthodox churches.

[59] National schools (for the poor).

[60] Peat (a cheap fuel) under his arm.

—Quite right, said Mr Power.

—No superfluities, said Mr Fogarty.

He enunciated the word and then drank gravely.

—I remember reading, said Mr Cunningham, that one of Pope Leo's poems was on the invention of the photograph—in Latin, of course.[61]

—On the photograph! exclaimed Mr Kernan.

—Yes, said Mr Cunningham.

He also drank from his glass.

—Well, you know, said Mr M'Coy, isn't the photograph wonderful when you come to think of it?

—O, of course, said Mr Power, great minds can see things.

—As the poet says: *Great minds are very near to madness*,[62] said Mr Fogarty.

Mr Kernan seemed to be troubled in mind. He made an effort to recall the Protestant theology on some thorny points and in the end addressed Mr Cunningham.

—Tell me, Martin, he said. Weren't some of the popes—of course, not our present man, or his predecessor, but some of the old popes—not exactly … you know … up to the knocker?[63]

There was a silence. Mr Cunningham said

—O, of course, there were some bad lots…. But the astonishing thing is this. Not one of them, not the biggest drunkard, not the most … out-and-out ruffian, not one of them ever preached *ex cathedra*[64] a word of false doctrine. Now isn't that an astonishing thing?

—That is, said Mr Kernan.

—Yes, because when the Pope speaks *ex cathedra*, Mr Fogarty explained, he is infallible.

—Yes, said Mr Cunningham.

—O, I know about the infallibility of the Pope. I remember I was younger then…. Or was it that—?

Mr Fogarty interrupted. He took up the bottle and helped the others to a little more. Mr M'Coy, seeing that there was not enough

---

[61] "Ars Photographica" ("Art of Photography"), 1867.

[62] See John Dryden, *Absalom and Achitophel* (1682): "Great wits are sure to madness near allied" (Part I, 1.163), a sentiment that dates to the Roman poet Horace.

[63] Standard.

[64] "From the throne" in Latin, meaning officially. The Pope's infallibility, however, was only decreed by the First Vatican Council in 1870 and this power had not yet been formally used when the story was published.

to go round, pleaded that he had not finished his first measure. The others accepted under protest. The light music of whisky falling into glasses made an agreeable interlude.

—What's that you were saying, Tom? asked Mr M'Coy.

—Papal infallibility, said Mr Cunningham, that was the greatest scene in the whole history of the Church.

—How was that, Martin? asked Mr Power.

Mr Cunningham held up two thick fingers.

—In the sacred college, you know, of cardinals and archbishops and bishops there were two men who held out against it while the others were all for it. The whole conclave except these two was unanimous. No! They wouldn't have it!

—Ha! said Mr M'Coy.

—And they were a German cardinal by the name of Dolling ... or Dowling ... or—

—Dowling was no German, and that's a sure five,[65] said Mr Power, laughing.

—Well, this great German cardinal, whatever his name was, was one; and the other was John MacHale.

—What? cried Mr Kernan. Is it John of Tuam?[66]

—Are you sure of that now? asked Mr Fogarty dubiously. I thought it was some Italian or American.[67]

—John of Tuam, repeated Mr Cunningham, was the man.

He drank and the other gentlemen followed his lead. Then he resumed:

—There they were at it, all the cardinals and bishops and archbishops from all the ends of the earth and these two fighting dog and devil until at last the Pope himself stood up and declared infallibility a dogma of the Church *ex cathedra*. On the very moment John MacHale, who had been arguing and arguing against it, stood up and shouted out with the voice of a lion: *Credo!*

—*I believe!* said Mr Fogarty.

—*Credo!* said Mr Cunningham That showed the faith he had. He submitted the moment the Pope spoke.

—And what about Dowling? asked Mr M'Coy.

[65] Billiards term meaning a sure thing. "Dowling" is an Irish name. German theologian Johann Döllinger (not, however, on the First Vatican Council) was excommunicated in 1871 for opposing Papal Infallibility.

[66] Irish Nationalist John MacHale, Archbishop of Tuam (1791–1881), absent at the Council vote, accepted the doctrine afterwards.

[67] These opponents were Bishop Riccio of Italy and Bishop Fitzgerald of the U.S.; they too accepted the majority vote.

—The German cardinal wouldn't submit. He left the church.

Mr Cunningham's words had built up the vast image of the church in the minds of his hearers. His deep raucous voice had thrilled them as it uttered the word of belief and submission. When Mrs Kernan came into the room drying her hands she came into a solemn company. She did not disturb the silence but leaned over the rail at the foot of the bed.

—I once saw John MacHale, said Mr Kernan, and I'll never forget it as long as I live.

He turned towards his wife to be confirmed.

—I often told you that?

Mrs Kernan nodded.

—It was at the unveiling of Sir John Gray's statue.[68] Edmund Dwyer Gray was speaking, blathering away, and here was this old fellow, crabbed-looking old chap, looking at him from under his bushy eyebrows.

Mr Kernan knitted his brows and, lowering his head like an angry bull, glared at his wife.

—God! he exclaimed, resuming his natural face, I never saw such an eye in a man's head. It was as much as to say: *I have you properly taped,*[69] *my lad.* He had an eye like a hawk.

—None of the Grays was any good, said Mr Power.

There was a pause again. Mr Power turned to Mrs Kernan and said with abrupt joviality:

—Well, Mrs Kernan, we're going to make your man here a good holy pious and God-fearing Roman Catholic.

He swept his arm round the company inclusively.

—We're all going to make a retreat together and confess our sins—and God knows we want it badly.

—I don't mind, said Mr Kernan, smiling a little nervously.

Mrs Kernan thought it would be wiser to conceal her satisfaction. So she said:

—I pity the poor priest that has to listen to your tale.

Mr Kernan's expression changed.

—If he doesn't like it, he said bluntly, he can ... do the other thing. I'll just tell him my little tale of woe. I'm not such a bad fellow—

Mr Cunningham intervened promptly.

[68] Gray (1816–75), though a Protestant, supported Home Rule and land reform; the statue was erected in 1879 on O'Connell St. to commemorate his efforts to bring clean water to Dublin.

[69] Measured.

—We'll all renounce the devil, he said, together, not forgetting his works and pomps.[70]

—Get behind me, Satan![71] said Mr Fogarty, laughing and looking at the others.

Mr Power said nothing. He felt completely out-generalled. But a pleased expression flickered across his face.

—All we have to do, said Mr Cunningham, is to stand up with lighted candles in our hands and renew our baptismal vows.[72]

—O, don't forget the candle, Tom, said Mr M'Coy, whatever you do.

—What? said Mr Kernan. Must I have a candle?

—O yes, said Mr Cunningham.

—No, damn it all, said Mr Kernan sensibly, I draw the line there. I'll do the job right enough. I'll do the retreat business and confession, and … all that business. But … no candles! No, damn it all, I bar the candles![73]

He shook his head with farcical gravity.

—Listen to that! said his wife.

—I bar the candles, said Mr Kernan, conscious of having created an effect on his audience and continuing to shake his head to and fro. I bar the magic-lantern[74] business.

Everyone laughed heartily.

—There's a nice Catholic for you! said his wife.

—No candles! repeated Mr Kernan obdurately. That's off!

* * *

The transept[75] of the Jesuit Church in Gardiner Street was almost full; and still at every moment gentlemen entered from the side door and, directed by the lay-brother,[76] walked on tiptoe along the aisles until they found seating accommodation. The gentlemen were all well dressed and orderly. The light of the lamps of the church fell upon an assembly of black clothes and white collars, relieved here

---

[70] A phrase in the rite of Baptism.

[71] Jesus's rebuke to Peter, who had urged him to avoid the fate of suffering and death when resurrection was promised (Matthew 16: 21–23).

[72] Originally made by godparents, they include the promise to reject Satan and embrace the Holy Spirit.

[73] Typical Protestant contempt of elaborate Catholic rituals.

[74] Precursor to the cinema.

[75] Central area.

[76] Secular assistant.

and there by tweeds, on dark mottled pillars of green marble and on lugubrious canvases.[77] The gentlemen sat in the benches, having hitched their trousers slightly above their knees and laid their hats in security. They sat well back and gazed formally at the distant speck of red light which was suspended before the high altar.

In one of the benches near the pulpit sat Mr Cunningham and Mr Kernan. In the bench behind sat Mr M'Coy alone: and in the bench behind him sat Mr Power and Mr Fogarty. Mr M'Coy had tried unsuccessfully to find a place in the bench with the others and, when the party had settled down in the form of a quincunx,[78] he had tried unsuccessfully to make comic remarks. As these had not been well received he had desisted. Even he was sensible of the decorous atmosphere and even he began to respond to the religious stimulus. In a whisper, Mr Cunningham drew Mr Kernan's attention to Mr Harford, the moneylender, who sat some distance off, and to Mr Fanning, the registration agent and mayor maker of the city,[79] who was sitting immediately under the pulpit beside one of the newly elected councillors of the ward. To the right sat old Michael Grimes, the owner of three pawnbroker's shops, and Dan Hogan's nephew, who was up for the job in the Town Clerk's office. Farther in front sat Mr Hendrick, the chief reporter of *The Freeman's Journal*, and poor O'Carroll, an old friend of Mr Kernan's, who had been at one time a considerable commercial figure. Gradually, as he recognised familiar faces, Mr Kernan began to feel more at home. His hat, which had been rehabilitated by his wife, rested upon his knees. Once or twice he pulled down his cuffs with one hand while he held the brim of his hat lightly, but firmly, with the other hand.

A powerful-looking figure, the upper part of which was draped with a white surplice,[80] was observed to be struggling into the pulpit. Simultaneously the congregation unsettled, produced handkerchiefs and knelt upon them with care. Mr Kernan followed the general example. The priest's figure now stood upright in the pulpit, two-thirds of its bulk, crowned by a massive red face, appearing above the balustrade.[81]

---

[77] Mournful paintings.

[78] A four-point rectangle with a fifth at its center (like a five on a die); the shape has many mystical and symbolic meanings and may refer here to the five wounds on the body of the crucified Jesus.

[79] The Sub-Sheriff of Dublin. See "Ivy Day" p.xxx n.32.

[80] Long linen vestment.

[81] Railing.

Father Purdon knelt down, turned towards the red speck of light and, covering his face with his hands, prayed. After an interval, he uncovered his face and rose. The congregation rose also and settled again on its benches. Mr Kernan restored his hat to its original position on his knee and presented an attentive face to the preacher. The preacher turned back each wide sleeve of his surplice with an elaborate large gesture and slowly surveyed the array of faces. Then he said:

—*For the children of this world are wiser in their generation than the children of light. Wherefore make unto yourselves friends out of the mammon of iniquity so that when you die they may receive you into everlasting dwellings.*[82]

Father Purdon developed the text with resonant assurance. It was one of the most difficult texts in all the Scriptures, he said, to interpret properly. It was a text which might seem to the casual observer at variance with the lofty morality elsewhere preached by Jesus Christ.[83] But, he told his hearers, the text had seemed to him specially adapted for the guidance of those whose lot it was to lead the life of the world and who yet wished to lead that life not in the manner of worldlings. It was a text for business men and professional men. Jesus Christ, with His divine understanding of every cranny of our human nature, understood that all men were not called to the religious life, that by far the vast majority were forced to live in the world and, to a certain extent, for the world: and in this sentence He designed to give them a word of counsel, setting before them as exemplars in the religious life those very worshippers of Mammon who were of all men the least solicitous in matters religious.

He told his hearers that he was there that evening for no terrifying, no extravagant purpose; but as a man of the world speaking to his fellow-men. He came to speak to business men and he would speak to them in a businesslike way. If he might use the metaphor, he said, he was their spiritual accountant; and he wished each and every one of his hearers to open his books, the books of his spiritual life, and see if they tallied accurately with conscience.[84]

Jesus Christ was not a hard taskmaster. He understood our little failings, understood the weakness of our poor fallen nature,

---

[82] Final lines of Jesus's parable of steward in Luke 16:1–9. See p. xxx.

[83] See, for example, Jesus's Sermon on the Mount: "Lay not up for yourselves treasures upon earth ... But lay up for yourselves treasure in heaven ... You cannot serve both God and Mammon" (Matthew 6:19–24). Mammon is the icon of worldly riches and avarice.

[84] A spiritual self-accounting undertaken in preparation for Confession.

understood the temptations of this life. We might have had, we all had from time to time, our temptations: we might have, we all had, our failings. But one thing only, he said, he would ask of his hearers. And that was: to be straight and manly with God. If their accounts tallied in every point to say:

—*Well, I have verified my accounts. I find all well.*

But if, as might happen, there were some discrepancies, to admit the truth, to be frank and say like a man:

—*Well, I have looked into my accounts. I find this wrong and this wrong. But, with God's grace, I will rectify this and this. I will set right my accounts.*

The Dead

LILY,[1] THE caretaker's daughter, was literally run off her feet. Hardly had she brought one gentleman into the little pantry behind the office on the ground floor and helped him off with his overcoat than the wheezy hall-door bell clanged again and she had to scamper along the bare hallway to let in another guest. It was well for her she had not to attend to the ladies also. But Miss Kate and Miss Julia had thought of that and had converted the bathroom upstairs into a ladies' dressing-room. Miss Kate and Miss Julia were there, gossiping and laughing and fussing, walking after each other to the head of the stairs, peering down over the banisters and calling down to Lily to ask her who had come.

It was always a great affair, the Misses Morkan's annual dance. Everybody who knew them came to it, members of the family, old friends of the family, the members of Julia's choir, any of Kate's pupils that were grown up enough, and even some of Mary Jane's pupils too. Never once had it fallen flat. For years and years it had gone off in splendid style, as long as anyone could remember; ever since Kate and Julia, after the death of their brother Pat, had left the house in Stoney Batter[2] and taken Mary Jane, their only niece, to live with them in the dark gaunt house on Usher's Island, the upper part of which they had rented from Mr Fulham, the corn-factor[3] on the ground floor. That was a good thirty years ago if it was a day. Mary Jane, who was then a little girl in short clothes, was now the main prop of the household, for she had the organ in Haddington Road.[4]

---

[1] The lily is associated with chastity as well as with the Virgin Mary and is placed on the graves of innocents. As the Easter flower, it is also symbolic of death and rebirth.

[2] A poorer section of Dublin.

[3] Grain dealer.

[4] Was the organist for St. Mary's Church.

She had been through the Academy[5] and gave a pupils' concert every year in the upper room of the Antient Concert Rooms.[6] Many of her pupils belonged to the better-class families on the Kingstown and Dalkey line. Old as they were, her aunts also did their share. Julia, though she was quite grey, was still the leading soprano in Adam and Eve's,[7] and Kate, being too feeble to go about much, gave music lessons to beginners on the old square piano in the back room. Lily, the caretaker's daughter, did housemaid's work for them. Though their life was modest they believed in eating well; the best of everything: diamond-bone sirloins, three-shilling tea and the best bottled stout. But Lily seldom made a mistake in the orders so that she got on well with her three mistresses. They were fussy, that was all. But the only thing they would not stand was back answers.[8]

Of course they had good reason to be fussy on such a night. And then it was long after ten o'clock and yet there was no sign of Gabriel[9] and his wife. Besides they were dreadfully afraid that Freddy Malins might turn up screwed.[10] They would not wish for worlds that any of Mary Jane's pupils should see him under the influence; and when he was like that it was sometimes very hard to manage him. Freddy Malins always came late but they wondered what could be keeping Gabriel: and that was what brought them every two minutes to the banisters to ask Lily had Gabriel or Freddy come.

—O, Mr Conroy, said Lily to Gabriel when she opened the door for him, Miss Kate and Miss Julia thought you were never coming. Good-night, Mrs Conroy.

—I'll engage they did, said Gabriel, but they forget that my wife here takes three mortal hours to dress herself.

He stood on the mat, scraping the snow from his goloshes, while Lily led his wife to the foot of the stairs and called out:

—Miss Kate, here's Mrs Conroy.

Kate and Julia came toddling down the dark stairs at once. Both of them kissed Gabriel's wife, said she must be perished alive and asked was Gabriel with her.

[5] The prestigious Royal Academy of Music.

[6] The site of Kathleen's recital in "A Mother," (p. xxx, n. 14).

[7] Nickname for the St. Francis of Assisi Church near Usher's Island.

[8] Sass or argument.

[9] "Man of God" in Hebrew. Archangel Gabriel announced the birth of Jesus to Mary.

[10] Drunk.

—Here I am as right as the mail,[11] Aunt Kate! Go on up. I'll follow, called out Gabriel from the dark.

He continued scraping his feet vigorously while the three women went upstairs, laughing, to the ladies' dressing-room. A light fringe of snow lay like a cape on the shoulders of his overcoat and like toecaps on the toes of his goloshes; and, as the buttons of his overcoat slipped with a squeaking noise through the snow-stiffened frieze,[12] a cold fragrant air from out-of-doors escaped from crevices and folds.

—Is it snowing again, Mr Conroy? asked Lily.

She had preceded him into the pantry to help him off with his overcoat. Gabriel smiled at the three syllables she had given his surname[13] and glanced at her. She was a slim, growing girl, pale in complexion and with hay-coloured hair. The gas[14] in the pantry made her look still paler. Gabriel had known her when she was a child and used to sit on the lowest step nursing a rag doll.

—Yes, Lily, he answered, and I think we're in for a night of it.

He looked up at the pantry ceiling, which was shaking with the stamping and shuffling of feet on the floor above, listened for a moment to the piano and then glanced at the girl, who was folding his overcoat carefully at the end of a shelf.

—Tell me, Lily, he said in a friendly tone, do you still go to school?

—O no, sir, she answered. I'm done schooling this year and more.

—O, then, said Gabriel gaily, I suppose we'll be going to your wedding one of these fine days with your young man, eh?

The girl glanced back at him over her shoulder and said with great bitterness:

—The men that is now is only all palaver[15] and what they can get out of you.

Gabriel coloured[16] as if he felt he had made a mistake and, without looking at her, kicked off his goloshes and flicked actively with his muffler[17] at his patent-leather shoes.

---

[11] Dependable.

[12] Coarse Irish wool cloth.

[13] *Con-nor-roy*—a lower-class accent.

[14] Gaslights.

[15] Chatter.

[16] Blushed.

[17] Heavy scarf.

He was a stout tallish young man. The high colour of his cheeks pushed upwards even to his forehead, where it scattered itself in a few formless patches of pale red; and on his hairless face there scintillated restlessly the polished lenses and the bright gilt rims of the glasses which screened his delicate and restless eyes. His glossy black hair was parted in the middle and brushed in a long curve behind his ears where it curled slightly beneath the groove left by his hat.

When he had flicked lustre[18] into his shoes he stood up and pulled his waistcoat down more tightly on his plump body. Then he took a coin rapidly from his pocket.

—O Lily, he said, thrusting it into her hands, it's Christmas-time, isn't it? Just ... here's a little....

He walked rapidly towards the door.

—O no, sir! cried the girl, following him. Really, sir, I wouldn't take it.

—Christmas-time! Christmas-time! said Gabriel, almost trotting to the stairs and waving his hand to her in deprecation.

The girl, seeing that he had gained the stairs, called out after him:

—Well, thank you, sir.

He waited outside the drawing-room door until the waltz should finish, listening to the skirts that swept against it and to the shuffling of feet. He was still discomposed by the girl's bitter and sudden retort. It had cast a gloom over him which he tried to dispel by arranging his cuffs and the bows of his tie. He then took from his waistcoat pocket a little paper and glanced at the headings he had made for his speech. He was undecided about the lines from Robert Browning[19] for he feared they would be above the heads of his hearers. Some quotation that they would recognise from Shakespeare or from the Melodies[20] would be better. The indelicate clacking of the men's heels and the shuffling of their soles reminded him that their grade of culture differed from his. He would only make himself ridiculous by quoting poetry to them which they could not understand. They would think that he was airing his superior education. He would fail with them just as he had failed with the girl in the pantry. He had taken up a wrong tone. His whole speech was a mistake from first to last, an utter failure.

[18] Shined or polished.

[19] Popular English poet (1812–89) widely known for his difficult, complex work, including often lengthy dramatic monologues.

[20] *Irish Melodies*: the much-loved poems of Thomas Moore (1779–1852); Joyce and other Irish artists disdained their easy sentimentalism.

Just then his aunts and his wife came out of the ladies' dressing-room. His aunts were two small plainly dressed old women. Aunt Julia was an inch or so the taller. Her hair, drawn low over the tops of her ears, was grey; and grey also, with darker shadows, was her large flaccid face. Though she was stout in build and stood erect her slow eyes and parted lips gave her the appearance of a woman who did not know where she was or where she was going. Aunt Kate was more vivacious. Her face, healthier than her sister's, was all puckers and creases, like a shrivelled red apple, and her hair, braided in the same old-fashioned way, had not lost its ripe nut colour.

They both kissed Gabriel frankly. He was their favourite nephew, the son of their dead elder sister, Ellen, who had married T. J. Conroy of the Port and Docks.[21]

—Gretta tells me you're not going to take a cab back to Monkstown[22] to-night, Gabriel, said Aunt Kate.

—No, said Gabriel, turning to his wife, we had quite enough of that last year, hadn't we? Don't you remember, Aunt Kate, what a cold Gretta got out of it? Cab windows rattling all the way, and the east wind blowing in after we passed Merrion. Very jolly it was. Gretta caught a dreadful cold.

Aunt Kate frowned severely and nodded her head at every word.

—Quite right, Gabriel, quite right, she said. You can't be too careful.

—But as for Gretta there, said Gabriel, she'd walk home in the snow if she were let.

Mrs Conroy laughed.

—Don't mind him, Aunt Kate, she said. He's really an awful bother, what with green shades for Tom's eyes at night and making him do the dumb-bells, and forcing Eva to eat the stirabout.[23] The poor child! And she simply hates the sight of it!... O, but you'll never guess what he makes me wear now!

She broke out into a peal of laughter and glanced at her husband, whose admiring and happy eyes had been wandering from her dress to her face and hair. The two aunts laughed heartily too, for Gabriel's solicitude was a standing joke with them.

—Goloshes! said Mrs Conroy. That's the latest. Whenever it's wet underfoot I must put on my goloshes. To-night even, he wanted

---

[21] The main office of waterfront management.

[22] Fashionable suburb south of Dublin.

[23] Oatmeal porridge.

me to put them on, but I wouldn't. The next thing he'll buy me will be a diving suit.

Gabriel laughed nervously and patted his tie reassuringly while Aunt Kate nearly doubled herself, so heartily did she enjoy the joke. The smile soon faded from Aunt Julia's face and her mirthless eyes were directed towards her nephew's face. After a pause she asked:

—And what are goloshes, Gabriel?

—Goloshes, Julia! exclaimed her sister. Goodness me, don't you know what goloshes are? You wear them over your ... over your boots, Gretta, isn't it?

—Yes, said Mrs Conroy. Guttapercha[24] things. We both have a pair now. Gabriel says everyone wears them on the Continent.

—O, on the Continent, murmured Aunt Julia, nodding her head slowly.

Gabriel knitted his brows and said, as if he were slightly angered:

—It's nothing very wonderful but Gretta thinks it very funny because she says the word reminds her of Christy Minstrels.[25]

—But tell me, Gabriel, said Aunt Kate, with brisk tact. Of course, you've seen about the room. Gretta was saying....

—O, the room is all right, replied Gabriel. I've taken one in the Gresham.[26]

—To be sure, said Aunt Kate, by far the best thing to do. And the children, Gretta, you're not anxious about them?

—O, for one night, said Mrs Conroy. Besides, Bessie will look after them.

—To be sure, said Aunt Kate again. What a comfort it is to have a girl[27] like that, one you can depend on! There's that Lily, I'm sure I don't know what has come over her lately. She's not the girl she was at all.

Gabriel was about to ask his aunt some questions on this point, but she broke off suddenly to gaze after her sister, who had wandered down the stairs and was craning her neck over the banisters.

—Now, I ask you, she said almost testily, where is Julia going? Julia! Julia! Where are you going?

[24] Like rubber.

[25] Popular 19th c. minstrel show, with actors in blackface staging racial stereotypes.

[26] Upscale hotel in central Dublin. See p. xxx.

[27] Servant.

Julia, who had gone half way down one flight, came back and announced blandly:

—Here's Freddy.

At the same moment a clapping of hands and a final flourish of the pianist told that the waltz had ended. The drawing-room door was opened from within and some couples came out. Aunt Kate drew Gabriel aside hurriedly and whispered into his ear:

—Slip down, Gabriel, like a good fellow and see if he's all right, and don't let him up if he's screwed. I'm sure he's screwed. I'm sure he is.

Gabriel went to the stairs and listened over the banisters. He could hear two persons talking in the pantry. Then he recognised Freddy Malins' laugh. He went down the stairs noisily.

—It's such a relief, said Aunt Kate to Mrs Conroy, that Gabriel is here. I always feel easier in my mind when he's here.... Julia, there's Miss Daly and Miss Power will take some refreshment. Thanks for your beautiful waltz, Miss Daly. It made lovely time.

A tall wizen-faced man, with a stiff grizzled moustache and swarthy skin, who was passing out with his partner, said:

—And may we have some refreshment, too, Miss Morkan?

—Julia, said Aunt Kate summarily, and here's Mr Browne and Miss Furlong. Take them in, Julia, with Miss Daly and Miss Power.

—I'm the man for the ladies, said Mr Browne, pursing his lips until his moustache bristled and smiling in all his wrinkles. You know, Miss Morkan, the reason they are so fond of me is—

He did not finish his sentence, but, seeing that Aunt Kate was out of earshot, at once led the three young ladies into the back room. The middle of the room was occupied by two square tables placed end to end, and on these Aunt Julia and the caretaker were straightening and smoothing a large cloth. On the sideboard were arrayed dishes and plates, and glasses and bundles of knives and forks and spoons. The top of the closed square piano served also as a sideboard for viands[28] and sweets. At a smaller sideboard in one corner two young men were standing, drinking hop-bitters.[29]

Mr Browne led his charges thither and invited them all, in jest, to some ladies' punch, hot, strong and sweet. As they said they never took anything strong he opened three bottles of lemonade for them. Then he asked one of the young men to move aside, and, taking hold of the decanter, filled out for himself a goodly measure of whisky. The young men eyed him respectfully while he took a trial sip.

[28] Food or provisions.
[29] Mild alcoholic drink.

—God help me, he said, smiling, it's the doctor's orders.

His wizened face broke into a broader smile, and the three young ladies laughed in musical echo to his pleasantry, swaying their bodies to and fro, with nervous jerks of their shoulders. The boldest said:

—O, now, Mr Browne, I'm sure the doctor never ordered anything of the kind.

Mr Browne took another sip of his whisky and said, with sidling mimicry:

—Well, you see, I'm like the famous Mrs Cassidy, who is reported to have said: *Now, Mary Grimes, if I don't take it, make me take it, for I feel I want it.*

His hot face had leaned forward a little too confidentially and he had assumed a very low[30] Dublin accent so that the young ladies, with one instinct, received his speech in silence. Miss Furlong, who was one of Mary Jane's pupils, asked Miss Daly what was the name of the pretty waltz she had played; and Mr Browne, seeing that he was ignored, turned promptly to the two young men who were more appreciative.

A red-faced young woman, dressed in pansy, came into the room, excitedly clapping her hands and crying:

—Quadrilles! Quadrilles![31]

Close on her heels came Aunt Kate, crying:

—Two gentlemen and three ladies, Mary Jane!

—O, here's Mr Bergin and Mr Kerrigan, said Mary Jane. Mr Kerrigan, will you take Miss Power? Miss Furlong, may I get you a partner, Mr Bergin. O, that'll just do now.

—Three ladies, Mary Jane, said Aunt Kate.

The two young gentlemen asked the ladies if they might have the pleasure, and Mary Jane turned to Miss Daly.

—O, Miss Daly, you're really awfully good, after playing for the last two dances, but really we're so short of ladies to-night.

—I don't mind in the least, Miss Morkan.

—But I've a nice partner for you, Mr Bartell D'Arcy, the tenor. I'll get him to sing later on. All Dublin is raving about him.

—Lovely voice, lovely voice! said Aunt Kate.

As the piano had twice begun the prelude to the first figure[32] Mary Jane led her recruits quickly from the room. They had hardly gone when Aunt Julia wandered slowly into the room, looking behind her at something.

[30] Lower class.

[31] Patterned square dancing.

[32] Part of the quadrille.

—What is the matter, Julia? asked Aunt Kate anxiously. Who is it?

Julia, who was carrying in a column of table-napkins, turned to her sister and said, simply, as if the question had surprised her:

—It's only Freddy, Kate, and Gabriel with him.

In fact right behind her Gabriel could be seen piloting Freddy Malins across the landing. The latter, a young man of about forty, was of Gabriel's size and build, with very round shoulders. His face was fleshy and pallid, touched with colour only at the thick hanging lobes of his ears and at the wide wings of his nose. He had coarse features, a blunt nose, a convex and receding brow, tumid[33] and protruded lips. His heavy-lidded eyes and the disorder of his scanty hair made him look sleepy. He was laughing heartily in a high key at a story which he had been telling Gabriel on the stairs and at the same time rubbing the knuckles of his left fist backwards and forwards into his left eye.

—Good-evening, Freddy, said Aunt Julia.

Freddy Malins bade the Misses Morkan good-evening in what seemed an offhand fashion by reason of the habitual catch in his voice and then, seeing that Mr Browne was grinning at him from the sideboard, crossed the room on rather shaky legs and began to repeat in an undertone the story he had just told to Gabriel.

—He's not so bad, is he? said Aunt Kate to Gabriel.

Gabriel's brows were dark but he raised them quickly and answered:

—O no, hardly noticeable.

—Now, isn't he a terrible fellow! she said. And his poor mother made him take the pledge[34] on New Year's Eve. But come on, Gabriel, into the drawing-room.

Before leaving the room with Gabriel she signalled to Mr Browne by frowning and shaking her forefinger in warning to and fro. Mr Browne nodded in answer and, when she had gone, said to Freddy Malins:

—Now, then, Teddy, I'm going to fill you out a good glass of lemonade just to buck you up.

Freddy Malins, who was nearing the climax of his story, waved the offer aside impatiently but Mr Browne, having first called Freddy Malins' attention to a disarray in his dress,[35] filled out and handed

[33] Swollen.

[34] In the temperance movement, a promise to stop drinking.

[35] Open fly.

him a full glass of lemonade. Freddy Malins' left hand accepted the glass mechanically, his right hand being engaged in the mechanical readjustment of his dress. Mr Browne, whose face was once more wrinkling with mirth, poured out for himself a glass of whisky while Freddy Malins exploded, before he had well reached the climax of his story, in a kink of high-pitched bronchitic laughter and, setting down his untasted and overflowing glass, began to rub the knuckles of his left fist backwards and forwards into his left eye, repeating words of his last phrase as well as his fit of laughter would allow him.

* * *

Gabriel could not listen while Mary Jane was playing her Academy piece,[1] full of runs and difficult passages, to the hushed drawing-room. He liked music but the piece she was playing had no melody for him and he doubted whether it had any melody for the other listeners, though they had begged Mary Jane to play something. Four young men, who had come from the refreshment-room to stand in the doorway at the sound of the piano, had gone away quietly in couples after a few minutes. The only persons who seemed to follow the music were Mary Jane herself, her hands racing along the key-board or lifted from it at the pauses like those of a priestess in momentary imprecation,[2] and Aunt Kate standing at her elbow to turn the page.

Gabriel's eyes, irritated by the floor, which glittered with beeswax[3] under the heavy chandelier, wandered to the wall above the piano. A picture of the balcony scene in *Romeo and Juliet* hung there and beside it was a picture of the two murdered princes in the Tower which Aunt Julia had worked[4] in red, blue and brown wools when she was a girl. Probably in the school they had gone to as girls that kind of work had been taught for one year. His mother had worked for him as a birthday present a waistcoat of purple tabinet,[5] with little foxes' heads upon it, lined with brown satin and having round mulberry buttons. It was strange that his mother had had no musical talent though Aunt Kate used to call her the brains carrier of

[1] Difficult piece of music used to demonstrate a student's technical mastery.

[2] Calling down a curse.

[3] Polish.

[4] Embroidered scenes from Shakespeare's plays. The second presents the the two sons of King Edward IV, who where murdered by their uncle, Richard III, so he could ascend to the throne.

[5] Irish fabric of silk and wool.

the Morkan family. Both she and Julia had always seemed a little proud of their serious and matronly sister. Her photograph stood before the pierglass.[6] She held an open book on her knees and was pointing out something in it to Constantine who, dressed in a man-o'-war suit,[7] lay at her feet. It was she who had chosen the name of her sons for she was very sensible of the dignity of family life. Thanks to her, Constantine was now senior curate in Balbrigan[8] and, thanks to her, Gabriel himself had taken his degree in the Royal University.[9] A shadow passed over his face as he remembered her sullen opposition to his marriage. Some slighting phrases she had used still rankled in his memory; she had once spoken of Gretta as being country cute[10] and that was not true of Gretta at all. It was Gretta who had nursed her during all her last long illness in their house at Monkstown.

He knew that Mary Jane must be near the end of her piece for she was playing again the opening melody with runs of scales after every bar and while he waited for the end the resentment died down in his heart. The piece ended with a trill of octaves in the treble and a final deep octave in the bass. Great applause greeted Mary Jane as, blushing and rolling up her music nervously, she escaped from the room. The most vigorous clapping came from the four young men in the doorway who had gone away to the refreshment-room at the beginning of the piece but had come back when the piano had stopped.

Lancers[11] were arranged. Gabriel found himself partnered with Miss Ivors. She was a frank-mannered talkative young lady, with a freckled face and prominent brown eyes. She did not wear a low-cut bodice and the large brooch which was fixed in the front of her collar bore on it an Irish device.[12]

When they had taken their places she said abruptly:

—I have a crow to pluck[13] with you.

[6] Mirror.

[7] A child's sailor-suit. Constantine was the first Roman emperor to convert to Christianity.

[8] Catholic clergyman in a town north of Dublin.

[9] Not a physical institution, but an examination board established in 1879 for Catholic students who were largely excluded from the Protestant universities.

[10] The full phrase "country cute and city clever" implies Gretta's cunning in securing an upwardly mobile marriage.

[11] Kind of quadrille.

[12] Her jewelry indicates her enthusiasm for the Irish Revival. See p. xxx.

[13] An argument to make.

—With me? said Gabriel.

She nodded her head gravely.

—What is it? asked Gabriel, smiling at her solemn manner.

—Who is G. C.? answered Miss Ivors, turning her eyes upon him.

Gabriel coloured and was about to knit his brows, as if he did not understand, when she said bluntly:

—O, innocent Amy! I have found out that you write for *The Daily Express*.[14] Now, aren't you ashamed of yourself?

—Why should I be ashamed of myself? asked Gabriel, blinking his eyes and trying to smile.

—Well, I'm ashamed of you, said Miss Ivors frankly. To say you'd write for a rag like that. I didn't think you were a West Briton.[15]

A look of perplexity appeared on Gabriel's face. It was true that he wrote a literary column every Wednesday in *The Daily Express*, for which he was paid fifteen shillings. But that did not make him a West Briton surely. The books he received for review were almost more welcome than the paltry cheque. He loved to feel the covers and turn over the pages of newly printed books. Nearly every day when his teaching in the college was ended he used to wander down the quays to the second-hand booksellers, to Hickey's on Bachelor's Walk, to Web's or Massey's on Aston's Quay, or to Clohissey's in the bystreet. He did not know how to meet her charge. He wanted to say that literature was above politics. But they were friends of many years' standing and their careers had been parallel, first at the University and then as teachers: he could not risk a grandiose phrase with her. He continued blinking his eyes and trying to smile and murmured lamely that he saw nothing political in writing reviews of books.

When their turn to cross had come he was still perplexed and inattentive. Miss Ivors promptly took his hand in a warm grasp and said in a soft friendly tone:

—Of course, I was only joking. Come, we cross now.

When they were together again she spoke of the University question[16] and Gabriel felt more at ease. A friend of hers had shown her his review of Browning's poems. That was how she had found

---

[14] This Dublin paper opposed Irish Home Rule; it was common practice to sign reviews with initials.

[15] Pejorative term for Irish people loyal to English rule who see the island as the western province of Great Britain.

[16] Complicated issue involving both whether women should be admitted to Irish universities and the sectarian divide between the elite Trinity College Dublin (primarily Protestant) and the smaller, poorer institutions recently created for Catholics.

out the secret: but she liked the review immensely. Then she said suddenly:

—O, Mr Conroy, will you come for an excursion to the Aran Isles[17] this summer? We're going to stay there a whole month. It will be splendid out in the Atlantic. You ought to come. Mr Clancy is coming, and Mr Kilkelly and Kathleen Kearney.[18] It would be splendid for Gretta too if she'd come. She's from Connacht,[19] isn't she?

—Her people are, said Gabriel shortly.

—But you will come, won't you? said Miss Ivors, laying her warm hand eagerly on his arm.

—The fact is, said Gabriel, I have already arranged to go—

—Go where? asked Miss Ivors.

—Well, you know, every year I go for a cycling tour with some fellows and so—

—But where? asked Miss Ivors.

—Well, we usually go to France or Belgium or perhaps Germany, said Gabriel awkwardly.

—And why do you go to France and Belgium, said Miss Ivors, instead of visiting your own land?

—Well, said Gabriel, it's partly to keep in touch with the languages and partly for a change.

—And haven't you your own language to keep in touch with— Irish? asked Miss Ivors.

—Well, said Gabriel, if it comes to that, you know, Irish is not my language.

Their neighbours had turned to listen to the cross-examination. Gabriel glanced right and left nervously and tried to keep his good humour under the ordeal which was making a blush invade his forehead.

—And haven't you your own land to visit, continued Miss Ivors, that you know nothing of, your own people, and your own country?

—O, to tell you the truth, retorted Gabriel suddenly, I'm sick of my own country, sick of it!

—Why? asked Miss Ivors.

Gabriel did not answer for his retort had heated him.

—Why? repeated Miss Ivors.

[17] Off the west coast, where the Irish language was spoken and old traditions maintained.

[18] The pianist from "A Mother."

[19] Ancient province on the western coast.

They had to go visiting together[20] and, as he had not answered her, Miss Ivors said warmly:

—Of course, you've no answer.

Gabriel tried to cover his agitation by taking part in the dance with great energy. He avoided her eyes for he had seen a sour expression on her face. But when they met in the long chain he was surprised to feel his hand firmly pressed. She looked at him from under her brows for a moment quizzically until he smiled. Then, just as the chain was about to start again, she stood on tiptoe and whispered into his ear:

—West Briton!

When the lancers were over Gabriel went away to a remote corner of the room where Freddy Malins' mother was sitting. She was a stout feeble old woman with white hair. Her voice had a catch in it like her son's and she stuttered slightly. She had been told that Freddy had come and that he was nearly all right. Gabriel asked her whether she had had a good crossing.[21] She lived with her married daughter in Glasgow and came to Dublin on a visit once a year. She answered placidly that she had had a beautiful crossing and that the captain had been most attentive to her. She spoke also of the beautiful house her daughter kept in Glasgow, and of all the nice friends they had there. While her tongue rambled on Gabriel tried to banish from his mind all memory of the unpleasant incident with Miss Ivors. Of course the girl or woman, or whatever she was, was an enthusiast but there was a time for all things. Perhaps he ought not to have answered her like that. But she had no right to call him a West Briton before people, even in joke. She had tried to make him ridiculous before people, heckling him and staring at him with her rabbit's eyes.

He saw his wife making her way towards him through the waltzing couples. When she reached him she said into his ear:

—Gabriel, Aunt Kate wants to know won't you carve the goose as usual. Miss Daly will carve the ham and I'll do the pudding.

—All right, said Gabriel.

—She's sending in the younger ones first as soon as this waltz is over so that we'll have the table to ourselves.

—Were you dancing? asked Gabriel.

—Of course I was. Didn't you see me? What words had you with Molly Ivors?

—No words. Why? Did she say so?

[20] A dance move that separates them.
[21] Sea voyage.

—Something like that. I'm trying to get that Mr D'Arcy to sing. He's full of conceit, I think.

—There were no words, said Gabriel moodily, only she wanted me to go for a trip to the west of Ireland and I said I wouldn't.

His wife clasped her hands excitedly and gave a little jump.

—O, do go, Gabriel, she cried. I'd love to see Galway[22] again.

—You can go if you like, said Gabriel coldly.

She looked at him for a moment, then turned to Mrs Malins and said:

—There's a nice husband for you, Mrs Malins.

While she was threading her way back across the room Mrs Malins, without adverting to the interruption, went on to tell Gabriel what beautiful places there were in Scotland and beautiful scenery. Her son-in-law brought them every year to the lakes and they used to go fishing. Her son-in-law was a splendid fisher. One day he caught a fish, a beautiful big big fish and the man in the hotel boiled it for their dinner.

Gabriel hardly heard what she said. Now that supper was coming near he began to think again about his speech and about the quotation. When he saw Freddy Malins coming across the room to visit his mother Gabriel left the chair free for him and retired into the embrasure[23] of the window. The room had already cleared and from the back room came the clatter of plates and knives. Those who still remained in the drawing-room seemed tired of dancing and were conversing quietly in little groups. Gabriel's warm trembling fingers tapped the cold pane of the window. How cool it must be outside! How pleasant it would be to walk out alone, first along by the river and then through the park! The snow would be lying on the branches of the trees and forming a bright cap on the top of the Wellington Monument.[24] How much more pleasant it would be there than at the supper-table!

He ran over the headings of his speech: Irish hospitality, sad memories, the Three Graces, Paris, the quotation from Browning. He repeated to himself a phrase he had written in his review: *One feels that one is listening to a thought-tormented music.* Miss Ivors had praised the review. Was she sincere? Had she really any life of

[22] County and a city in the far west of Ireland.

[23] Recessed sill.

[24] Erected in honor of Dublin-born Arthur Wellesley, the Duke of Wellington (1769-1852) who defeated Napoleon at Waterloo (1815). As Prime Minister, he granted Irish Catholics civil rights in 1829, but was a strong opponent of Home Rule.

her own behind all her propagandism? There had never been any ill-feeling between them until that night. It unnerved him to think that she would be at the supper-table, looking up at him while he spoke with her critical quizzing eyes. Perhaps she would not be sorry to see him fail in his speech. An idea came into his mind and gave him courage. He would say, alluding to Aunt Kate and Aunt Julia: *Ladies and Gentlemen, the generation which is now on the wane among us may have had its faults but for my part I think it had certain qualities of hospitality, of humour, of humanity, which the new and very serious and hypereducated generation that is growing up around us seems to me to lack.* Very good: that was one for Miss Ivors. What did he care that his aunts were only two ignorant old women?

A murmur in the room attracted his attention. Mr Browne was advancing from the door, gallantly escorting Aunt Julia, who leaned upon his arm, smiling and hanging her head. An irregular musketry of applause escorted her also as far as the piano and then, as Mary Jane seated herself on the stool, and Aunt Julia, no longer smiling, half turned so as to pitch her voice fairly into the room, gradually ceased. Gabriel recognised the prelude. It was that of an old song of Aunt Julia's—*Arrayed for the Bridal*.[25] Her voice, strong and clear in tone, attacked with great spirit the runs which embellish the air and though she sang very rapidly, she did not miss even the smallest of the grace notes. To follow the voice, without looking at the singer's face, was to feel and share the excitement of swift and secure flight. Gabriel applauded loudly with all the others at the close of the song and loud applause was borne in from the invisible supper-table. It sounded so genuine that a little colour struggled into Aunt Julia's face as she bent to replace in the music-stand the old leather-bound songbook that had her initials on the cover. Freddy Malins, who had listened with his head perched sideways to hear her better, was still applauding when everyone else had ceased and talking animatedly to his mother who nodded her head gravely and slowly in acquiescence. At last, when he could clap no more, he stood up suddenly and hurried across the room to Aunt Julia whose hand he seized and held in both his hands, shaking it when words failed him or the catch in his voice proved too much for him.

—I was just telling my mother, he said, I never heard you sing so well, never. No, I never heard your voice so good as it is tonight. Now! Would you believe that now? That's the truth. Upon my

[25] A technically complex song set to an aria from Bellini's opera *I Puritani* (1835). See p. xxx.

word and honour that's the truth. I never heard your voice sound so fresh and so ... so clear and fresh, never.

Aunt Julia smiled broadly and murmured something about compliments as she released her hand from his grasp. Mr Browne extended his open hand towards her and said to those who were near him in the manner of a showman introducing a prodigy to an audience:

—Miss Julia Morkan, my latest discovery!

He was laughing very heartily at this himself when Freddy Malins turned to him and said:

—Well, Browne, if you're serious you might make a worse discovery. All I can say is I never heard her sing half so well as long as I am coming here. And that's the honest truth.

—Neither did I, said Mr Browne. I think her voice has greatly improved.

Aunt Julia shrugged her shoulders and said with meek pride:

—Thirty years ago I hadn't a bad voice as voices go.

—I often told Julia, said Aunt Kate emphatically, that she was simply thrown away in that choir. But she never would be said by me.

She turned as if to appeal to the good sense of the others against a refractory[26] child while Aunt Julia gazed in front of her, a vague smile of reminiscence playing on her face.

—No, continued Aunt Kate, she wouldn't be said or led by anyone, slaving there in that choir night and day, night and day. Six o'clock on Christmas morning! And all for what?

—Well, isn't it for the honour of God, Aunt Kate? asked Mary Jane, twisting round on the piano-stool and smiling.

Aunt Kate turned fiercely on her niece and said:

—I know all about the honour of God, Mary Jane, but I think it's not at all honourable for the pope to turn out the women out of the choirs that have slaved there all their lives and put little whipper-snappers of boys over their heads.[27] I suppose it is for the good of the Church if the pope does it. But it's not just, Mary Jane, and it's not right.

She had worked herself into a passion and would have continued in defence of her sister for it was a sore subject with her but Mary Jane, seeing that all the dancers had come back, intervened pacifically:

[26] Stubborn.

[27] A genuine grievance: In November 1903 Pope Pius X banned women from church choirs; boys sang the parts instead.

—Now, Aunt Kate, you're giving scandal to Mr Browne who is of the other persuasion.[28]

Aunt Kate turned to Mr Browne, who was grinning at this allusion to his religion, and said hastily:

—O, I don't question the pope's being right. I'm only a stupid old woman and I wouldn't presume to do such a thing. But there's such a thing as common everyday politeness and gratitude. And if I were in Julia's place I'd tell that Father Healey straight up to his face....

—And besides, Aunt Kate, said Mary Jane, we really are all hungry and when we are hungry we are all very quarrelsome.

—And when we are thirsty we are also quarrelsome, added Mr Browne.

—So that we had better go to supper, said Mary Jane, and finish the discussion afterwards.

On the landing outside the drawing-room Gabriel found his wife and Mary Jane trying to persuade Miss Ivors to stay for supper. But Miss Ivors, who had put on her hat and was buttoning her cloak, would not stay. She did not feel in the least hungry and she had already overstayed her time.

—But only for ten minutes, Molly, said Mrs Conroy. That won't delay you.

—To take a pick[29] itself, said Mary Jane, after all your dancing.

—I really couldn't, said Miss Ivors.

—I am afraid you didn't enjoy yourself at all, said Mary Jane hopelessly.

—Ever so much, I assure you, said Miss Ivors, but you really must let me run off now.

—But how can you get home? asked Mrs Conroy.

—O, it's only two steps up the quay.

Gabriel hesitated a moment and said:

—If you will allow me, Miss Ivors, I'll see you home if you are really obliged to go.

But Miss Ivors broke away from them.

—I won't hear of it, she cried. For goodness' sake go in to your suppers and don't mind me. I'm quite well able to take care of myself.

—Well, you're the comical girl, Molly, said Mrs Conroy frankly.

—*Beannacht libh,*[30] cried Miss Ivors, with a laugh, as she ran down the staircase.

[28] Protestant.

[29] Have a bit.

[30] "Bless you" in Irish—a typical farewell.

Mary Jane gazed after her, a moody puzzled expression on her face, while Mrs Conroy leaned over the banisters to listen for the hall-door. Gabriel asked himself was he the cause of her abrupt departure. But she did not seem to be in ill humour: she had gone away laughing. He stared blankly down the staircase.

At the moment Aunt Kate came toddling out of the supper-room, almost wringing her hands in despair.

—Where is Gabriel? she cried. Where on earth is Gabriel? There's everyone waiting in there, stage to let,[31] and nobody to carve the goose!

—Here I am, Aunt Kate! cried Gabriel, with sudden animation, ready to carve a flock of geese, if necessary.

A fat brown goose lay at one end of the table and at the other end, on a bed of creased paper strewn with sprigs of parsley, lay a great ham, stripped of its outer skin and peppered over with crust crumbs, a neat paper frill round its shin and beside this was a round of spiced beef. Between these rival ends ran parallel lines of side-dishes: two little minsters[32] of jelly, red and yellow; a shallow dish full of blocks of blancmange[33] and red jam, a large green leaf-shaped dish with a stalk-shaped handle, on which lay bunches of purple raisins and peeled almonds, a companion dish on which lay a solid rectangle of Smyrna figs, a dish of custard topped with grated nutmeg, a small bowl full of chocolates and sweets wrapped in gold and silver papers and a glass vase in which stood some tall celery stalks. In the centre of the table there stood, as sentries to a fruit-stand which upheld a pyramid of oranges and American apples, two squat old-fashioned decanters of cut glass, one containing port and the other dark sherry. On the closed square piano a pudding in a huge yellow dish lay in waiting and behind it were three squads of bottles of stout and ale and minerals,[34] drawn up according to the colours of their uniforms, the first two black, with brown and red labels, the third and smallest squad white, with transverse green sashes.

Gabriel took his seat boldly at the head of the table and, having looked to the edge of the carver, plunged his fork firmly into the

---

[31] Ready.

[32] Containers, though technically a temple or cathedral.

[33] Jellied sweetmeat.

[34] Mineral water.

goose. He felt quite at ease now for he was an expert carver and liked nothing better than to find himself at the head of a well-laden table.

—Miss Furlong, what shall I send you? he asked. A wing or a slice of the breast?

—Just a small slice of the breast.

—Miss Higgins, what for you?

—O, anything at all, Mr Conroy.

While Gabriel and Miss Daly exchanged plates of goose and plates of ham and spiced beef Lily went from guest to guest with a dish of hot floury potatoes wrapped in a white napkin. This was Mary Jane's idea and she had also suggested apple sauce for the goose but Aunt Kate had said that plain roast goose without any apple sauce had always been good enough for her and she hoped she might never eat worse. Mary Jane waited on her pupils and saw that they got the best slices and Aunt Kate and Aunt Julia opened and carried across from the piano bottles of stout and ale for the gentlemen and bottles of minerals for the ladies. There was a great deal of confusion and laughter and noise, the noise of orders and counterorders, of knives and forks, of corks and glass-stoppers. Gabriel began to carve second helpings as soon as he had finished the first round without serving himself. Everyone protested loudly so that he compromised by taking a long draught of stout for he had found the carving hot work. Mary Jane settled down quietly to her supper but Aunt Kate and Aunt Julia were still toddling round the table, walking on each other's heels, getting in each other's way and giving each other unheeded orders. Mr Browne begged of them to sit down and eat their suppers and so did Gabriel but they said there was time enough, so that, at last, Freddy Malins stood up and, capturing Aunt Kate, plumped her down on her chair amid general laughter.

When everyone had been well served Gabriel said, smiling:

—Now, if anyone wants a little more of what vulgar people call stuffing let him or her speak.

A chorus of voices invited him to begin his own supper and Lily came forward with three potatoes which she had reserved for him.

—Very well, said Gabriel amiably, as he took another preparatory draught, kindly forget my existence, ladies and gentlemen, for a few minutes.

He set to his supper and took no part in the conversation with which the table covered Lily's removal of the plates. The subject of talk was the opera company which was then at the Theatre Royal. Mr Bartell D'Arcy, the tenor, a dark-complexioned young man with a smart moustache, praised very highly the leading contralto[35] of the company but Miss Furlong thought she had a rather vulgar style of production. Freddy Malins said there was a Negro chieftain singing in the second part of the Gaiety pantomime[36] who had one of the finest tenor voices he had ever heard.

—Have you heard him? he asked Mr Bartell D'Arcy across the table.

—No, answered Mr Bartell D'Arcy carelessly.

—Because, Freddy Malins explained, now I'd be curious to hear your opinion of him. I think he has a grand voice.

—It takes Teddy to find out the really good things, said Mr Browne familiarly to the table.

—And why couldn't he have a voice too? asked Freddy Malins sharply. Is it because he's only a black?

Nobody answered this question and Mary Jane led the table back to the legitimate opera. One of her pupils had given her a pass for *Mignon*.[37] Of course it was very fine, she said, but it made her think of poor Georgina Burns.[38] Mr Browne could go back farther still, to the old Italian companies that used to come to Dublin— Tietjens, Ilma de Murzka, Campanini, the great Giuglini, Ravelli, Aramburo. Those were the days, he said, when there was something like singing to be heard in Dublin. He told too of how the top gallery of the old Royal used to be packed night after night, of how one night an Italian tenor had sung five encores to *Let me like a Soldier fall*,[39] introducing a high C every time, and of how the gallery boys would sometimes in their enthusiasm unyoke the horses from the carriage of some great *prima donna*[40] and pull her themselves through the streets to her hotel. Why did they never play the grand old operas now, he asked, *Dinorah, Lucrezia Borgia*?[41] Because they could not get the voices to sing them: that was why.

---

[35] Lowest alto voice: can be sung by either a man or a woman.

[36] Popular entertainments, with songs, dances, theatricals, and jokes that often involved racial stereotypes. The Gaiety was a Dublin theater.

[37] Sentimental French opera by Ambroise Thomas (1811-1896) first performed in Paris, in 1866.

[38] A famous opera singer whose husband had recently died.

[39] Aria from *Maritana*. See "A Mother," p. xxx, n. 26.

[40] Star singer.

[41] The first is a popular name for the French opera *Le Pardon de Poërmel* with music by Giacomo Meyerbeer (1791-1864); the second, an Italian opera by Gaetano Donizetti (1797-1848), features a dinner party at which all the guests are poisoned.

—Oh, well, said Mr Bartell D'Arcy, I presume there are as good singers to-day as there were then.

—Where are they? asked Mr Browne defiantly.

—In London, Paris, Milan, said Mr Bartell D'Arcy warmly. I suppose Caruso,[42] for example, is quite as good, if not better than any of the men you have mentioned.

—Maybe so, said Mr Browne. But I may tell you I doubt it strongly.

—O, I'd give anything to hear Caruso sing, said Mary Jane.

—For me, said Aunt Kate, who had been picking a bone, there was only one tenor. To please me, I mean. But I suppose none of you ever heard of him.

—Who was he, Miss Morkan? asked Mr Bartell D'Arcy politely.

—His name, said Aunt Kate, was Parkinson.[43] I heard him when he was in his prime and I think he had then the purest tenor voice that was ever put into a man's throat.

—Strange, said Mr Bartell D'Arcy. I never even heard of him.

—Yes, yes, Miss Morkan is right, said Mr Browne. I remember hearing of old Parkinson but he's too far back for me.

—A beautiful pure sweet mellow English tenor, said Aunt Kate with enthusiasm.

Gabriel having finished, the huge pudding was transferred to the table. The clatter of forks and spoons began again. Gabriel's wife served out spoonfuls of the pudding and passed the plates down the table. Midway down they were held up by Mary Jane, who replenished them with raspberry or orange jelly or with blanc-mange and jam. The pudding was of Aunt Julia's making and she received praises for it from all quarters. She herself said that it was not quite brown enough.

—Well, I hope, Miss Morkan, said Mr Browne, that I'm brown enough for you because, you know, I'm all brown.

All the gentlemen, except Gabriel, ate some of the pudding out of compliment to Aunt Julia. As Gabriel never ate sweets the celery had been left for him. Freddy Malins also took a stalk of celery and ate it with his pudding. He had been told that celery was a capital thing for the blood and he was just then under doctor's care. Mrs Malins, who had been silent all through the supper, said that her son was going down to Mount Melleray[44] in a week or so. The table then spoke of

---

[42] Famed Italian tenor Enrico Caruso (1873–1921).

[43] English singer William Parkinson.

[44] A retreat in the southeast run by Trappist monks for the rehabilitation of alcoholics.

Mount Melleray, how bracing the air was down there, how hospitable the monks were and how they never asked for a penny-piece from their guests.

—And do you mean to say, asked Mr Browne incredulously, that a chap can go down there and put up there as if it were a hotel and live on the fat of the land and then come away without paying a farthing?

—O, most people give some donation to the monastery when they leave, said Mary Jane.

—I wish we had an institution like that in our Church, said Mr Browne candidly.

He was astonished to hear that the monks never spoke, got up at two in the morning and slept in their coffins. He asked what they did it for.

—That's the rule of the order,[45] said Aunt Kate firmly.

—Yes, but why? asked Mr Browne.

Aunt Kate repeated that it was the rule, that was all. Mr Browne still seemed not to understand. Freddy Malins explained to him, as best he could, that the monks were trying to make up for the sins committed by all the sinners in the outside world. The explanation was not very clear for Mr Browne grinned and said:

—I like that idea very much but wouldn't a comfortable spring bed do them as well as a coffin?

—The coffin, said Mary Jane, is to remind them of their last end.

As the subject had grown lugubrious it was buried in a silence of the table during which Mrs Malins could be heard saying to her neighbour in an indistinct undertone:

—They are very good men, the monks, very pious men.

The raisins and almonds and figs and apples and oranges and chocolates and sweets were now passed about the table and Aunt Julia invited all the guests to have either port or sherry. At first Mr Bartell D'Arcy refused to take either but one of his neighbours nudged him and whispered something to him upon which he allowed his glass to be filled. Gradually as the last glasses were being filled the conversation ceased. A pause followed, broken only by the noise of the wine and by unsettlings of chairs. The Misses Morkan, all three, looked down at the tablecloth. Someone coughed once or twice and then a few gentlemen patted the table gently as a signal for silence. The silence came and Gabriel pushed back his chair.

---

[45] Not quite; but this was a real discipline.

The patting at once grew louder in encouragement and then ceased altogether. Gabriel leaned his ten trembling fingers on the tablecloth and smiled nervously at the company. Meeting a row of upturned faces he raised his eyes to the chandelier. The piano was playing a waltz tune and he could hear the skirts sweeping against the drawing-room door. People, perhaps, were standing in the snow on the quay outside, gazing up at the lighted windows and listening to the waltz music. The air was pure there. In the distance lay the park where the trees were weighted with snow. The Wellington Monument wore a gleaming cap of snow that flashed westward over the white field of Fifteen Acres.[46]

He began:

—Ladies and Gentlemen.

—It has fallen to my lot this evening, as in years past, to perform a very pleasing task but a task for which I am afraid my poor powers as a speaker are all too inadequate.

—No, no! said Mr Browne.

—But, however that may be, I can only ask you to-night to take the will for the deed and to lend me your attention for a few moments while I endeavour to express to you in words what my feelings are on this occasion.

—Ladies and Gentlemen. It is not the first time that we have gathered together under this hospitable roof, around this hospitable board. It is not the first time that we have been the recipients—or perhaps, I had better say, the victims—of the hospitality of certain good ladies.

He made a circle in the air with his arm and paused. Everyone laughed or smiled at Aunt Kate and Aunt Julia and Mary Jane who all turned crimson with pleasure. Gabriel went on more boldly:

—I feel more strongly with every recurring year that our country has no tradition which does it so much honour and which it should guard so jealously as that of its hospitality. It is a tradition that is unique as far as my experience goes (and I have visited not a few places abroad) among the modern nations. Some would say, perhaps, that with us it is rather a failing than anything to be boasted of. But granted even that, it is, to my mind, a princely failing, and one that I trust will long be cultivated among us. Of one thing, at least, I am sure. As long as this one roof shelters the good ladies aforesaid—and I wish from my heart it may do so for many and

---

[46] Phoenix Park lawn used for military drills and displays.

many a long year to come—the tradition of genuine warm-hearted courteous Irish hospitality, which our forefathers have handed down to us and which we in turn must hand down to our descendants, is still alive among us.

A hearty murmur of assent ran round the table. It shot through Gabriel's mind that Miss Ivors was not there and that she had gone away discourteously: and he said with confidence in himself:

—Ladies and Gentlemen.

—A new generation is growing up in our midst, a generation actuated by new ideas and new principles. It is serious and enthusiastic for these new ideas and its enthusiasm, even when it is misdirected, is, I believe, in the main sincere. But we are living in a sceptical and, if I may use the phrase, a thought-tormented age: and sometimes I fear that this new generation, educated or hypereducated as it is, will lack those qualities of humanity, of hospitality, of kindly humour which belonged to an older day. Listening to-night to the names of all those great singers of the past it seemed to me, I must confess, that we were living in a less spacious age. Those days might, without exaggeration, be called spacious days: and if they are gone beyond recall let us hope, at least, that in gatherings such as this we shall still speak of them with pride and affection, still cherish in our hearts the memory of those dead and gone great ones whose fame the world will not willingly let die.[47]

—Hear, hear! said Mr Browne loudly.

—But yet, continued Gabriel, his voice falling into a softer inflection, there are always in gatherings such as this sadder thoughts that will recur to our minds: thoughts of the past, of youth, of changes, of absent faces that we miss here to-night. Our path through life is strewn with many such sad memories: and were we to brood upon them always we could not find the heart to go on bravely with our work among the living. We have all of us living duties and living affections which claim, and rightly claim, our strenuous endeavours.

—Therefore, I will not linger on the past. I will not let any gloomy moralising intrude upon us here to-night. Here we are gathered together for a brief moment from the bustle and rush of our everyday routine. We are met here as friends, in the spirit of good-fellowship, as colleagues, also to a certain extent, in the true spirit

---

[47] Echoing John Milton's (1608-1674) dedication to a career as poet in *The Reason of Church Government* (1642): "I might perhaps leave something so written to after times as they should not willingly let it die."

of *camaraderie*, and as the guests of—what shall I call them?—the Three Graces[48] of the Dublin musical world.

The table burst into applause and laughter at this sally. Aunt Julia vainly asked each of her neighbours in turn to tell her what Gabriel had said.

—He says we are the Three Graces, Aunt Julia, said Mary Jane.

Aunt Julia did not understand but she looked up, smiling, at Gabriel, who continued in the same vein:

—Ladies and Gentlemen.

—I will not attempt to play to-night the part that Paris[49] played on another occasion. I will not attempt to choose between them. The task would be an invidious one and one beyond my poor powers. For when I view them in turn, whether it be our chief hostess herself, whose good heart, whose too good heart, has become a byword with all who know her, or her sister, who seems to be gifted with perennial youth and whose singing must have been a surprise and a revelation to us all to-night, or, last but not least, when I consider our youngest hostess, talented, cheerful, hard-working and the best of nieces, I confess, Ladies and Gentlemen, that I do not know to which of them I should award the prize.

Gabriel glanced down at his aunts and, seeing the large smile on Aunt Julia's face and the tears which had risen to Aunt Kate's eyes, hastened to his close. He raised his glass of port gallantly, while every member of the company fingered a glass expectantly, and said loudly:

—Let us toast them all three together. Let us drink to their health, wealth, long life, happiness and prosperity and may they long continue to hold the proud and self-won position which they hold in their profession and the position of honour and affection which they hold in our hearts.

All the guests stood up, glass in hand, and, turning towards the three seated ladies, sang in unison, with Mr Browne as leader:

> —For they are jolly gay fellows,
> For they are jolly gay fellows,
> For they are jolly gay fellows,
> Which nobody can deny.

Aunt Kate was making frank use of her handkerchief and even Aunt Julia seemed moved. Freddy Malins beat time with his

---

[48] Greek goddesses who personify charm, creativity, and beauty.

[49] In Greek myth, Trojan prince Paris was asked to judge which of three goddesses—Hera, Venus, or Aphrodite—was the most beautiful.

pudding-fork and the singers turned towards one another, as if in melodious conference, while they sang with emphasis:

—Unless he tells a lie,
Unless he tells a lie.

Then, turning once more towards their hostesses, they sang:

—For they are jolly gay fellows,
For they are jolly gay fellows,
For they are jolly gay fellows,
Which nobody can deny.

The acclamation which followed was taken up beyond the door of the supper-room by many of the other guests and renewed time after time, Freddy Malins acting as officer with his fork on high.

* * *

The piercing morning air came into the hall where they were standing so that Aunt Kate said:

—Close the door, somebody. Mrs Malins will get her death of cold.

—Browne is out there, Aunt Kate, said Mary Jane.

—Browne is everywhere, said Aunt Kate, lowering her voice.

Mary Jane laughed at her tone.

—Really, she said archly, he is very attentive.

—He has been laid on here like the gas,[1] said Aunt Kate in the same tone, all during the Christmas.

She laughed herself this time good-humouredly and then added quickly:

—But tell him to come in, Mary Jane, and close the door. I hope to goodness he didn't hear me.

At that moment the hall-door was opened and Mr Browne came in from the doorstep, laughing as if his heart would break. He was dressed in a long green overcoat with mock astrakhan[2] cuffs and collar and wore on his head an oval fur cap. He pointed down the snow-covered quay from where the sound of shrill prolonged whistling was borne in.

—Teddy will have all the cabs in Dublin out, he said.

Gabriel advanced from the little pantry behind the office, struggling into his overcoat and, looking round the hall, said:

—Gretta not down yet?

---

[1] Like gas lighting: everywhere in the house.
[2] Soft wool.

—She's getting on her things, Gabriel, said Aunt Kate.

—Who's playing up there? asked Gabriel.

—Nobody. They're all gone.

—O no, Aunt Kate, said Mary Jane. Bartell D'Arcy and Miss O'Callaghan aren't gone yet.

—Someone is fooling at the piano anyhow, said Gabriel.

Mary Jane glanced at Gabriel and Mr Browne and said with a shiver:

—It makes me feel cold to look at you two gentlemen muffled up like that. I wouldn't like to face your journey home at this hour.

—I'd like nothing better this minute, said Mr Browne stoutly, than a rattling fine walk in the country or a fast drive with a good spanking goer between the shafts.[3]

—We used to have a very good horse and trap[4] at home, said Aunt Julia sadly.

—The never-to-be-forgotten Johnny, said Mary Jane, laughing.

Aunt Kate and Gabriel laughed too.

—Why, what was wonderful about Johnny? asked Mr Browne.

—The late lamented Patrick Morkan, our grandfather, that is, explained Gabriel, commonly known in his later years as the old gentleman, was a glue-boiler.[5]

—O, now, Gabriel, said Aunt Kate, laughing, he had a starch mill.[6]

—Well, glue or starch, said Gabriel, the old gentleman had a horse by the name of Johnny. And Johnny used to work in the old gentleman's mill, walking round and round in order to drive the mill. That was all very well; but now comes the tragic part about Johnny. One fine day the old gentleman thought he'd like to drive out with the quality to a military review in the park.

—The Lord have mercy on his soul, said Aunt Kate compassionately.

—Amen, said Gabriel. So the old gentleman, as I said, harnessed Johnny and put on his very best tall hat and his very best stock collar and drove out in grand style from his ancestral mansion somewhere near Back Lane,[7] I think.

---

[3] Strong horse pulling a carriage.

[4] Light carriage: a sign of modest affluence.

[5] Glue was made from horse-hooves and other offal.

[6] More dignified profession, creating starch from the husks of various grains.

[7] Unfashionable address in the city's center.

Everyone laughed, even Mrs Malins, at Gabriel's manner and Aunt Kate said:

—O, now, Gabriel, he didn't live in Back Lane, really. Only the mill was there.

—Out from the mansion of his forefathers, continued Gabriel, he drove with Johnny. And everything went on beautifully until Johnny came in sight of King Billy's statue:[8] and whether he fell in love with the horse King Billy sits on or whether he thought he was back again in the mill, anyhow he began to walk round the statue.

Gabriel paced in a circle round the hall in his goloshes amid the laughter of the others.

—Round and round he went, said Gabriel, and the old gentleman, who was a very pompous old gentleman, was highly indignant. *Go on, sir! What do you mean, sir? Johnny! Johnny! Most extraordinary conduct! Can't understand the horse!*

The peals of laughter which followed Gabriel's imitation of the incident was interrupted by a resounding knock at the hall door. Mary Jane ran to open it and let in Freddy Malins. Freddy Malins, with his hat well back on his head and his shoulders humped with cold, was puffing and steaming after his exertions.

—I could only get one cab, he said.

—O, we'll find another along the quay, said Gabriel.

—Yes, said Aunt Kate. Better not keep Mrs Malins standing in the draught.

Mrs Malins was helped down the front steps by her son and Mr Browne and, after many manoeuvres, hoisted into the cab. Freddy Malins clambered in after her and spent a long time settling her on the seat, Mr Browne helping him with advice. At last she was settled comfortably and Freddy Malins invited Mr Browne into the cab. There was a good deal of confused talk, and then Mr Browne got into the cab. The cabman settled his rug over his knees, and bent down for the address. The confusion grew greater and the cabman was directed differently by Freddy Malins and Mr Browne, each of whom had his head out through a window of the cab. The difficulty was to know where to drop Mr Browne along the route and Aunt Kate, Aunt Julia and Mary Jane helped the discussion from the doorstep with cross-directions and contradictions and

---

[8] Statue near Trinity College of King William III (1650–1702), also known as William of Orange; he secured his claim to the English throne with the brutal subjugation of Ireland.

abundance of laughter. As for Freddy Malins he was speechless with laughter. He popped his head in and out of the window every moment to the great danger of his hat, and told his mother how the discussion was progressing, till at last Mr Browne shouted to the bewildered cabman above the din of everybody's laughter:

—Do you know Trinity College?

—Yes, sir, said the cabman.

—Well, drive bang up against Trinity College gates, said Mr Browne, and then we'll tell you where to go. You understand now?

—Yes, sir, said the cabman.

—Make like a bird for Trinity College.

—Right, sir, said the cabman.

The horse was whipped up and the cab rattled off along the quay amid a chorus of laughter and adieus.

Gabriel had not gone to the door with the others. He was in a dark part of the hall gazing up the staircase. A woman was standing near the top of the first flight, in the shadow also. He could not see her face but he could see the terra-cotta and salmon-pink panels of her skirt which the shadow made appear black and white. It was his wife. She was leaning on the banisters, listening to something. Gabriel was surprised at her stillness and strained his ear to listen also. But he could hear little save the noise of laughter and dispute on the front steps, a few chords struck on the piano and a few notes of a man's voice singing.

He stood still in the gloom of the hall, trying to catch the air that the voice was singing and gazing up at his wife. There was grace and mystery in her attitude as if she were a symbol of something. He asked himself what is a woman standing on the stairs in the shadow, listening to distant music, a symbol of. If he were a painter he would paint her in that attitude. Her blue felt hat would show off the bronze of her hair against the darkness and the dark panels of her skirt would show off the light ones. *Distant Music* he would call the picture if he were a painter.

The hall-door was closed; and Aunt Kate, Aunt Julia and Mary Jane came down the hall, still laughing.

—Well, isn't Freddy terrible? said Mary Jane. He's really terrible.

Gabriel said nothing but pointed up the stairs towards where his wife was standing. Now that the hall-door was closed the voice and the piano could be heard more clearly. Gabriel held up his hand for them to be silent. The song seemed to be in the old Irish tonality[9] and

[9] Using a five-note scale rather than the more familiar eight-note one.

the singer seemed uncertain both of his words and of his voice. The voice, made plaintive by distance and by the singer's hoarseness, faintly illuminated the cadence of the air with words expressing grief:

—O, the rain falls on my heavy locks
And the dew wets my skin,
My babe lies cold ...[10]

—O, exclaimed Mary Jane. It's Bartell D'Arcy singing and he wouldn't sing all the night. O, I'll get him to sing a song before he goes.

—O, do, Mary Jane, said Aunt Kate.

Mary Jane brushed past the others and ran to the staircase but before she reached it the singing stopped and the piano was closed abruptly.

—O, what a pity! she cried. Is he coming down, Gretta?

Gabriel heard his wife answer yes and saw her come down towards them. A few steps behind her were Mr Bartell D'Arcy and Miss O'Callaghan.

—O, Mr D'Arcy, cried Mary Jane, it's downright mean of you to break off like that when we were all in raptures listening to you.

—I have been at him all the evening, said Miss O'Callaghan, and Mrs Conroy, too, and he told us he had a dreadful cold and couldn't sing.

—O, Mr D'Arcy, said Aunt Kate, now that was a great fib to tell.

—Can't you see that I'm as hoarse as a crow? said Mr D'Arcy roughly.

He went into the pantry hastily and put on his overcoat. The others, taken aback by his rude speech, could find nothing to say. Aunt Kate wrinkled her brows and made signs to the others to drop the subject. Mr D'Arcy stood swathing his neck carefully and frowning.

—It's the weather, said Aunt Julia, after a pause.

—Yes, everybody has colds, said Aunt Kate readily, everybody.

—They say, said Mary Jane, we haven't had snow like it for thirty years; and I read this morning in the newspapers that the snow is general all over Ireland.

—I love the look of snow, said Aunt Julia sadly.

---

[10] From the opening lines of *The Lass of Aughrim* about a poor Irish girl who begs admittance to the manor house of Lord Gregory with his (presumably illegitimate) child dying in her arms. See p. xxx.

—So do I, said Miss O'Callaghan. I think Christmas is never really Christmas unless we have the snow on the ground.

—But poor Mr D'Arcy doesn't like the snow, said Aunt Kate, smiling.

Mr D'Arcy came from the pantry, fully swathed and buttoned, and in a repentant tone told them the history of his cold. Everyone gave him advice and said it was a great pity and urged him to be very careful of his throat in the night air. Gabriel watched his wife who did not join in the conversation. She was standing right under the dusty fanlight[11] and the flame of the gas lit up the rich bronze of her hair which he had seen her drying at the fire a few days before. She was in the same attitude and seemed unaware of the talk about her. At last she turned towards them and Gabriel saw that there was colour on her cheeks and that her eyes were shining. A sudden tide of joy went leaping out of his heart.

—Mr D'Arcy, she said, what is the name of that song you were singing?

—It's called *The Lass of Aughrim*, said Mr D'Arcy, but I couldn't remember it properly. Why? Do you know it?

—*The Lass of Aughrim*, she repeated. I couldn't think of the name.

—It's a very nice air, said Mary Jane. I'm sorry you were not in voice to-night.

—Now, Mary Jane, said Aunt Kate, don't annoy Mr D'Arcy. I won't have him annoyed.

Seeing that all were ready to start she shepherded them to the door, where good-night was said:

—Well, good-night, Aunt Kate, and thanks for the pleasant evening.

—Good-night, Gabriel. Good-night, Gretta!

—Good-night, Aunt Kate, and thanks ever so much. Good-night, Aunt Julia.

—O, good-night, Gretta, I didn't see you.

—Good-night, Mr D'Arcy. Good-night, Miss O'Callaghan.

—Good-night, Miss Morkan.

—Good-night, again.

—Good-night, all. Safe home.

—Good-night. Good-night.

[11] A semi-circular window at the top of the front door—a common feature of Dublin's Georgian homes.

The morning was still dark. A dull yellow light brooded over the houses and the river; and the sky seemed to be descending. It was slushy underfoot; and only streaks and patches of snow lay on the roofs, on the parapets[12] of the quay and on the area railings. The lamps were still burning redly in the murky air and, across the river, the palace of the Four Courts[13] stood out menacingly against the heavy sky.

She was walking on before him with Mr Bartell D'Arcy, her shoes in a brown parcel tucked under one arm and her hands holding her skirt up from the slush. She had no longer any grace of attitude but Gabriel's eyes were still bright with happiness. The blood went bounding along his veins; and the thoughts went rioting through his brain, proud, joyful, tender, valorous.

She was walking on before him so lightly and so erect that he longed to run after her noiselessly, catch her by the shoulders and say something foolish and affectionate into her ear. She seemed to him so frail that he longed to defend her against something and then to be alone with her. Moments of their secret life together burst like stars upon his memory. A heliotrope[14] envelope was lying beside his breakfast-cup and he was caressing it with his hand. Birds were twittering in the ivy and the sunny web of the curtain was shimmering along the floor: he could not eat for happiness. They were standing on the crowded platform and he was placing a ticket inside the warm palm of her glove. He was standing with her in the cold, looking in through a grated window at a man making bottles in a roaring furnace. It was very cold. Her face, fragrant in the cold air, was quite close to his; and suddenly she called out to the man at the furnace:

—Is the fire hot, sir?

But the man could not hear her with the noise of the furnace. It was just as well. He might have answered rudely.

A wave of yet more tender joy escaped from his heart and went coursing in warm flood along his arteries. Like the tender fire of stars moments of their life together, that no one knew of or would ever know of, broke upon and illumined his memory. He longed to recall to her those moments, to make her forget the years of their dull existence together and remember only their moments of ecstasy. For the years, he felt, had not quenched his soul or hers. Their children, his

[12] Low walls.

[13] Law courts.

[14] Purple.

writing, her household cares had not quenched all their souls' tender fire. In one letter that he had written to her then he had said: *Why is it that words like these seem to me so dull and cold? Is it because there is no word tender enough to be your name?*

Like distant music these words that he had written years before were borne towards him from the past. He longed to be alone with her. When the others had gone away, when he and she were in the room in the hotel, then they would be alone together. He would call her softly:

—Gretta!

Perhaps she would not hear at once: she would be undressing. Then something in his voice would strike her. She would turn and look at him....

At the corner of Winetavern Street they met a cab. He was glad of its rattling noise as it saved him from conversation. She was looking out of the window and seemed tired. The others spoke only a few words, pointing out some building or street. The horse galloped along wearily under the murky morning sky, dragging his old rattling box after his heels, and Gabriel was again in a cab with her, galloping to catch the boat, galloping to their honeymoon.

As the cab drove across O'Connell Bridge Miss O'Callaghan said:

—They say you never cross O'Connell Bridge without seeing a white horse.

—I see a white man this time, said Gabriel.

—Where? asked Mr Bartell D'Arcy.

Gabriel pointed to the statue,[15] on which lay patches of snow. Then he nodded familiarly to it and waved his hand.

—Good-night, Dan, he said gaily.

When the cab drew up before the hotel Gabriel jumped out and, in spite of Mr Bartell D'Arcy's protest, paid the driver. He gave the man a shilling over his fare.[16] The man saluted and said:

—A prosperous New Year to you, sir.

—The same to you, said Gabriel cordially.

She leaned for a moment on his arm in getting out of the cab and while standing at the curbstone, bidding the others good-night. She leaned lightly on his arm, as lightly as when she had danced with him a few hours before. He had felt proud and happy then, happy that she

[15] Of Daniel O'Connell (1775–1847), "The Liberator" who helped secure civil rights for Catholics in Ireland.

[16] A generous tip.

was his, proud of her grace and wifely carriage. But now, after the kindling again of so many memories, the first touch of her body, musical and strange and perfumed, sent through him a keen pang of lust. Under cover of her silence he pressed her arm closely to his side; and, as they stood at the hotel door, he felt that they had escaped from their lives and duties, escaped from home and friends and run away together with wild and radiant hearts to a new adventure.

An old man[17] was dozing in a great hooded chair in the hall. He lit a candle in the office and went before them to the stairs. They followed him in silence, their feet falling in soft thuds on the thickly carpeted stairs. She mounted the stairs behind the porter, her head bowed in the ascent, her frail shoulders curved as with a burden, her skirt girt tightly about her. He could have flung his arms about her hips and held her still for his arms were trembling with desire to seize her and only the stress of his nails against the palms of his hands held the wild impulse of his body in check. The porter halted on the stairs to settle his guttering[18] candle. They halted too on the steps below him. In the silence Gabriel could hear the falling of the molten wax into the tray and the thumping of his own heart against his ribs.

The porter led them along a corridor and opened a door. Then he set his unstable candle down on a toilet-table[19] and asked at what hour they were to be called in the morning.

—Eight, said Gabriel.

The porter pointed to the tap[20] of the electric-light and began a muttered apology, but Gabriel cut him short.

—We don't want any light. We have light enough from the street. And I say, he added, pointing to the candle, you might remove that handsome article, like a good man.

The porter took up his candle again, but slowly for he was surprised by such a novel idea. Then he mumbled good-night and went out. Gabriel shot the lock to.

A ghostly[21] light from the street lamp lay in a long shaft from one window to the door. Gabriel threw his overcoat and hat on a couch and crossed the room towards the window. He looked down into the street in order that his emotion might calm a little. Then he turned and leaned against a chest of drawers with his back to the light. She had taken off her hat and cloak and was standing before a

[17] The hotel porter.

[18] Melting through a hole in the side.

[19] Dressing table.

[20] Switch.

[21] In an earlier version of the story, this reads "ghastly."

large swinging mirror, unhooking her waist. Gabriel paused for a few moments, watching her, and then said:

—Gretta!

She turned away from the mirror slowly and walked along the shaft of light towards him. Her face looked so serious and weary that the words would not pass Gabriel's lips. No, it was not the moment yet.

—You looked tired, he said.

—I am a little, she answered.

—You don't feel ill or weak?

—No, tired: that's all.

She went on to the window and stood there, looking out. Gabriel waited again and then, fearing that diffidence[22] was about to conquer him, he said abruptly:

—By the way, Gretta!

—What is it?

—You know that poor fellow Malins? he said quickly.

—Yes. What about him?

—Well, poor fellow, he's a decent sort of chap, after all, continued Gabriel in a false voice. He gave me back that sovereign I lent him and I didn't expect it really. It's a pity he wouldn't keep away from that Browne, because he's not a bad fellow at heart.

He was trembling now with annoyance. Why did she seem so abstracted? He did not know how he could begin. Was she annoyed, too, about something? If she would only turn to him or come to him of her own accord! To take her as she was would be brutal. No, he must see some ardour in her eyes first. He longed to be master of her strange mood.

—When did you lend him the pound? she asked, after a pause.

Gabriel strove to restrain himself from breaking out into brutal language about the sottish[23] Malins and his pound. He longed to cry to her from his soul, to crush her body against his, to overmaster her. But he said:

—O, at Christmas, when he opened that little Christmas-card shop in Henry Street.

He was in such a fever of rage and desire that he did not hear her come from the window. She stood before him for an instant, looking at him strangely. Then, suddenly raising herself on tiptoe and resting her hands lightly on his shoulders, she kissed him.

—You are a very generous person, Gabriel, she said.

[22] Self-doubt.

[23] Drunken or stupid.

Gabriel, trembling with delight at her sudden kiss and at the quaintness of her phrase, put his hands on her hair and began smoothing it back, scarcely touching it with his fingers. The washing had made it fine and brilliant. His heart was brimming over with happiness. Just when he was wishing for it she had come to him of her own accord. Perhaps her thoughts had been running with his. Perhaps she had felt the impetuous desire that was in him and then the yielding mood had come upon her. Now that she had fallen to him so easily, he wondered why he had been so diffident.

He stood, holding her head between his hands. Then, slipping one arm swiftly about her body and drawing her towards him, he said softly:

—Gretta dear, what are you thinking about?

She did not answer nor yield wholly to his arm. He said again, softly:

—Tell me what it is, Gretta. I think I know what is the matter. Do I know?

She did not answer at once. Then she said in an outburst of tears:

—O, I am thinking about that song, *The Lass of Aughrim.*

She broke loose from him and ran to the bed and, throwing her arms across the bed-rail, hid her face. Gabriel stood stock-still for a moment in astonishment and then followed her. As he passed in the way of the cheval-glass[24] he caught sight of himself in full length, his broad, well-filled shirt-front, the face whose expression always puzzled him when he saw it in a mirror, and his glimmering gilt-rimmed eyeglasses. He halted a few paces from her and said:

—What about the song? Why does that make you cry?

She raised her head from her arms and dried her eyes with the back of her hand like a child. A kinder note than he had intended went into his voice.

—Why, Gretta? he asked.

—I am thinking about a person long ago who used to sing that song.

—And who was the person long ago? asked Gabriel, smiling.

—It was a person I used to know in Galway when I was living with my grandmother, she said.

The smile passed away from Gabriel's face. A dull anger began to gather again at the back of his mind and the dull fires of his lust began to glow angrily in his veins.

—Someone you were in love with? he asked ironically.

---

[24] Free-standing hinged mirror.

—It was a young boy I used to know, she answered, named Michael Furey. He used to sing that song, *The Lass of Aughrim*. He was very delicate.[25]

Gabriel was silent. He did not wish her to think that he was interested in this delicate boy.

—I can see him so plainly, she said after a moment. Such eyes as he had: big dark eyes! And such an expression in them—an expression!

—O then, you were in love with him? said Gabriel.

—I used to go out walking with him,[26] she said, when I was in Galway.

A thought flew across Gabriel's mind.

—Perhaps that was why you wanted to go to Galway with that Ivors girl? he said coldly.

She looked at him and asked in surprise:

—What for?

Her eyes made Gabriel feel awkward. He shrugged his shoulders and said:

—How do I know? To see him perhaps.

She looked away from him along the shaft of light towards the window in silence.

—He is dead, she said at length. He died when he was only seventeen. Isn't it a terrible thing to die so young as that?

—What was he? asked Gabriel, still ironically.

—He was in the gasworks,[27] she said.

Gabriel felt humiliated by the failure of his irony and by the evocation of this figure from the dead, a boy in the gasworks. While he had been full of memories of their secret life together, full of tenderness and joy and desire, she had been comparing him in her mind with another. A shameful consciousness of his own person assailed him. He saw himself as a ludicrous figure, acting as a pennyboy[28] for his aunts, a nervous well-meaning sentimentalist, orating to vulgarians and idealising his own clownish lusts, the pitiable fatuous fellow he had caught a glimpse of in the mirror. Instinctively he turned his back more to the light lest she might see the shame that burned upon his forehead.

He tried to keep up his tone of cold interrogation but his voice when he spoke was humble and indifferent.

—I suppose you were in love with this Michael Furey, Gretta, he said.

[25] Of frail health.
[26] An intimate date.
[27] Power plant.
[28] Errand-boy.

—I was great[29] with him at that time, she said.

Her voice was veiled and sad. Gabriel, feeling now how vain it would be to try to lead her whither he had purposed, caressed one of her hands and said, also sadly:

—And what did he die of so young, Gretta? Consumption,[30] was it?

—I think he died for me, she answered.

A vague terror seized Gabriel at this answer as if, at that hour when he had hoped to triumph, some impalpable and vindictive being was coming against him, gathering forces against him in its vague world. But he shook himself free of it with an effort of reason and continued to caress her hand. He did not question her again, for he felt that she would tell him of herself. Her hand was warm and moist: it did not respond to his touc, but he continued to caress it just as he had caressed her first letter to him that spring morning.

—It was in the winter, she said, about the beginning of the winter when I was going to leave my grandmother's and come up here to the convent.[31] And he was ill at the time in his lodgings[32] in Galway and wouldn't be let out and his people in Oughterard[33] were written to. He was in decline, they said, or something like that. I never knew rightly.

She paused for a moment and sighed.

—Poor fellow, she said. He was very fond of me and he was such a gentle boy. We used to go out together, walking, you know, Gabriel, like the way they do in the country. He was going to study singing only for his health. He had a very good voice, poor Michael Furey.

—Well, and then? asked Gabriel.

—And then when it came to the time for me to leave Galway and come up to the convent he was much worse and I wouldn't be let see him so I wrote him a letter saying I was going up to Dublin and would be back in the summer and hoping he would be better then.

She paused for a moment to get her voice under control and then went on:

—Then the night before I left, I was in my grandmother's house in Nun's Island,[34] packing up, and I heard gravel thrown up against the

---

[29] Intimate.

[30] Tuberculosis: a common, wasting disease.

[31] A convent school.

[32] Rented rooms.

[33] Village outside Galway.

[34] In the middle of Galway—about 17 miles from Furey's lodgings.

window. The window was so wet I couldn't see so I ran downstairs as I was and slipped out the back into the garden and there was the poor fellow at the end of the garden, shivering.

—And did you not tell him to go back? asked Gabriel.

—I implored of him to go home at once and told him he would get his death in the rain. But he said he did not want to live. I can see his eyes as well as well! He was standing at the end of the wall where there was a tree.

—And did he go home? asked Gabriel.

—Yes, he went home. And when I was only a week in the convent he died and he was buried in Oughterar, where his people came from. O, the day I heard that, that he was dead!

She stopped, choking with sobs, and, overcome by emotion, flung herself face downward on the bed, sobbing in the quilt. Gabriel held her hand for a moment longer, irresolutely, and then, shy of intruding on her grief, let it fall gently and walked quietly to the window.

She was fast asleep.

Gabriel, leaning on his elbow, looked for a few moments unresentfully on her tangled hair and half-open mouth, listening to her deep-drawn breath. So she had had that romance in her life: a man had died for her sake. It hardly pained him now to think how poor a part he, her husband, had played in her life. He watched her while she slept as though he and she had never lived together as man and wife. His curious eyes rested long upon her face and on her hair: and, as he thought of what she must have been then, in that time of her first girlish beauty, a strange, friendly pity for her entered his soul. He did not like to say even to himself that her face was no longer beautiful but he knew that it was no longer the face for which Michael Furey had braved death.

Perhaps she had not told him all the story. His eyes moved to the chair over which she had thrown some of her clothes. A petticoat string dangled to the floor. One boot stood upright, its limp upper fallen down: the fellow of it lay upon its side. He wondered at his riot of emotions of an hour before. From what had it proceeded? From his aunt's supper, from his own foolish speech, from the wine and dancing, the merry-making when saying good-night in the hall, the pleasure of the walk along the river in the snow. Poor Aunt Julia! She, too, would soon be a shade with the shade of Patrick Morkan and his horse. He had caught that haggard look upon her face for a moment when she was singing *Arrayed for the Bridal*. Soon, perhaps, he would be sitting in that same drawing-room, dressed in black, his silk hat on his knees. The blinds would be drawn down and Aunt Kate would be sitting beside him, crying and blowing her nose and telling him how Julia had died. He would cast about in his mind for some words that might console her, and would find only lame and useless ones. Yes, yes: that would happen very soon.

The air of the room chilled his shoulders. He stretched himself cautiously along under the sheets and lay down beside his wife. One by one they were all becoming shades. Better pass boldly into that other world, in the full glory of some passion, than fade and wither dismally with age. He thought of how she who lay beside him had locked in her heart for so many years that image of her lover's eyes when he had told her that he did not wish to live.

Generous tears filled Gabriel's eyes. He had never felt like that himself towards any woman but he knew that such a feeling must be love. The tears gathered more thickly in his eyes and in the partial darkness he imagined he saw the form of a young man standing under a dripping tree. Other forms were near. His soul had approached that region where dwell the vast hosts of the dead. He was conscious of, but could not apprehend, their wayward and flickering existence. His own identity was fading out into a grey impalpable world: the solid world itself which these dead had one time reared and lived in was dissolving and dwindling.

A few light taps upon the pane made him turn to the window. It had begun to snow again. He watched sleepily the flakes, silver and dark, falling obliquely against the lamplight. The time had come for him to set out on his journey westward.[35] Yes, the newspapers were right: snow was general all over Ireland. It was falling on every part of the dark central plain, on the treeless hills, falling softly upon the Bog of Allen[36] and, farther westward, softly falling into the dark mutinous Shannon[37] waves. It was falling, too, upon every part of the lonely churchyard on the hill where Michael Furey lay buried. It lay thickly drifted on the crooked crosses and headstones, on the spears of the little gate, on the barren thorns. His soul swooned slowly as he heard the snow falling faintly through the universe and faintly falling, like the descent of their last end, upon all the living and the dead.

[35] Towards his own sunset, but with an echo of Miss Ivors' earlier invitation to visit western Ireland.

[36] A soggy, eerie land west of Dublin.

[37] Major western river.

Contexts

Life in Edwardian Dublin

CURRENCY

A colony of Great Britain, Ireland used English currency from 1826 until 1928. The pound sterling (£) was its basic unit and broke down as follows:

> one pound = twenty shillings
> one shilling ("bob") = twelve pence (or pennies)
> one guinea = twenty one shillings (though this gold coin was obsolete, the unit was still widely used, especially for upscale pricing)

These coins were in circulation:

> sovereign—gold coin worth £1
> crown—silver coin worth five shillings
> half-crown—silver coin worth two shillings, six pence
> florin—silver coin worth two shillings
> sixpence ("tanner")—silver coin worth six pennies
> copper—copper coin worth one penny
> farthing—bronze (sometimes copper) coin worth one-fourth of a penny

INCOMES AND LIVING EXPENSES

Dubliners focuses primarily on the lives of the city's middle class, though we do see examples of both poverty ("Two Gallants") and affluence ("After the Race"). Many characters are beset by money troubles and seem to be struggling to make ends meet. Farrington in

"Counterparts," for example pawns his watch to buy a drink and Tom Kernan in "Grace" has become entangled with a loan shark. The threat of poverty hovers near almost all of the stories, a fact made clear when we look at just how fragile the financial lives of Joyce's Dubliners might be.

A 1904 Royal Commission on the poor found that the minimum weekly income necessary to maintain a Dublin family of four with the bare necessities of life in was £1. More than two-thirds of this wage would have been spent on a meager diet and the rest would go to rent, leaving nothing for entertainment, education, or other luxuries like alcohol. This accounted for the spread of tenements throughout the city (glimpsed often in the stories) as well as a reliance on pawn shops to survive from one paycheck to the next. Called "the poor-man's banker," these shops took in items of value (like Farrington's watch) as collateral against small loans. Wages were paid on Saturday, which is also when weekly grocery accounts had to be paid up and when pawned objects could be redeemed. Rents were then due on Monday, leaving families little money to make it through the week. Thus, in a story like "Eveline" we see characters trying to get money from the head of household before it would be spent on a weekend night of drinking and revelry.

Real weekly wages in the city often fell below £1 a week; it's estimated that one-quarter of Dubliners survived below the poverty level. Eveline, for example, makes only seven shillings a week as a store cler, and according to government surveys, wages ranged from ten shillings per week for a menial tailor to twenty shillings for a general laborer. The ten shillings or so that Maria spends on gifts in "Clay," therefore, was likely more than her weekly wages, and the golden sovereign Corley receives from the slavey in "Two Gallants" is far above what she could readily earn or easily save. Thus, although many of the characters in these stories consider themselves members of the middle class, they actually live at or near the poverty line, struggling constantly to find money for rent, food, and drink.

The middle class was a relatively narrow social group in turn-of-the-century Dublin. The 1900 census found that of the city's approximately 290,000 people, only about 19,000 were in professional or commercial professions. These were not only the civil servants, lawyers, clergymen, doctors, and merchants who lived generally comfortable lives, but also the often poorly paid shop-owners, clerks, and salesmen around whom most of Joyce's stories revolve. Unemployment was a constant threat, and without any kind of social insurance the loss of a job could quickly be followed by the loss of a home. Joyce understood the fragile nature of economic life at this end of the middle class: as the fortunes of his own family declined, they moved from house to house, running up debts, dodging landlords, and gradually pawning their possessions. In 1902, to salvage his middle-class life, Joyce's father cashed in half his pension to purchase a house, but this left the large family with an income of just over £5 a month—barely enough to reach the subsistence level. Within three years, the new house had been so often mortgaged that the Joyces succumbed to the exhausting poverty reflected everywhere in *Dubliners*.

Pubs

Alcohol and drunkenness thread their way through *Dubliners* from the uncle who forgets about the fair in "Araby" to the pitiable Freddy Malins who will soon leave for treatment at a monastery in "The Dead." The problem was more pressing in Ireland at the time than elsewhere in Britain. Arrest rates in Dublin for public intoxication involved 2% of the population—more than twice that of any English city. Dubliners also suffered unusually high rates of arrest for disorderly conduct and child mistreatment—both likely symptoms of alcohol abuse. We see the direct connection between drink and violence in "Counterparts," and Joyce's father's problems with drink contributed to the family's ruin.

The high rate of alcohol abuse was related to the importance of the "pub" or public house in Irish social life. According to a 1925 government survey there were nearly twice as many pubs per capita in Ireland as in Britain and alcohol was relatively inexpensive. The glass of porter (a kind of beer) Farrington orders in "Counterparts," for example, costs only a penny, and beer was consumed by both men and women. Its relatively high caloric content helped offset deficiencies in diet. Indeed, the Guinness brewing company in Dublin launched a famous advertising campaign in the 1920s built on the informally shared belief that it contributed to strength and good health. Whiskey, a much stronger drink, is linked throughout the stories to drunkenness. The temperance movements of the day focused on the physical and moral problems of drink, as well as on its domestic consequences: ruined homes, beaten wives and children, lost wages, lost hopes. The growing influence of these movements is marked by the several characters considering "the pledge," a public oath to renounce alcohol.

This was harder to do than it may seem because Irish pubs were important social spaces governed by an array of informal rules and rituals. The most significant of these was the practice of "rounds," which transformed the consumption of alcohol from an individual indulgence to a public display of generosity. In this practice, members of a group take turns in "standing" (that is, treating) everyone to drinks, continuing until everyone with money has paid at least once—at which point the round might continue. This creates a sense of public obligation readily on display in "Counterparts," where Farrington runs quickly through all his money. In the process, he and O'Halloran (the other character with money) buy almost all of the drinks consumed by the party, but end up drinking only half of them. The practice of rounds also affords those without money the chance to drink for free—as we see not only in "Counterparts" but also in "Two Gallants," where Lenehan has the practice down to a fine art. In these drinking rituals, full servings of whiskey or other hard liquor were the preferred "manly" rounds. Half measures and the addition of mixers like mineral water were generally regarded as effeminate, needlessly expensive, or both. Thus characters like Weathers and Chandler subtly disrupt the gendered rituals of the pub.

THE CATHOLIC CHURCH

The Catholic Church was woven through nearly every aspect of Dublin life at the turn of the twentieth century and exercised considerable power over education, politics, and social life. In 1900, Catholics comprised about three-fourths of Ireland's population and an even larger fraction of Dublin's. Passage of the Catholic Relief Act by the British Parliament in 1829 had lifted long-standing restrictions on Catholic civil rights (such as voting and the opportunity to hold office), and helped to build a small middle class while increasing the influence of the Church. Although generally supportive of Home Rule, the Church broke with many nationalists when its leader, Charles Stewart Parnell, was named in a divorce case (see p. xxx). The deep schism between religious and political identity that followed forms an important subtext for *Dubliners* where ecclesiastical authority is often cast as a suspect and even corrupting influence.

Church authority was considerable and extended deep into the realm of education. Girls were typically sent away to convent schools run by nuns while boys studied either at private Catholic schools or at National Schools—the latter funded by the government but managed by parish priests. The Christian Brothers, a lay organization, also administered Catholic schools for the city's poor. Lessons were learned by rote and included a heavy dose of theology taught by catechism—a question-and-answer form students were expected to memorize. Subjects included math, science, and history as well as Latin, the official language of the Church. Clergy were held in high regard and bright students might aspire to the priesthood, a choice sometimes made out of necessity in a city where middle-class employment was scarce and unstable. Access to higher education for Catholics was extremely limited. Dublin's prestigious Trinity College was primarily for the Protestant Anglo-Irish elite. Although there were Catholic and non-denominational universities, degrees from the Catholic schools were not recognized by the civil authorities, and the nondenominational institutions were deemed "godless." The 1879 University Education Act created the Royal University of Ireland, not a physical campus, but an examining and degree-awarding body for Catholic students, including women.

Catholic practice involved numerous sacred rituals. The mass, recited in Latin by a priest facing the altar with his back to the congregation, focused on the miraculous transformation of wine and bread into the body and blood of Christ. Regular attendance at mass was expected as was regular confession of one's sins to a priest who prescribed penance and offered the absolution necessary for attaining heaven in the afterlife. Other rituals and icons were important too, including the Sacred Heart of Jesus, a graphic symbol of divine suffering found in many Irish homes. The Virgin Mary was just as important, not only for her promise of intercession for those who prayed to her, but also for her symbolic kinship to the iconic symbol of Ireland as a virginal woman.

Catholic practice in *Dubliners* is varied and subject to subtle yet often biting ironies, from the materialist sermon in "Grace" to the suspect behavior of Father Flynn in "The Sisters." Joyce himself had once been devout, and as a poor but bright student had even considered entering the priesthood. Though he would turn away from the Church, Catholic thought and theology continued to shape his writing and imagination. As one character in *Ulysses* says of Stephen Dedalus (Joyce's alter ego): "you have the cursed Jesuit strain in you, only it's injected the wrong way." So too Catholicism is injected in *Dubliners*, albeit in ways that often disrupt the stories and disorient the interpretive efforts of its readers.

Home Rule and Empire

JOYCE COMPOSED most of *Dubliners* as hopes for Irish independence from the British Empire seemed diminished. When the 1800 Act of Union dissolved the independent Irish Parliament, Ireland became, in effect, a colony—albeit one with elected representatives in the British House of Commons. Over the nineteenth century, Irish nationalists fought intermittently for independence while working to secure civil and electoral rights for the Catholics who made up some 90% of the island's population. This struggle reached a climax at the end of the century when a charismatic young Anglo-Irish parliamentarian, Charles Stuart Parnell, began to transform the loosely linked Irish representatives into a powerfully organized voting bloc. Under his leadership, this bloc controlled the balance of power in the British Parliament and helped propel the British Liberal Party and its leader, William Gladstone, to power on the promise that the new government would pursue Home Rule, the ideal of Irish autonomy over its domestic affairs. In 1893 success seemed imminent when the House of Commons passed the Irish Government Bill, but the measure was rejected by the House of Lords.

This defeat, ending immediate hope for Home Rule, was compounded by the collapse of Parnell's leadership. Cherished as the "Uncrowned King of Ireland" and "The Chief," Parnell was named in a divorce suit as the lover of Katherine O'Shea, a woman long separated from her husband. Their affair was openly known, and O'Shea's husband may have timed the divorce case to frustrate the drive toward Home Rule. The scandal split Ireland in two, pitting secular nationalists against a highly conservative, outraged Catholic majority. When Parnell was ejected from the leadership of the Irish Parliamentary Party on December 1, 1890, nine-year-old Joyce wrote a short poem, "Et Tu, Healy," lamenting Parnell's betrayal by his confidant, Timothy Healy. Broken and angry, Parnell died in 1891, shortly after marrying O'Shea.

In 1904, when Joyce wrote the first story of *Dubliners*, these events remained fresh in his mind, their tumult still regularly evoked by his father, who linked Parnell's fall to the Joyce family's own financial collapse. Hopes for Home Rule seemed nearly dead, with the Liberal politician (and future prime minister) Herbert Asquith assuring his constituents that he would not support it. Ireland remained, in effect, a colony, ruled from London by an appointed viceroy with order maintained by armed force. The political energy and activism of the Parnell period had given way to the frustrated quietism and cynicism Joyce caustically satirizes in "Ivy Day in the Committee Room" as well as in a brief essay, "When Home Rule Comes of Age." When *Dubliners* appeared in 1914, however, the political situation had changed entirely: John Redmond had re-energized the Irish Parliamentary Party and, with Liberal allies, secured passage of a Home Rule bill immune to veto by the Lords. Its enactment, however, was stalled with the abrupt onset of World War I, setting the stage for a much more violent and protracted struggle for Irish independence.

The documents here illuminate the political energies that drove Home Rule at the end of the nineteenth century as well as the chaos and sense of betrayal that followed Parnell's fall. The excerpt from Parnell's speech to his constituents in Cork during the elections of 1885 emphasizes not only political liberty, but also the spirit of cultural independence fueling the Irish Revival. Cork, in southern Ireland, was a center of nationalist sympathies, and one that still bore the signs and memories of the Great Famine—an event many blamed on England. Parnell's fall from power and subsequent death came as a great shock to Home Rule supporters, and Joyce's own emotional engagement with these events can be gleaned from an arresting vignette drawn from his semi-autobiographical novel, *A Portrait of the Artist as a Young Man* (1916). The scene describes a stormy holiday dinner, which descends into bitter argument when the protagonist's father and his friend, both ardent Parnellites, defend their fallen leader against Dante Riordan, a staunch Catholic woman.

CHARLES STUART PARNELL'S SPEECH

Delivered in Cork, from the *Cork Examiner*,
January 22, 1885.

… At the election in 1880 I laid certain principles before you and you accepted them (applause, and cries of "we do"). I said and I pledged myself, that I should form one of an independent Irish party to act in opposition to every English government which refused to concede the just rights of Ireland (applause). And in the longer time which is gone by since then, the more I am convinced that that is the true policy to pursue so far as parliamentary policy is concerned, and that it will be impossible for either or both of the English parties to contend for any long time against a determined band of Irishmen acting honestly upon these principles, and backed by the Irish people (cheers).

But we have not alone had that object in view—we have always been very careful not to fetter or control the people at home in any way, not to prevent them from doing anything by their own strength which it is possible for them to do. Sometimes, perhaps, in our anxiety in this direction we have asked them to do what is beyond their strength, but I hold that it is better even to encourage you to do what is beyond your strength even should you fail sometimes in the attempt than to teach you to be subservient and unreliant (applause). You have been encouraged to organise yourselves, to depend upon the rectitude of your cause for your justification, and to depend upon the determination which has helped Irishmen through many centuries to retain the name of Ireland and to retain her nationhood.

Nobody could point to any single action of ours in the House of Commons or out of it which was not based upon the knowledge that behind us existed a strong and brave people, that without the help of the people our exertions would be as nothing, and that with their help and with their confidence we should be, as I believe we shall prove to be in the near future, invincible and unconquerable (great applause)....

We shall struggle, as we have been struggling, for the great and important interests of the Irish tenant farmer.[1] We shall ask that his industry shall not be fettered by rent. We shall ask also from the farmer in return that he shall do what in him lies to encourage the struggling manufactures of Ireland, and that he shall not think it too great a sacrifice to be called upon when he wants anything, when he has to purchase anything, to consider how he may get it of Irish material and manufacture ("hear, hear"), even supposing he has to pay a little more for it (cheers). I am sorry if the agricultural population has shown itself somewhat deficient in its sense of duty in this respect up to the present time, but I feel convinced that the matter has only to be put before them to secure the opening up of most important markets in this country for those manufactures which have always existed, and for those which have been reopened

---

[1] Land ownership was a major political issue, particularly in the countryside where many small farmers rented their fields from absent landlords.

anew, as a consequence of the recent exhibitions, the great exhibition in Dublin and the other equally great one in Cork, which have been recently held (cheers).

We shall also endeavour to secure for the labourer some recognition and some right in the land of his country (applause). We don't care whether it be the prejudices of the farmer or of the landlord that stands in his way ("hear, hear"). We consider that whatever class tries to obstruct the labourer in the possession of those fair and just rights to which he is entitled, that class should be putdown, and coerced if you will, into doing justice to the labourer....

Well, but gentlemen, I go back from the consideration of these questions to the Land Question, in which the labourers' question is also involved and the manufacturers' question. I come back—and every Irish politician must be forcibly driven back—to the consideration of the great question of National Self-Government for Ireland (cheers). I do not know how this great question will be eventually settled. I do not know whether England will be wise in time and concede to constitutional arguments and methods the restitution of that which was stolen from us towards the close of the last century (cheers).[2] It is given to none of us to forecast the future, and just as it is impossible for us to say in what way or by what means the National question may be settled, in what way full justice may be done to Ireland, so it is impossible for us to say to what extent that justice should be done. We cannot ask for less than restitution of Grattan's Parliament[3] (renewed cheering). But no man has the right to fix the boundary to the march of a nation (great cheers). No man has a right to say to his country: "Thus far shalt thou go, and no further"; and we have never attempted to fix the *ne plus ultra*[4] to the progress of Ireland's nationhood, and we never shall (cheers).

But gentlemen, while we leave those things to time, circumstances, and the future, we must each one of us resolve in our own hearts that we shall at all times do everything which within us lies to obtain for Ireland the fullest measure of her rights (applause). In this way we shall avoid difficulties and contentions amongst each other. In this way we shall not give up anything which the future may put in favour of our country, and while we struggle today for that which

[2] With the 1800 Act of Union.

[3] Under the leadership of Henry Grattan, the Irish parliament exercised considerable power and autonomy at the end of the 18th c., until the Act of Union.

[4] Highest achievement.

may seem possible for us with our combination, we must struggle for it with the proud consciousness that we shall not do anything to hinder or prevent better men who may come after us from gaining better things than those for which we now contend (prolonged applause).

JAMES JOYCE, *A PORTRAIT OF THE ARTIST AS A YOUNG MAN* (1916)

[T]he warm heavy smell of turkey and ham and celery rose from the plates and dishes and the great fire was banked high and red in the grate and the green ivy and red holly made you feel so happy and when dinner was ended the big plum pudding would be carried in, studded with peeled almonds and sprigs of holly, with bluish fire running around it and a little green flag flying from the top.

It was his first Christmas dinner and he thought of his little brothers and sisters who were waiting in the nursery, as he had often waited, till the pudding came. The deep low collar and the Eton jacket made him feel queer and oldish: and that morning when his mother had brought him down to the parlour, dressed for mass, his father had cried. That was because he was thinking of his own father. And uncle Charles had said so too.

Mr Dedalus covered the dish and began to eat hungrily. Then he said:

—Poor old Christy, he's nearly lopsided now with roguery.

—Simon, said Mrs Dedalus, you haven't given Mrs Riordan any sauce.

Mr Dedalus seized the sauceboat.

—Haven't I? he cried. Mrs Riordan, pity the poor blind. Dante covered her plate with her hands and said:

—No, thanks.

Mr Dedalus turned to Uncle Charles.

—How are you off, sir?

—Right as the mail, Simon.

—You, John?

—I'm all right. Go on yourself.

—Mary? Here, Stephen, here's something to make your hair curl.

He poured sauce freely over Stephen's plate and set the boat again on the table. Then he asked uncle Charles was it tender. Uncle Charles could not speak because his mouth was full; but he nodded that it was.

—That was a good answer our friend made to the canon.[1]
What? said Mr Dedalus.

—I didn't think he had that much in him, said Mr Casey.

—*I'll pay your dues, father, when you cease turning the house
of God into a polling-booth.*

—A nice answer, said Dante, for any man calling himself a
catholic to give to his priest.

—They have only themselves to blame, said Mr Dedalus
suavely. If they took a fool's advice they would confine their attention to religion.

—It is religion, Dante said. They are doing their duty in warning the people.

—We go to the house of God, Mr Casey said, in all humility to
pray to our Maker and not to hear election addresses.

—It is religion, Dante said again. They are right. They must
direct their flocks.

—And preach politics from the altar, is it? asked Mr Dedalus.

—Certainly, said Dante. It is a question of public morality.
A priest would not be a priest if he did not tell his flock what is right
and what is wrong.

Mrs Dedalus laid down her knife and fork, saying:

—For pity' sake and for pity' sake let us have no political discussion on this day of all days in the year.

—Quite right, ma'am, said uncle Charles. Now, Simon, that's
quite enough now. Not another word now.

—Yes, yes, said Mr Dedalus quickly.

He uncovered the dish boldly and said:

—Now then, who's for more turkey?

Nobody answered. Dante said:

—Nice language for any catholic to use!

—Mrs Riordan, I appeal to you, said Mrs Dedalus, to let the
matter drop now.

Dante turned on her and said:

—And am I to sit here and listen to the pastors of my church
being flouted?

—Nobody is saying a word against them, said Mr Dedalus, so
long as they don't meddle in politics.

—The bishops and priests of Ireland have spoken, said Dante,
and they must be obeyed.

---

[1] Catholic priest.

—Let them leave politics alone, said Mr Casey, or the people may leave their church alone.

—You hear? said Dante, turning to Mrs Dedalus.

—Mr Casey! Simon! said Mrs Dedalus, let it end now.

—Too bad! Too bad! said uncle Charles.

—What? cried Mr Dedalus. Were we to desert him[2] at the bidding of the English people?

—He was no longer worthy to lead, said Dante. He was a public sinner.

—We are all sinners and black sinners, said Mr Casey coldly.

—*Woe be to the man by whom the scandal cometh!* said Mrs Riordan. *It would be better for him that a millstone were tied about his neck and that he were cast into the depths of the sea rather than that he should scandalise one of these, my least little ones.* That is the language of the Holy Ghost.

—And very bad language, if you ask me, said Mr Dedalus coolly.

—Simon! Simon! said uncle Charles. The boy.

—Yes, yes, said Mr Dedalus. I meant about the.... I was thinking about the bad language of that railway porter. Well now, that's all right. Here, Stephen, show me your plate, old chap. Eat away now. Here.

He heaped up the food on Stephen's plate and served uncle Charles and Mr Casey to large pieces of turkey and splashes of sauce. Mrs Dedalus was eating little and Dante sat with her hands in her lap. She was red in the face. Mr Dedalus rooted with the carvers at the end of the dish and said:

—There's a tasty bit here we call the pope's nose. If any lady or gentleman ...

He held a piece of fowl up on the prong of the carving fork. Nobody spoke. He put it on his own plate, saying:

—Well, you can't say but you were asked. I think I had better eat it myself because I'm not well in my health lately.

He winked at Stephen and, replacing the dish-cover, began to eat again.

There was a silence while he ate. Then he said:

—Well now, the day kept up fine after all. There were plenty of strangers down too.

[2] Parnell.

Nobody spoke. He said again:

—I think there were more strangers down than last Christmas.

He looked round at the others whose faces were bent towards their plates and, receiving no reply, waited for a moment and said bitterly:

—Well, my Christmas dinner has been spoiled anyhow.

—There could be neither luck nor grace, Dante said, in a house where there is no respect for the pastors of the church.

Mr Dedalus threw his knife and fork noisily on his plate.

—Respect! he said. Is it for Billy with the lip or for the tub of guts up in Armagh?[3] Respect!

—Princes of the church, said Mr Casey with slow scorn.

—Lord Leitrim's coachman,[4] yes, said Mr Dedalus.

—They are the Lord's anointed, Dante said. They are an honour to their country.

—Tub of guts, said Mr Dedalus coarsely. He has a handsome face, mind you, in repose. You should see that fellow lapping up his bacon and cabbage of a cold winter's day. O Johnny!

He twisted his features into a grimace of heavy bestiality and made a lapping noise with his lips.

—Really, Simon, you should not speak that way before Stephen. It's not right.

—O, he'll remember all this when he grows up, said Dante hotly, the language he heard against God and religion and priests in his own home.

—Let him remember too, cried Mr Casey to her from across the table, the language with which the priests and the priests' pawns broke Parnell's heart and hounded him into his grave. Let him remember that too when he grows up.

—Sons of bitches! cried Mr Dedalus. When he was down they turned on him to betray him and rend him like rats in a sewer. Low-lived dogs! And they look it! By Christ, they look it!

—They behaved rightly, cried Dante. They obeyed their bishops and their priests. Honour to them!

—Well, it is perfectly dreadful to say that not even for one day in the year, said Mrs Dedalus, can we be free from these dreadful disputes!

---

[3] William Walsh (1841-1921), archbishop of Dublin and Michael Logue (1840-1924), archbishop of Armagh—the top-ranking Irish clergy.

[4] Slang for collaborators (from a servant who tried to defend an Anglo-Irish landlord from assassination in 1878).

Uncle Charles raised his hands mildly and said:

—Come now, come now, come now! Can we not have our opinions whatever they are without this bad temper and this bad language? It is too bad surely.

Mrs Dedalus spoke to Dante in a low voice but Dante said loudly:

—I will not say nothing. I will defend my church and my religion when it is insulted and spit on by renegade catholics.

Mr Casey pushed his plate rudely into the middle of the table and, resting his elbows before him, said in a hoarse voice to his host:

—Tell me, did I tell you that story about a very famous spit?

—You did not, John, said Mr Dedalus.

—Why then, said Mr Casey, it is a most instructive story. It happened not long ago in the county Wicklow where we are now.

He broke off and, turning towards Dante, said with quiet indignation:

—And I may tell you, ma'am, that I, if you mean me, am no renegade catholic. I am a catholic as my father was and his father before him and his father before him again, when we gave up our lives rather than sell our faith.

—The more shame to you now, Dante said, to speak as you do.

—The story, John, said Mr Dedalus smiling. Let us have the story anyhow.

—Catholic indeed! repeated Dante ironically. The blackest protestant in the land would not speak the language I have heard this evening.

Mr Dedalus began to sway his head to and fro, crooning like a country singer.

—I am no protestant, I tell you again, said Mr Casey, flushing.

Mr Dedalus, still crooning and swaying his head, began to sing in a grunting nasal tone:

> *O, come all you Roman catholics*
> *That never went to mass.*

He took up his knife and fork again in good humour and set to eating, saying to Mr Casey:

—Let us have the story, John. It will help us to digest.

[...]

—The story is very short and sweet, Mr Casey said. It was one day down in Arklow, a cold bitter day, not long before the chief died. May God have mercy on him!

He closed his eyes wearily and paused. Mr Dedalus took a bone from his plate and tore some meat from it with his teeth, saying:

—Before he was killed, you mean.

Mr Casey opened his eyes, sighed and went on:

—It was down in Arklow one day. We were down there at a meeting and after the meeting was over we had to make our way to the railway station through the crowd. Such booing and baaing, man, you never heard. They called us all the names in the world. Well there was one old lady, and a drunken old harridan she was surely, that paid all her attention to me. She kept dancing along beside me in the mud bawling and screaming into my face: *Priesthunter! The Paris Funds! Mr Fox! Kitty O'Shea!*

—And what did you do, John? asked Mr Dedalus.

—I let her bawl away, said Mr Casey. It was a cold day and to keep up my heart I had (saving your presence, ma'am) a quid of Tullamore⁵ in my mouth and sure I couldn't say a word in any case because my mouth was full of tobacco juice.

—Well, John?

—Well. I let her bawl away, to her heart's content, *Kitty O'Shea* and the rest of it till at last she called that lady a name that I won't sully this Christmas board nor your ears, ma'am, nor my own lips by repeating.

He paused. Mr Dedalus, lifting his head from the bone, asked:

—And what did you do, John?

—Do! said Mr Casey. She stuck her ugly old face up at me when she said it and I had my mouth full of tobacco juice. I bent down to her and *Phth*! says I to her like that.

He turned aside and made the act of spitting.

—*Phth*! says I to her like that, right into her eye.

He clapped his hand to his eye and gave a hoarse scream of pain.

—*O Jesus, Mary, and Joseph!* says she. *I'm blinded! I'm blinded and drowned!*

He stopped in a fit of coughing and laughter, repeating:

—*I'm blinded entirely.*

Mr Dedalus laughed loudly and lay back in his chair while uncle Charles swayed his head to and fro.

Dante looked terribly angry and repeated while they laughed:

—Very nice! Ha! Very nice!

It was not nice about the spit in the woman's eye.

⁵ Tobacco.

But what was the name the woman had called Kitty O'Shea that Mr Casey would not repeat? He thought of Mr Casey walking through the crowds of people and making speeches from a wagonette. That was what he had been in prison for and he remembered that one night Sergeant O'Neill had come to the house and had stood in the hall, talking in a low voice with his father and chewing nervously at the chinstrap of his cap. And that night Mr Casey had not gone to Dublin by train but a car had come to the door and he had heard his father say something about the Cabinteely road.

He was for Ireland and Parnell and so was his father: and so was Dante too for one night at the band on the esplanade she had hit a gentleman on the head with her umbrella because he had taken off his hat when the band played *God Save the Queen* at the end.

Mr Dedalus gave a snort of contempt.

—Ah, John, he said. It is true for them. We are an unfortunate priestridden race and always were and always will be till the end of the chapter.

Uncle Charles shook his head, saying:

—A bad business! A bad business!

Mr Dedalus repeated:

—A priestridden Godforsaken race!

He pointed to the portrait of his grandfather on the wall to his right.

—Do you see that old chap up there, John? he said. He was a good Irishman when there was no money in the job. He was condemned to death as a whiteboy[6]. But he had a saying about our clerical friends, that he would never let one of them put his two feet under his mahogany.

Dante broke in angrily:

—If we are a priestridden race we ought to be proud of it! They are the apple of God's eye. *Touch them not*, says Christ, *for they are the apple of My eye.*

—And can we not love our country then? asked Mr Casey. Are we not to follow the man that was born to lead us?

—A traitor to his country! replied Dante. A traitor, an adulterer! The priests were right to abandon him. The priests were always the true friends of Ireland.

—Were they, faith? said Mr Casey.

[6] Protestors who often fought violently for the rights of tenant farmers.

He threw his fist on the table and, frowning angrily, protruded one finger after another.

—Didn't the bishops of Ireland betray us in the time of the union when Bishop Lanigan presented an address of loyalty to the Marquess Cornwallis? Didn't the bishops and priests sell the aspirations of their country in 1829 in return for catholic emancipation? Didn't they denounce the fenian movement from the pulpit and in the confession box? And didn't they dishonour the ashes of Terence Bellew MacManus?[7]

His face was glowing with anger and Stephen felt the glow rise to his own cheek as the spoken words thrilled him. Mr Dedalus uttered a guffaw of coarse scorn.

—O, by God, he cried, I forgot little old Paul Cullen![8] Another apple of God's eye!

Dante bent across the table and cried to Mr Casey:

—Right! Right! They were always right! God and morality and religion come first.

Mrs Dedalus, seeing her excitement, said to her:

—Mrs Riordan, don't excite yourself answering them.

—God and religion before everything! Dante cried. God and religion before the world.

Mr Casey raised his clenched fist and brought it down on the table with a crash.

—Very well then, he shouted hoarsely, if it comes to that, no God for Ireland!

—John! John! cried Mr Dedalus, seizing his guest by the coat sleeve.

Dante stared across the table, her cheeks shaking. Mr Casey struggled up from his chair and bent across the table towards her, scraping the air from before his eyes with one hand as though he were tearing aside a cobweb.

—No God for Ireland! he cried. We have had too much God In Ireland. Away with God!

—Blasphemer! Devil! screamed Dante, starting to her feet and almost spitting in his face.

---

[7] Incidents throughout the 19th c. in which nationalist demands were compromised to secure Catholic civil rights and preserve peace in Ireland.

[8] Archbishop of Dublin in the 19th c. who condemned revolutionary Irish nationalism.

Uncle Charles and Mr Dedalus pulled Mr Casey back into his chair again, talking to him from both sides reasonably. He stared before him out of his dark flaming eyes, repeating:

—Away with God, I say!

Dante shoved her chair violently aside and left the table, upsetting her napkinring which rolled slowly along the carpet and came to rest against the foot of an easychair. Mrs Dedalus rose quickly and followed her towards the door. At the door Dante turned round violently and shouted down the room, her cheeks flushed and quivering with rage:

—Devil out of hell! We won! We crushed him to death! Fiend!

The door slammed behind her.

Mr Casey, freeing his arms from his holders, suddenly bowed his head on his hands with a sob of pain.

—Poor Parnell! he cried loudly. My dead king!

He sobbed loudly and bitterly.

Stephen, raising his terror-stricken face, saw that his father's eyes were full of tears.

The Irish Revival

FOLLOWING THE fall of Parnell and the defeat of the Irish Government Bill at the end of the nineteenth century, the movement for autonomy shifted from parliamentary politics to art and culture. From roughly the 1890s to the outbreak of Word War One, a disparate array of writers, scholars, actors, entrepreneurs, amateur anthropologists, and community organizers set out to define an "Irish" culture, distinct from the impositions of the English. Known as the Irish Revival, this work took various forms, ranging from attempts to propagate the Irish language and popularize Gaelic sports (like hurley) to anthropological and aesthetic studies of folklore and the ancient bardic tradition. Anglo-Irish artists—among them, W. B. Yeats, Lady Augusta Gregory, George Moore, J. M. Synge, and Edward Martyn—played key roles in these efforts.

The movement's popularity and influence depended not only on the stature and talents of its supporters, but upon its ready accommodation with popular images of Ireland as a mythic, pre-modern place still shot through with primitive beliefs and energies. Many scholars and writers—both Irish and English—traced the island's language and culture to the ancient Phonecians (an ancient Mediterranean people) rather than to Europe and the West. This resulted in a distinctive Irish Orientalism that took shape, even before the Revival, in the dreamy epic verses of Thomas Moore, whose long poem, *Lala Rookh* (1817) and series of *Irish Melodies* (1808-1834), make this connection explicit. These texts are frequent targets of Joyce's satire throughout *Dubliners*, their wistful abstractions a far cry from the "style of scrupulous meanness" pervading the collection. Although the poems in Joyce's earliest work, *Chamber Music*, share many of these influences, *Dubliners* is conspicuously at odds with this sensibility, reflecting Joyce's staunch resistance to its sentimental nativism and anachronistic themes. This critique is evident not only in the crass *Eire Abu* Society of "A Mother," but in the stinted imagination of the aspiring poet in "A Little Cloud" and in the aborted romances at the heart of "Araby" and "An Encounter." Most notably, Gabriel struggles in "The Dead" to strike some balance between his own cosmopolitanism and the ghostly past that rises to meet him from the mythic west of Ireland.

The Revival itself, however, cannot be easily reduced to a single aesthetic or philosophy, nor do Joyce's frequent parodies of it give a full sense of its richness. It marked a period of intense artistic creativity, cultural recovery, and intellectual exploration that looked not only to a mythic Oriental past but also to an emergent cosmopolitan future. Young intellectuals looked to European writers like Friedrich Nietzsche and Henrik Ibsen, both of whom find their way into the pages of *Dubliners*. In Dublin, little magazines like *Dana* and *Samhain* sought to cultivate an intellectual independence capable of both recording and escaping Ireland's colonial repression.

The selections in this section reflect the diverse, often contradictory impulses of the Revival, and then Joyce's acerbic response to it in some early critical writing. In the opening pages of his collection of Irish folklore, *The Celtic Twilight* (1893), W. B. Yeats, an Anglo-Irishman descended from British settlers, embraces Irish identity and Ireland's ancient culture. The stories he collects do more than convey a native tradition of myth and storytelling; they also present an alternative to a modernity that Yeats found spiritually empty and imaginatively destitute. Yeats's energies also extended beyond his own writings and with other leaders of the Revival—including Lady Gregory and J. M. Synge—he helped found the Irish National Theatre Society in 1903 at the Abbey Theatre in Dublin. Created to promote works about and by the Irish, it quickly became a site of both political debate and aesthetic innovation. Its first program, shown here, features the richly symbolic image of Queen Maeve, a mythic Irish warrior queen, hunting at dawn with her Irish wolfhound.

Like Yeats, Anglo-Irishman Douglas Hyde played a key role in the Revival, helping to found the Gaelic League in 1893 and becoming the first president of the Irish Republic (a largely ceremonial position) in 1938. A scholar rather than a poet or folklorist, he advocated the preservation of the Irish language, a cause famously advanced in "The Necessity for De-Anglicising Ireland" (1892), a pamphlet whose insistence on the value, dignity, and imaginative power of a long-repressed native language would be echoed in other post-colonial movements.

But for all this energy, there were drawbacks: Not only did Revivalism court stereotypes of Irish primitivism that could be as destructive as they were romantic, but the focus on western Ireland, depopulated by the Great Famine of the 1840s and ensuing economic decline, also entailed a kind of enervated parochialism. Thus other Revivalists sought to forge links to the new politics and art abroad. One brief-lived outlet was *Dana*, the magazine in which Joyce published his first poem. Its inaugural issue in 1904 carried a provocative essay by its co-founder, playwright and journalist Frederick Ryan, "Political and Intellectual Freedom," a powerful critique of religious and national sectarianism that Joyce would echo.

These echoes play across *Dubliners* and Joyce's early journalism, heralding his eventual decision to leave Ireland permanently for the continent. The short newspaper review "The Soul of Ireland" is a stinging critique of Lady Gregory's collection of folktales and stories, *Poets and Dreamers: Studies and Translations from the Irish* (1903). With it Joyce effectively announced his break with this branch of the Revival, turning on the very woman who had generously helped him secure work as a newspaper reviewer. Although Joyce rejected the Irish Revival, he did not reject Ireland. Seeking to forge his own aesthetic, he set about imagining a national revival on his own terms.

FROM W. B. YEATS, *THE CELTIC TWILIGHT* (1893)[1]

The Hosting of the Sidhe

> *The host is riding from Knocknarea.[2]*
> *And over the grave of Clooth-na-bare:[3]*
> *Caolte[4] tossing his burning hair.*
> *And Niamh[5] calling, "Away, come away:*
> *Empty your heart of its mortal dream.*
> *The winds awaken, the leaves whirl round.*
> *Our cheeks are pale, our hair is unbound.*
> *Our breasts are heaving, our eyes are a-gleam.*
> *Our arms are waving, our lips are apart.*
> *And if any gaze on our rushing band.*
> *We come between him and the deed of his hand.*
> *We come between him and the hope of his heart. "*

---

[1] Fairies.

[2] A mountain in Sligo, in the west of Ireland.

[3] *Cailleach Bhéirre* (Irish for "The Old Woman of Beare")—a goddess who attempted to destroy her fairy life by drowning herself in a lake.

[4] Ancient Irish warrior known for speed and poetic skill.

[5] Beautiful Irish goddess who lured an Irish hero into the land of eternal youth.

The host is rushing 'twixt night and day:
And where is there hope or deed as fair?
Caolte tossing his burning hair,
And Niamh calling, "Away, come away."

This Book

I

I have desired, like every artist, to create a little world out of the beautiful, pleasant, and significant things of this marred and clumsy world, and to show in a vision something of the face of Ireland to any of my own people who would look where I bid them. I have therefore written down accurately and candidly much that I have heard and seen, and, except by way of commentary, nothing that I have merely imagined. I have, however, been at no pains to separate my own beliefs from those of the peasantry, but have rather let my men and women, dhouls and faeries, go their way unoffended or defended by any argument of mine. The things a man has heard and seen are threads of life, and if he pull them carefully from the confused distaff of memory, any who will can weave them into whatever garments of belief please them best. I too have woven my garment like another, but I shall try to keep warm in it, and shall be well content if it do not unbecome me.

Hope and Memory have one daughter and her name is Art, and she has built her dwelling far from the desperate field where men hang out their garments upon forked boughs to be banners of battle. O beloved daughter of Hope and Memory, be with me for a little.

A Teller of Tales

Many of the tales in this book were told me by one Paddy Flynn, a little bright-eyed old man, who lived in a leaky and one-roomed cabin in the village of Ballisodare, which is, he was wont to say, "the most gentle"—whereby he meant faery—"place in the whole of County Sligo."[6] Others hold it, however, but second to Drumcliff and Drumahair. The first time I saw him he was cooking mushrooms for himself; the next time he was asleep under a hedge, smiling in his sleep. He was indeed always cheerful, though I thought I could see in his eyes (swift as the eyes of a rabbit, when they peered out of their wrinkled holes) a

---

[6] In Western Ireland where Yeats found much of his folkloric sources and poetic inspiration.

melancholy which was well-nigh a portion of their joy; the visionary melancholy of purely instinctive natures and of all animals.

And yet there was much in his life to depress him, for in the triple solitude of age, eccentricity, and deafness, he went about much pestered by children. It was for this very reason perhaps that he ever recommended mirth and hopefulness. He was fond, for instance, of telling how Collumcille[7] cheered up his mother. "How are you to-day, mother?" said the saint. "Worse," replied the mother. "May you be worse to-morrow," said the saint. The next day Collumcille came again, and exactly the same conversation took place, but the third day the mother said, "Better, thank God." And the saint replied, "May you be better to-morrow." He was fond too of telling how the Judge smiles at the last day alike when he rewards the good and condemns the lost to unceasing flames. He had many strange sights to keep him cheerful or to make him sad. I asked him had he ever seen the faeries, and got the reply, "Am I not annoyed with them?" I asked too if he had ever seen the banshee.[8] "I have seen it," he said, "down there by the water, batting the river with its hands."

I have copied this account of Paddy Flynn, with a few verbal alterations, from a note-book which I almost filled with his tales and sayings, shortly after seeing him. I look now at the note-book regretfully, for the blank pages at the end will never be filled up. Paddy Flynn is dead; a friend of mine gave him a large bottle of whiskey, and though a sober man at most times, the sight of so much liquor filled him with a great enthusiasm, and he lived upon it for some days and then died. His body, worn out with old age and hard times, could not bear the drink as in his young days. He was a great teller of tales, and unlike our common romancers, knew how to empty heaven, hell, and purgatory, faeryland and earth, to people his stories. He did not live in a shrunken world, but knew of no less ample circumstance than did Homer himself. Perhaps the Gaelic people shall by his like bring back again the ancient simplicity and amplitude of imagination. What is literature but the expression of moods by the vehicle of symbol and incident? And are there not moods which need heaven, hell, purgatory, and faeryland for their expression, no less than this dilapidated earth? Nay, are there not moods which shall find no expression unless there be men who dare to mix heaven, hell, purgatory, and faeryland together, or even to set the

[7] Famous 6th-c. Irish saint who helped spread Christianity from Ireland to Northern Europe.

[8] Fairy creature that wails outside a house where someone is soon to die.

heads of beasts to the bodies of men, or to thrust the souls of men into the heart of rocks? Let us go forth, the tellers of tales, and seize whatever prey the heart long for, and have no fear. Everything exists, everything is true, and the earth is only a little dust under our feet.

Belief and Unbelief

There are some doubters even in the western villages. One woman told me last Christmas that she did not believe either in hell or in ghosts. Hell she thought was merely an invention got up by the priest to keep people good; and ghosts would not be permitted, she held, to go "trapsin about the earth" at their own free will; "but there are faeries," she added, "and little leprechauns, and water-horses, and fallen angels." I have met also a man with a mohawk Indian tattooed upon his arm, who held exactly similar beliefs and unbeliefs. No matter what one doubts one never doubts the faeries, for, as the man with the mohawk Indian on his arm said to me, "they stand to reason." Even the official mind does not escape this faith.

A little girl who was at service[9] in the village of Grange, close under the seaward slopes of Ben Bulben,[10] suddenly disappeared one night about three years ago. There was at once great excitement in the neighbourhood, because it was rumoured that the faeries had taken her. A villager was said to have long struggled to hold her from them, but at last they prevailed, and he found nothing in his hands but a broomstick. The local constable was applied to, and he at once instituted a house-to-house search, and at the same time advised the people to burn all the *bucalauns* (ragweed) on the field she vanished from, because *bucalauns* are sacred to the faeries. They spent the whole night burning them, the constable repeating spells the while. In the morning the little girl was found, the story goes, wandering in the field. She said the faeries had taken her away a great distance, riding on a faery horse. At last she saw a big river, and the man who had tried to keep her from being carried off was drifting down it—such are the topsy-turvydoms of faery glamour—in a cockleshell. On the way her companions had mentioned the names of several people who were about to die shortly in the village.

Perhaps the constable was right. It is better doubtless to believe much unreason and a little truth than to deny for denial's sake truth and unreason alike, for when we do this we have not even a rush

---

[9] Domestic servant.

[10] Mountain in Sligo.

First Program of the Irish National Theater Society (1904)

candle to guide our steps, not even a poor sowlth[11] to dance before us on the marsh, and must needs fumble our way into the great emptiness where dwell the mis-shapen dhouls. And after all, can we come to so great evil if we keep a little fire on our hearths and in our

---

[11] Formless ghost.

souls, and welcome with open hand whatever of excellent come to warm itself, whether it be man or phantom, and do not say too fiercely, even to the dhouls themselves, "Be ye gone"? When all is said and done, how do we not know but that our own unreason may be better than another's truth? for it has been warmed on our hearths and in our souls, and is ready for the wild bees of truth to hive in it, and make their sweet honey. Come into the world again, wild bees, wild bees!

Douglas Hyde's Speech, "The Necessity for De-Anglicising Ireland"

Delivered before the Irish National Literary Society in Dublin, 25 November 1892.

When we speak of "The Necessity for De-Anglicising the Irish Nation," we mean it, not as a protest against imitating what is best in the English people, for that would be absurd, but rather to show the folly of neglecting what is Irish, and hastening to adopt, pell-mell, and indiscriminately, everything that is English, simply because it is English. This is a question which most Irishmen will naturally look at from a National point of view, but it is one which ought also to claim the sympathies of every intelligent Unionist, and which, as I know, does claim the sympathy of many.

If we take a bird's-eye view of our island today, and compare it with what it used to be, we must be struck by the extraordinary fact that the nation which was once, as every one admits, one of the most classically learned and cultured nations in Europe, is now one of the least so; how one of the most reading and literary peoples has become one of the least studious and most un-literary, and how the present art products of one of the quickest, most sensitive, and most artistic races on earth are now only distinguished for their hideousness.

I shall endeavour to show that this failure of the Irish people in recent times has been largely brought about by the race diverging during this century from the right path, and ceasing to be Irish without becoming English. I shall attempt to show that with the bulk of the people this change took place quite recently, much more recently than most people imagine, and is, in fact, still going on. I should also like to call attention to the illogical position of men who drop their own language to speak English, of men who translate their euphonious Irish names into English monosyllables, of men who read English books, and know nothing about Gaelic literature, nevertheless protesting as a matter of sentiment that they hate the country which at every hand's turn they rush to imitate.

I wish to show you that in Anglicising ourselves wholesale we have thrown away with a light heart the best claim which we have upon the world's recognition of us as a separate nationality. What did Mazzini[1] say? What is Goldwin Smith[2] never tired of declaiming? What do the *Spectator* and *Saturday Review* harp on? That we ought to be content as an integral part of the United Kingdom because we have lost the notes of nationality, our language and customs.

It has always been very curious to me how Irish sentiment sticks in this half-way house—how it continues to apparently hate the English, and at the same time continues to imitate them; how it continues to clamour for recognition as a distinct nationality, and at the same time throws away with both hands what would make it so. If Irishmen only went a little farther they would become good Englishmen in sentiment also. But—illogical as it appears—there seems not the slightest sign or probability of their taking that step. It is the curious certainty that come what may Irishmen will continue to resist English rule, even though it should be for their good, which prevents many of our nation from becoming Unionists upon the spot. It is a fact, and we must face it as a fact, that although they adopt English habits and copy England in every way, the great bulk of Irishmen and Irishwomen over the whole world are known to be filled with a dull, ever-abiding animosity against her, and—right or wrong—to grieve when she prospers, and joy when she is hurt. Such movements as Young Irelandism, Fenianism, Land Leagueism, and Parliamentary obstruction[3] seem always to gain their sympathy and support. It is just because there appears no earthly chance of their becoming good members of the Empire that I urge that they should not remain in the anomalous position they are in, but since they absolutely refuse to become the one thing, that they become the other; cultivate what they have rejected, and build up an Irish nation on Irish lines.

But you ask, why should we wish to make Ireland more Celtic than it is—why should we de-Anglicise it at all?

I answer because the Irish race is at present in a most anomalous position, imitating England and yet apparently hating it. How can it produce anything good in literature, art, or institutions as long as it is actuated by motives so contradictory? Besides, I believe it is our Gaelic past which, though the Irish race does not recognise it just at

---

[1] Giuseppe Mazzini, 19th c. Italian nationalist, politician, and philosopher.

[2] British biographer, historian, and journalist who supported Catholic civil rights but opposed Home Rule.

[3] 19th c. movements for Irish political independence.

present, is really at the bottom of the Irish heart, and prevents us becoming citizens of the Empire, as, I think, can be easily proved.

To say that Ireland has not prospered under English rule is simply a truism; all the world admits it, England does not deny it. But the English retort is ready. You have not prospered, they say, because you would not settle down contentedly, like the Scotch, and form part of the Empire. "Twenty years of good, resolute, grandfatherly government," said a well-known Englishman, will solve the Irish question. He possibly made the period too short, but let us suppose this. Let us suppose for a moment—which is impossible—that there were to arise a series of Cromwells[4] in England for the space of one hundred years, able administrators of the Empire, careful rulers of Ireland, developing to the utmost our national resources, whilst they unremittingly stamped out every spark of national feeling, making Ireland a land of wealth and factories, whilst they extinguished every thought and every idea that was Irish, and left us, at last, after a hundred years of good government, fat, wealthy, and populous, but with all our characteristics gone, with every external that at present differentiates us from the English lost or dropped; all our Irish names of places and people turned into English names; the Irish language completely extinct; the O's and the Macs dropped; our Irish intonation changed, as far as possible by English schoolmasters into something English; our history no longer remembered or taught; the names of our rebels and martyrs blotted out; our battlefields and traditions forgotten; the fact that we were not of Saxon origin dropped out of sight and memory, and let me now put the question—How many Irishmen are there who would purchase material prosperity at such a price? It is exactly such a question as this and the answer to it that shows the difference between the English and Irish race. Nine Englishmen out of ten would jump to make the exchange, and I as firmly believe that nine Irishmen out of ten would indignantly refuse it.

And yet this awful idea of complete Anglicisation, which I have here put before you in all its crudity is, and has been, making silent inroads upon us for nearly a century.

Its inroads have been silent, because, had the Gaelic race perceived what was being done, or had they been once warned of what was taking place in their own midst, they would, I think, never have allowed it. When the picture of complete Anglicisation is drawn for

---

[4] Oliver Cromwell: 16th c. English general and political leader who brutally suppressed Irish Catholics in order to consolidate his power over the island and integrate it into the Commonwealth of England.

them in all its nakedness, Irish sentimentality becomes suddenly a power and refuses to surrender its birthright. [...]

I have often heard people thank God that if the English gave us nothing else they gave us at least their language. In this way they put a bold face upon the matter, and pretend that the Irish language is not worth knowing, and has no literature. But the Irish language is worth knowing, or why would the greatest philologists[5] of Germany, France, and Italy be emulously studying it, and it does possess a literature, or why would a German savant have made the calculation that the books written in Irish between the eleventh and seventeenth centuries, and still extant, would fill a thousand octavo volumes.

I have no hesitation at all in saying that every Irish-feeling Irishman, who hates the reproach of West-Britonism,[6] should set himself to encourage the efforts, which are being made to keep alive our once great national tongue. The losing of it is our greatest blow, and the sorest stroke that the rapid Anglicisation of Ireland has inflicted upon us. In order to de-Anglicise ourselves we must at once arrest the decay of the language. We must bring pressure upon our politicians not to snuff it out by their tacit discouragement merely because they do not happen themselves to understand it. We must arouse some spark of patriotic inspiration among the peasantry who still use the language, and put an end to the shameful state of feeling—a thousand-tongued reproach to our leaders and statesmen—which makes young men and women blush and hang their heads when overheard speaking their own language. Maynooth[7] has at last come splendidly to the front, and it is now incumbent upon every clerical student to attend lectures in the Irish language and history during the first three years of his course. But in order to keep the Irish language alive where it is still spoken—which is the utmost we can at present aspire to—nothing less than a house-to-house visitation and exhortation of the people themselves will do, something—though with a very different purpose—analogous to the procedure that James Stephens[8] adopted throughout Ireland when he found her like a corpse on the dissecting table. This and some system of giving medals or badges of honour to every family who will guarantee that

---

[5] Scholars of language.

[6] Derisive term for Irish who identify with Britain. (See "The Dead," p. xxx n. 50)

[7] The Royal College of St. Patrick at Maynooth—a prominent Catholic seminary offering courses in the Irish language.

[8] 19th c. Irish nationalist who helped found the Feinian movement while taking a walking tour of Ireland to assess its readiness for revolt.

they have always spoken Irish amongst themselves during the year. But unfortunately, distracted as we are and torn by contending factions, it is impossible to find either men or money to carry out this simple remedy, although [...] this is of greater importance than whether Mr. Redmond or Mr. MacCarthy lead the largest wing of the Irish party for the moment, or Mr. So-and-So succeed with his election petition. To a person taking a bird's eye view of the situation a hundred or five hundred years hence, believe me, it will also appear of greater importance than any mere temporary wrangle, but, unhappily, our countrymen cannot be brought to see this.

We can, however, insist, and we shall insist if Home Rule be carried, that the Irish language, which so many foreign scholars of the first calibre find so worthy of study, shall be placed on a par with—or even above—Greek, Latin, and modern languages, in all examinations held under the Irish Government. We can also insist, and we shall insist, that in those baronies where the children speak Irish, Irish shall be taught, and that Irish-speaking schoolmasters, petty sessions clerks, and even magistrates be appointed in Irish-speaking districts. If all this were done, it should not be very difficult, with the aid of the foremost foreign scholars, to bring about a tone of thought which would make it disgraceful for an educated Irishman especially of the old Celtic race, MacDermotts, O'Conors, O'Sullivans, MacCarthys, O'Neills—to be ignorant of his own language—would make it at least as disgraceful as for an educated Jew to be quite ignorant of Hebrew. [...]

I have now mentioned a few of the principal points on which it would be desirable for us to move, with a view to de-Anglicising ourselves; but perhaps the principal point of all I have taken for granted. That is the necessity for encouraging the use of Anglo-Irish literature instead of English books, especially instead of English periodicals. We must set our face sternly against penny dreadfuls, shilling shockers,[9] and still more, the garbage of vulgar English weeklies like *Bow Bells* and the *Police Intelligence*. Every house should have a copy of Moore[10] and Davis.[11] In a word, we must strive to cultivate everything that is most racial, most smacking of the soil, most Gaelic, most Irish, because in spite of the little admixture of Saxon blood in the north-east corner, this island is and will ever remain Celtic at the core. [...] On racial lines, then, we shall best develop, following the bent of

---

[9] Cheap popular literature (see "An Encounter" p. xxx n.1).

[10] Irish poet Thomas Moore.

[11] Thomas Davis, 19th c. Irish poet and politician who helped found the Young Ireland movement.

our own natures; and, in order to do this, we must create a strong feeling against West-Britonism, for it—if we give it the least chance, or show it the smallest quarter—will overwhelm us like a flood, and we shall find ourselves toiling painfully behind the English at each step following the same fashions, only six months behind the English ones; reading the same books, only months behind them; taking up the same fads, after they have become stale there; following them in our dress, literature, music, games, and ideas, only a long time after them and a vast way behind. We will become, what, I fear, we are largely at present, a nation of imitators, the Japanese of Western Europe, lost to the power of native initiative and alive only to second-hand assimilation. [...] We must teach ourselves to be less sensitive, we must teach ourselves not to be ashamed of ourselves, because the Gaelic people can never produce its best before the world as long as it remains tied to the apron-strings of another race and another island, waiting for it to move before it will venture to take any step itself.

In conclusion, I would earnestly appeal to every one, whether Unionist or Nationalist, who wishes to see the Irish nation produce its best—surely whatever our politics are we all wish that—to set his face against this constant running to England for our books, literature, music, games, fashions, and ideas. I appeal to every one whatever his politics—for this is no political matter—to do his best to help the Irish race to develop in future upon Irish lines, even at the risk of encouraging national aspirations, because upon Irish lines alone can the Irish race once more become what it was of yore—one of the most original, artistic, literary, and charming peoples of Europe.

FREDERICK RYAN, "POLITICAL AND INTELLECTUAL FREEDOM"

Published in *Dana: An Irish Magazine of Independent Thought*, May 1904.

I

More than one recent incident has set up the fear in many minds that Ireland is about to experience another attack of that religious fever which has so often afflicted her in the past, at a time when other indications went to show that saner and more pacific ideals were gaining in strength. We continually suffer in Ireland from rival bigotries which, so far from injuring, positively help one another and stimulate each other. There is, firstly, the Orange and ascendancy party,[1]

---

[1] Supporters of the Union with Great Britain.

continually waging a political war against the people and against the policy of self-government which is the chief cure for Orange and Catholic bigotry alike. That Orange party, with the vices which peculiarly attach to every such faction, maintained by outside political support and kept in countenance by outside authority, actuated by base and bigoted ideas, has the strength which all such minorities possess. It is comparatively compact, unimaginative, self-centred. Its boycott, of course, is chiefly political, but it also serves to set up a counter bigotry on the other side. That is the fate of all countries so situated as Ireland. The vices of the dominant faction, ruling without consent and without sympathy, corrupt the whole body politic, so that in such a soil, race and religious passion waxes strong, and political science is at a discount.

This seems to me the simple explanation of such incidents as the campaign started a year or so ago by a weekly Dublin journal to accentuate and embitter Catholic feeling, to make Catholics particularly sensitive as to their Catholicism, and to urge them to demand rights, not as citizens, nor in the interests of national well-being, but to demand them as Catholics in the interests of Catholicity. This campaign, it is true, was carried on at a level of vulgarity and with a wealth of epithet that would have excited the envy of Mr. Chamberlain,[2] and was of that "will-you-take-it-lying-down" order which peculiarly appeals to the uneducated and semi-educated mob, since it touches that natural and even healthy egoism which lies so near the surface in any crowd. The formula of that mob-appeal is now fairly familiar to most of us. When England with a quarter of a million of men set out to conquer two little peasant states in Africa,[3] the English Jingo politicians and journals appealed to the English mob in a fashion that would lead an observer to imagine that they were fighting a desperate battle for their very existence against tremendous odds. The race or religious bigot generally paints the conditions of those whom he is addressing in the worst colours, tells them they are in a very perilous state, and that they are being trampled upon by a wily and treacherous enemy, against whom any and every means of defence is permissible. The "enemy"—or the worst elements on its side—may easily be trusted to better the example, and, if all goes well, the bigot will soon be at the summit of his ambition: rival

[2] Joseph Chamberlain (1836–1914), English political leader and member of the Liberal Unionist Party; an ardent opponent of Home Rule.

[3] The Boer War (1899–1902) in which Britain struggled to maintain control of its colonies in South Africa.

mobs will glare at each other, mob-newspapers will hurl abuse at one another, and every member of the community will have a keen consciousness of every other member's sins.

A case by which the ethical standard of the leaders of this Catholic campaign might be tested arose in the matter of the anti-Jewish outburst in Limerick. An ignorant priest in Limerick preached a sermon retailing old and exploded libels against Jews in general and urging the people to boycott the Jews in Limerick, a sermon which, by the way, evoked a humane and admirable protest from Mr. Michael Davitt,[4] which justifies the high place he holds in the esteem of Irish democrats. What was the conduct of those who are so loud in their demand for "justice" to Catholics? They supported the priest. When Catholics are boycotted it is an outrageous injustice; when Catholics boycott others it is all right and proper, being merely a process of recovering their own. On many to whom this conduct appears defensible, probably nothing that is here written will have any effect. But to others the question may be put: on what principle is any lawless egoism to be condemned, if this be justified?

II.

Let us, however, seek a clear intellectual outlook. Philosophically, of course, the conduct of the religionists all round is absurd. According to the Christian view, this world is a "vale of tears," a vestibule of eternity, a mere halting place on a road that stretches into the illimitable future. Yet amongst the people who profess this belief, the fight is waged with a bitterness which seems to suggest that the combatants are determined to stay in the "vestibule" as long as they can, and are determined to make it as comfortable, in the meantime, as possible.

The contrast between Christian precept and practice is certainly amusing. Yet far be it from me to press the precepts mentioned on the various combatants. The only modern Christian to profess the doctrine of non-resistance is Count Tolstoy,[5] and even with him it is only a profession since he maintains a continuous and vigorous propaganda against what he considers the evils of modern society. Indeed his English admirers keep up a supply of books, pamphlets and leaflets

---

[4] Irish politician (1846-1906) who helped found the Land League and fought for Home Rule.

[5] 19th c. Russian novelist and philosopher Leo Tolstoy (1828-1910), widely admired for his rationalist moral philosophy of non-violence.

from his pen in such bewildering profusion that one never knows exactly whether one is reading a new pronouncement or merely a new edition of an old one.

Yet Tolstoy's example surely sets us on the right path. The method of redressing the sectarian bitterness in Ireland is not by counter bitterness. We shall never cure matters by boycotting, or intimidation, or abuse. It is by science and by moral appeal that progress is always to be permanently won. The first and absolutely necessary step is the winning of self-government. And it is the failure to recognise this that vitiates otherwise capable surveys like Mr. Filson Young's and Sir Horace Plunkett's.[6] Indeed the latter book, in this respect, considering its title and pretensions, is almost rendered worthless. A man sets out to describe the condition of a patient suffering from cancer, and the one thing he will not discuss is—cancer. He will dispassionately and even illuminatingly discuss every by-effect of the malady, but he is ignorant of the fact of the malady itself, or else is professionally precluded from dealing with it. For many of the evils that many recent writers discuss have their proximate cause in the lack of political wisdom. And the only road to political wisdom is by way of political responsibility. A people long suffering from political servitude have the vices of slavery: lack of constructive political faculty, lack of initiative, lack of the wise compromise that comes of action; though notwithstanding these defects the Irish people, on the whole, have shown at the least as much political sagacity as the English.

But to recognise and proclaim these things does not by any means preclude the right or the propriety of internal criticism. Rather does that criticism come the more appropriately from those who are alive to the main political evil. And whilst demanding the redress of that evil, it becomes necessary, concurrently, to raise our own canons of conduct and scrutinise our own standards of thinking. Sir Horace Plunkett in one passage in his book observes:—

"The revolution in the industrial order, and its consequences, such as the concentration of immense populations within restricted areas, have brought with them social and moral evils that must be met with new weapons. In the interests of religion itself, principles first expounded to a Syrian community with the most elementary physical needs and the simplest of avocations, have to be taught in

---

[6] Important commentators on Irish life and politics. Plunkett published *Ireland in the New Century* in 1904; for Young, see p. xxx.

their application to the conditions of the most complex social organisation and economic life. Taking people as we find them, it may be said with truth that their lives must be wholesome before they can be holy; and while a voluntary asceticism may hate its justification, it behoves a Church to see that its members, while fully acknowledging the claims of another life, should develop the qualities which make for well-being in this life."—*Ireland in the New Century*, pp. 103–104.

Some of us, of course might cavil at Sir Horace's implication that it is possible to really combine concern for "another life" with effective regard for the well-being of this. The essential business of the Churches all round and the essence of the Church ideal is to prepare men for the "hereafter"; and the affairs of this world are only treated as incidental to such preparation. The true logical antithesis of this view is the positivist and scientific ideal which, taking humanity as the highest we know, regards the well-being of humanity here as the greatest end for which we can work, and frankly accepting the fact that this life is the only one of which we have real knowledge, ignores all distracting hypothesis.

None the less, however, is it well and courageous for Sir Horace Plunkett to put the secular ideal in his own words and fashion. It is easy for the popular press to sneer at him on this score, for it is sure of a response from the religious multitude. But it is precisely in a country where the "principles" [of Christianity] are professed on all sides with a heartiness almost unknown elsewhere, that we have the eternal sectarian wrangles, here over the creed of a dispensary doctor or an inspector of schools, there over the religion of an unfortunate foundling who may be "damned" without its knowledge by the votes of a Board of Guardians[7] consisting for the most part of publicans and slum-owners.

One would on first thought conclude that the spectacle of such sectarian squabbling would perforce raise in an ordinarily intelligent people doubts of the genuineness of the creeds that could stimulate it. But such is not the case; it seems to require a definitely humanist philosophy and a humanitarian enthusiasm to realise that the welfare of humanity as such is the greatest and noblest end for which humanity can work. But humanity in Ireland has not yet come into its inheritance. In a recent review of Mr. Filson Young's book *Ireland at the*

---

[7] Elected officials charged with dispensing aid for the poor. See "Ivy Day in the Committee Room" p.xxx n.5.

Cross Roads the Rev. Dr. McDonald in an article in the *Freeman's Journal* wrote: "Consider the real Ireland too. In that sad country one thing only has prospered, as Mr. Young admits, the Church; and she is based on a system of almost absolute self-government." So far as Dr. McDonald intended this as an argument for self-government, as against Mr. Young, I am with him. But he does not seem to have realized the ominous significance of his analogy. The Church has flourished amidst universal decay. Precisely. In a country warped and injured by lack of political freedom, it would be curious if intellectual freedom prospered. The Irish people, trampled by alien and unsympathetic rule, have looked with aching eyes to a heaven of bliss, and they have, more or less contentedly, lain down in their chains soothed by the hope of after-reward. If Ireland is to be saved we must surely change all that; the people must turn their energies from dreaming of another world to the task of bettering and beautifying the things of this. It is nobler to make a happy human home than to raise a dozen granite temples for a worship which does not need them; it is a greater thing to rescue one human heart from despair than to have kept every letter of the religious law. We need in Ireland a spirit of intellectual freedom, and a recognition of the supremacy of humanity. And so far from this prescription being offered as a substitute for national freedom it is urged as a necessity of a true national ideal. For the synthesis of much recent criticism is this: intellectual freedom and political freedom are not opposites. Rightly understood, intellectual freedom and political freedom are one.

JAMES JOYCE, "THE SOUL OF IRELAND"

From the *Daily Express* (Dublin), 26 March 1903.

Aristotle finds at the beginning of all speculation the feeling of wonder, a feeling proper to childhood, and if speculation be proper to the middle period of life it is natural that one should look to the crowning period of life for the fruit of speculation, wisdom itself. But nowadays people have greatly confused childhood and middle life and old age; those who succeed in spite of civilisation in reaching old age seem to have less and less wisdom, and children who are usually put to some business as soon as they can walk and talk, seem to have more and more "common sense;" and, perhaps, in the future little boys with long beards will stand aside and applaud, while old men in short trousers play hand-ball against the side of a house.

This may even happen in Ireland, if Lady Gregory has truly set forth the old age of her country. In her new book she has left legends and heroic youth far behind, and has explored in a land almost fabulous in its sorrow and senility. Half of her book is an account of old men and old women in the West of Ireland. These old people are full of stories about giants and witches, and dogs and black-handled knives, and they tell their stories one after another at great length and with many repetitions (for they are people of leisure) by the fire or in the yard of a workhouse. It is difficult to judge well of their charms and herb-healing, for that is the province of those who are learned in these matters and can compare the customs of countries, and, indeed, it is well not to know these magical-sciences, for if the wind changes while you are cutting wild camomile you will lose your mind.

But one can judge more easily of their stories. These stories appeal to some feeling which is certainly not that feeling of wonder which is the beginning of all speculation. The story-tellers are old, and their imagination is not the imagination of childhood. The story-teller preserves the strange machinery of fairyland, but his mind is feeble and sleepy. He begins one story and wanders from it into another story, and none of the stories has any satisfying imaginative wholeness, none of them is like Sir John Daw's poem that cried tink in the close.[1] Lady Gregory is conscious of this, for she often tries to lead the speaker back to his story by questions, and when the story has become hopelessly involved, she tries to establish some wholeness by keeping only the less involved part; sometimes she listens "half interested and half impatient." In fine, her book, wherever it treats of the "folk," sets forth in the fulness of its senility a class of mind which Mr. Yeats has set forth with such delicate scepticism in his happiest book, "The Celtic Twilight."

Something of health and naturalness, however, enters with Raftery, the poet.[2] He had a terrible tongue, it seems and would make a satirical poem for a very small offence. He could make love-poems, too (though Lady Gregory finds a certain falseness in the western love-poems), and repentant poems. Raftery though he be the last of the great bardic procession, has much of the bardic tradition about him. He took shelter one day from the rain under a bush; at first the bush kept out the rain, and he made verses praising it, but after a while it let the rain through, and he made verses dispraising it.

---

[1] Reference to Ben Johnson's comedy, *Epicoene, or The Silent Woman* (1609). Here a satirical reference to having good form ("tink" means tinkles or rhymes).

[2] Anthony Raftery (or Antaine Ó Reachtaire, 1784-1835) was an Iris-language poet considered one of the last of the traditional Irish bards. He did not write out his texts, but they survived in oral tradition and were first collected by Douglas Hyde and Lady Gregory.

Lady Gregory translates some of his verses, and she also translates some West Irish ballads and some poems by Dr. Douglas Hyde. She completes her book with translations of four one-act plays by Dr. Douglas Hyde, three of which have for their central figure that legendary person, who is vagabond and poet, and even saint at times, while the fourth play is called a "nativity" play. The dwarf-drama (if one may use that term) is a form of art which is improper and ineffectual, but it is easy to understand why it finds favour with an age which has pictures that are "nocturnes," and writers like Mallarmé and the composer of "Recapitulation."[3] The dwarf-drama is accordingly to be judged as an entertainment, and Dr. Douglas Hyde is certainly entertaining in the "Twisting of the Rope," and Lady Gregory has succeeded better with her verse-translations here than elsewhere, as these four lines may show:

> *I have heard the melodious harp*
> *On the streets of Cork playing to us:*
> *More melodious by far I thought your voice,*
> *More melodious by far your mouth than that.*

This book, like so many other books of our time, is in part picturesque and in part an indirect or direct utterance of the central belief of Ireland. Out of the material and spiritual battle which has gone so hardly with her Ireland has emerged with many memories of beliefs, and with one belief—a belief in the incurable ignobility of the forces that have overcome her—and Lady Gregory, whose old men and women seem to be almost their own judges when they tell their wandering stories, might add to the passage from Whitman which forms her dedication, Whitman's ambiguous word for the vanquished—"Battles are lost in the spirit in which they are won."[4]

---

[3] James McNeil Whistler (1834–1903) was an American painter of impressionist night scenes; Stéphane Mallarmé (1842–1898) and Catulle Mendès (1841–1909) were French Symbolist poets.

[4] From Walt Whitman (1819–1892) *Leaves of Grass* (1855).

After the Famine: Emigration and Exile

JOYCE IS often celebrated for his courage in leaving Ireland in 1904, casting off what Stephen Dedalus (in *A Portrait of the Artist as a Young Man*) calls the "nets" of nation, family, and religion. His decision, however, was hardly unique: Joyce and his partner, Nora Barnacle, were among the thousands who left that year—the tail end of the massive waves of emigration that transformed the island. From 1841 to 1851, Ireland lost 20% of its population—the result of a potato blight that decimated the agrarian economy and led to the Great Famine of 1845–1849. Forced evictions, poverty, and starvation led to as many as one million deaths, creating a widespread hostility toward the imperial government in London that many considered indifferent or ineffective in its response to the disaster. As rural populations streamed into the cities, agricultural communities collapsed and desperate families emigrated across the globe, in what amounted to an Irish diaspora. These departures became such a regular and permanent part of life that families regularly held what were known as "American wakes," adapting the traditional Irish funeral ceremony to bid farewell to emigrants. Those who set sail left behind empty cottages and vacant fields as well as a growing sense of alarm that Ireland itself was gradually being emptied. The population finally stabilized at about three million in 1904, just as Joyce bid farewell.

Dubliners chronicles this sense of lack, exile, and even failure—themes that featured prominently in the writings of other novelists, journalists, and social reformers at the time. Indeed, that odd word "gnomon" at the beginning of "The Sisters," which describes a kind of gap or missing piece, gestures subtly toward the more pronounced absences visible all across Ireland. Although the stories rarely make direct reference to the Famine and its aftermath, the sense of emptiness, despair, and paralysis it generated is pervasive. Joyce wrote many of these stories after he had left Ireland, and despite being set in the city, they almost all contain references to those who have vanished, from the shades who stalk through the pages of "The Dead" to the dying mother in "Eveline" whose mysterious and untranslatable command helps arrest her daughter's flight. Those who remain behind, furthermore, find themselves in often untenable and even disastrous situations, casualties of what Joyce called "the soul of that hemiplegia or paralysis which many consider a city."

This unit opens with excerpts from accounts of the Famine in newspapers and magazines as the disaster unfolded. Tales of terror and tragedy like the one recorded dispassionately by the *Cork Examiner* were commonplace in 1846 and 1847 as the poor and starving sought relief in ports and cities. Entire villages, like Moveen, were abandoned, deserted to become ghost towns. Across the half century from 1841 to 1891, as the graph makes dramatically evident, the region that would become the Republic of Ireland lost nearly half of its population. Filson Young takes a stark measure of the situation in 1903 in *Ireland at the Cross Roads: An Essay in Explanation*—a deft, often devastating picture of decline, leavened with tenuous hope for a cultural and economic revival. Young, a novelist as well as a critic and journalist, read *Dubliners* for his own publisher Grant Richards and recommended publication, likely seeing in Joyce's narratives of "hemiplegia" the cultural illness he sought to diagnose.

"MORE STARVATION"

From the *Cork Examiner*, December 4, 1846.

William J. Maher, Esq., one of our County Coroners, held an inquest at Corbetstown, in this county (midway between this city and Castlecomer) on view of the bodies of four individuals, found drowned in a dyke on the townsland of Webbsborough, on Sunday last. It appeared from the evidence at the inquest that the mother and three children had been in that neighbourhood for some days in a state of very great destitution. On Friday last they had been relieved[1] at the house of Hugh Muldowney, a respectable farmer living at Corbetstown; they were subsequently seen loitering on the road at Webbsborough—the mother, about 30 years old, appeared to be in an unconscious state, probably from mental anxiety and hunger.

---

[1] Fed.

The bodies were brought to a house on the road side, the nearest that could be procured, by the police—they presented a truly heart-rending spectacle, partially covered with filthy rags saturated with mud, and frozen, having been exposed to the inclemency of the weather. The hand of one child, and part of the foot of another, had been devoured by rats. Doctor Gwydir, of Freshford, made a minute post mortem examination of the bodies of the mother and eldest daughter, a child about 9 years old. The Doctor was unable to detect in the stomach or the bowels of the mother a trace of food having entered for more than twenty hours before death. The child's stomach contained a very small quantity of half-digested potatoes. The following was the verdict of the jury:— "We find that deceased and her three children's death's were caused by drowning, and we find from the post mortem examinations made by Doctor Gwydir on two of the bodies, that they were in a state of hunger bordering on starvation, but how the bodies came into the dyke of water, whether by accident or design on the part of the mother, we have no evidence to show."—*Kilkenny Journal.*

"The Depopulation of Ireland"

From the *Illustrated London News*, May 10, 1851.

The Census Returns, when published, will enable us to ascertain, in some degree, the extent of the combined ravages of famine and pestilence, in the first place, and of despair and emigration, in the second, in the depopulation of Ireland. But even these returns, authentic as they will be, cannot be complete; for the emigration that has gone on since the census was taken, and which still continues, will compel the statist to make large deductions from the amount which the census will yield, if he wishto ascertain the real number of the Irish people. The annals of the modern world offer no such record as that presented in the history of Ireland, since the memorable and deplorable years of the potato famine, and of the pestilence that followed in its track. The splendid emigrant ships that ply between Liverpool and New York, and which have sufficed in previous years to carry to the shores of America an Irish emigration, amounting on the average to 250,000 souls per annum, have, during the present spring, been found insufficient to transport to the States the increasing swarms of Irish who have resolved to try in the New World to gain the independence which has been denied them in the old.

"Emigration," says a letter dated a few days back, "is proceeding to an extent altogether unprecedented; but much less, in proportion, from Ulster[1] than the other provinces. From most of the southern counties, the small farmers are hastening in vast numbers; and even in Leinster the mania for emigration prevails far and wide. The remittances from America are far greater in amount than in any previous year, and considerable sums are paid by the banks and by private commercial establishments, from day to day, on orders from the United States. From some districts in Ulster, numbers of the smaller tenantry are taking their departure. From one of the principle estates in Monaghan nearly one thousand persons of the cottier class[2] are about to be sent to Canada at the expense of the landlord, who, it is stated, has made arrangements for providing them with a comfortable passage, and some small allowance of money to each family after reaching the port of their destination."

The number of emigrant vessels proceeding to America direct from Irish ports is quite unprecedented, and is one of the most extraordinary circumstances of the time. Within eight days, the following eleven vessels, carrying 1568 passengers, sailed from the single port of Cork:— *the Dominique*, for Quebec, 150 passengers; the *Don*, for New York, 160; the *Lockwoods*, for New York, 280; the *Marchioness of Bute*, for Quebec, 120; the *Sara*, for Boston, 104; the *Solway*, for New York, 196; the *Try Again*, for Quebec, 130; the *Favourite*, for Boston, 120; the *Clarinda*, for New York, 100; the *Swift*, for Boston, 120; the *Field Marshal Radetzsky*, for New York, 88 passengers. In addition to those vessels, the *Hotspur* went down the Cork river, on Tuesday, with 100 paupers on board, from the Kenmare Union-house.

But what is most remarkable is, that, while this enormous emigration is going on, leading to a fear in some parts of the country that sufficient people will not be left to cultivate the land, the owners or mortgagees of Irish estates continue to evict their tenantry with as much virulence as ever. The *Galway Vindicator* states:—"There were 195 ejectments entered—13 at the suit of the trustees of A. H. Lynch, one of Mathew S. Coneys, and 181 were brought by the Law Life Insurance Company; and of 183 entries of civil bills, 87 were at the suit of the insurance company. With the exception of three or four, the ejectments were all undefended. They were disposed of at the rate of one each minute; so that, taking an average of five souls to each family ejected, we will have 300 per hour, and in the entire 905 human beings cast upon poor-house relief."

---

[1] A predominantly Protestant and pro-Union district in North Ireland, partially shielded by its manufacturing base from the worst effects of the Famine.

[2] Tenant farmers.

The same journal estimates the total evictions in Connemara during the present season at upwards of 4000. In Limerick and Kerry the same system is carried on; the evicted remaining in the union workhouse until remittances arrive from their friends in America, when they shake from their feet the dust of their native land, and rejoin their friends and relations across the Atlantic.

The deserted village of Moveen, *London Illustrated News*, December 22, 1849.

Population of Ireland (Republic), 1841–1946

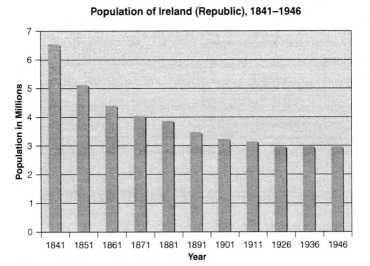

Population of Ireland (Republic), 1841–1946
Data from the Central Statistics Office of Ireland

FILSON YOUNG, "THE DOUBLE LEAK"

From *Ireland at the Cross Roads: An Essay in Explanation*
(London: Grant Richards, 1903).

The decrease in the population in Ireland is a gross fact which the simplest mind can lay hold of as an indication of something seriously amiss in the national condition; but the causes that lie at the root of it are a fruitful subject of difference among sociologists of the profoundest thought. The train of causes on the economic side do not take one back very far. The population diminishes because the people emigrate; they emigrate because there is not work for them to do in their own country; there is not work for them to do because—and here the reasons spread out into a variety of figures and statistics which, however accurate and convincing they may be, cannot but leave one with the feeling that the last word has not been said on the subject. In an earlier chapter I mentioned what every one who knows the country knows as a matter of course; that the Irish are not discontented by nature, do not want money for its own sake, and are all too capable of dwelling happily even in extreme poverty. The prospect of lucrative employment and high wages is not enough to account for the continual stream of emigration amongst a people who bear a passionate devotion to the soil that bred them; we must look deeper for the moving causes of their discontent. We shall find that it is more spiritual than material, that the hunger which drives them westward is a diviner and more compelling thing than the hunger of the body, and that when they go forth from their own poor and beloved soil it is in quest not so much of ampler means of life as of life itself.

Queenstown[1] is the great physical leak in Ireland through which, during the last fifty years, her life has been steadily drained, and through which it is still draining, although on a decreasing scale. The decrease is not yet because of any considerable improvement in the conditions of life, but because the source of the outgoing stream has fallen so low that it cannot continue to flow at the same pressure. The emigrant himself has been the subject of innumerable poems and outpourings of sympathy, and it is still customary for those who like to have their feelings harrowed to go to Queenstown and see the departure of ships carrying emigrants. But it is not by the emigrant himself that our sympathies are most needed. He, at any rate, when the pangs of parting are over, is going

---

[1] Renamed Cobh in 1922—a major seaport on the southern coast.

to a new life, how new, how full, and how rich in wide possibilities he cannot know until he has plunged into it. The Irishman in America is not so picturesque a person as the Irishman in his own country, and undoubtedly he loses some of those qualities which flourish abundantly in the poorer soil of his life at home; but still he goes to a world in which he can live, in which his energies and hopes are encouraged, and which does not stifle and wither his growth as a human being. The truly melancholy prospect is that of the place which he leaves, the people whom he leaves, and the conditions which cast him out. He is right to go; and the country that wishes to keep him must first of all make life possible.

But there is another leakage in the life of Ireland, strangely involved as regards its causes with the physical emigration, and that is the mental leakage, the increase of lunacy. It is not a subject which lends itself to picturesque treatment, and it has none of the obviously pathetic and dramatic qualities that inspire the writers of patriotic poems and wailful songs. But as surely and as steadily as the physical life of Ireland has been drained out of her by emigration, just so surely and steadily is her mental and intellectual vigour being tapped and drained off into the vacant world of lunacy. The healthy mind is apt to revolt at the thought, and to assert with loud assurance that the thing is untrue and exaggerated. Exaggerated it may be by some people, but when all exaggeration has been allowed for, the cold fact remains that lunacy in Ireland is on the increase, and that it is already in excessive proportion even as compared with other Western countries in which lunacy is also increasing. There is always a tendency amongst people not to credit things like this; they are so hateful and mysterious that we tend to persuade ourselves into the comfortable belief that matters are not so bad as they are represented to be. The whole subject is one which sane people instinctively avoid; and yet all those gloomy buildings with their inhabitants of vacant and perverted mind are a part of the burden of our civilisation, and are a result of certain causes which we cannot afford to ignore.

In Ireland particularly, the whole subject of lunacy is one which I think demands a very full and expert inquiry. The methods adopted in the certifying of lunatics seem to me far from satisfactory. I think I am right in saying that the names of two dispensary doctors are required on a certificate; they receive a fee if a certificate of lunacy is granted, but if after examination of the patient they decide that he or she is not a lunatic and that no certificate is required, they get no fee. This is surely an unwise and dangerous way of conducting such important inquiries in a country where medical men find it hard to make even a modest livelihood. Such a suggestion does not involve any reflection upon medical men as a whole; but the line which divides a lunatic from a sane person is admittedly a very narrow one, and it is not always an easy matter to decide whether or not a certificate ought to be granted. A full inquiry might possibly reveal the fact that in Ireland we are even manufacturing lunatics by the very machinery which is designed for their treatment; for once a person whose mind is at all disturbed in balance is confined in a county lunatic asylum, there is not much chance of his sanity being saved or preserved. It is a ghastly suggestion, and one would gladly think that it was without foundation; but that, at any rate, is a point which expert inquiry could easily settle.

Even this is but a small thing compared with the greater social causes which go to produce this mental blight in Ireland. There are various theories with regard to the principal causes of the disease. Some attribute it to the constant drinking of bad and fiery spirits; but then the men are the chief consumers of spirits, and the men are in a minority amongst the lunatics. Others attribute it to excessive indulgence in tea, a beverage which among the Irish is quite poisonous owing to their method of keeping it for ever stewing and brewing until it is thick and black and bitter. Others, again, regard lunacy in Ireland not so much as an increasing disease as a phenomenon presented by the survival of the unfittest[2]—that is to say, a remainder of the less robust and capable left when all the strong-minded and able-bodied have emigrated. All these, I think, may be contributing causes, but none of them seems like a primary cause. The third view would account satisfactorily enough for a large ratio of the lunacy in proportion to the remaining population of the country. But it would hardly account satisfactorily for the fact that the gross annual number of lunatics certified increases, while the number of emigrants, as well as the gross population of the country, diminishes.

At the risk of appearing to be governed by an obsession, I must go back and say that the chief cause of this mental rot appears to me to be the social desolation of the people, working upon minds weakened

---

[2] Play on the phrase coined by Herbert Spencer (1820-1903) after reading Charles Darwin's *Origin of Species* (1864): "This survival of the fittest ... is that which Mr. Darwin has called 'natural selection,' or the preservation of favoured races in the struggle for life."

and demoralised by religion. The physical body of Ireland is frail and weak, but its religious heart is strong, nervous, and vital; there are no restraints or checks upon it; it feeds upon the mind and the emotions; and being admittedly the stronger life, it wastes and devours the already enfeebled independent life of the mind. The perfect lunatic is a person whose mind is entirely occupied by abstractions, who has lost his touch with material things, in whom all ideas are detached, or, at any rate, do not bear that ordered relation to each other which by common consent we regard as sanity. And that is exactly the condition of mind which peasant life in Ireland tends to produce. It must be clearly understood that I do not refer to religious mania, but to ordinary lunacy. Some people would expect to find religious mania prevalent in a social condition such as I have been describing, but it is not so in Ireland. The reason, I take it, is twofold. The Roman Catholic religion does not produce, even in unbalanced minds, that revolting form of melancholia which induces people to sing hymns and divest themselves of all their clothing; that comes from religious systems which merely excite emotion, and do not satisfy it. But the Catholic religion, like all well-organised religions, is too protective and satisfying to excite religious mania; it at least takes care of its subjects, and provides them with all emotional necessaries. But there are, I have no doubt, hundreds of people in convents and monasteries who are really religious lunatics, and would be certified as such if they were in the outer world. As it is, they are honoured for their remarkable piety.

I have spoken of social isolation; that is one great cause of mental weakness. The contact of human minds with each other, the exchange of ideas, the development of knowledge, observation, and mental activity induced by human intercourse, are among the great strengthening forces which thousands of Irish people are virtually deprived of. Added to this social sterility, you have absence of occupation for the individual mind and initiative, for the mere business of living from hand to mouth occupies only a very small portion of a healthy man's activities. And in the pastoral counties, where the ratio of lunatics is higher than in any other part of Ireland, both these conditions are extreme. The life of a human being who spends his time drowsing in a field and watching the cattle feeding furnishes no grist for his intellectual mill; and when, in addition, he has no social life or intercourse to provide him with human interest, his mind must necessarily tend to vacancy. And then comes religion and plants itself in this fallow soil, filling it with ideas which bear no relationship to its material environment, teaching it that the very earth by which, if it were alive, it might educate and develop itself, is an unreal and

passing dream; and that the true life is revealed in a series of statements and dogmas, and, above all, in that most dangerous and weak-
ening of all influences, a blind faith in things which are to be taken on
trust like a physical dose taken with eyes shut and nostrils held. You
have there an ideal condition for the production of those melancholy
phantasms which constitute the mental world of the lunatic.

There is another and still more unpleasant side to the question
which I have only the heart to touch upon lightly, and that is to be
found in the effect of the rigid sexual discipline imposed by the
Church. For this absorbing, compelling, and inspiring influence is
choked from its very birth in the Irish people. That divine force
which can sweep us entirely outside ourselves, which builds the his-
tories of empires and of races, is in this case shackled and directed
by the ecclesiastical police force. Like the Danish king sitting before
the great flood of the sea and commanding its movements,[3] the Irish
priests have commanded that this great primitive force of nature
shall hold back its tides at their bidding, or flow only in the chan-
nels ordained for it by the Church.

The letter of their ordinances seems to be obeyed; but the great
spirit of nature still breathes and moves according to her intention,
unchanged and unweakened by all the incantations of all the
churches. Its human results they do in a way dam up and divert; but,
like all interferences with the course of nature, it is but a diversion
that they produce, and one that makes for a greater and more tragic
unhappiness than that which they sought to prevent. For the frustrated sexual life of this unhappy community, weakened as it may be
by discipline, must ultimately find its escape and effluence. It but
turns from a beneficent to a bitter power when its purpose is denied
it, but it is only the quality and not the power itself that changes.
There may be no bastards[4] in Ireland, but a hundred bastards would
be a more gracious and healthy sign than one lunatic; and if you follow back the course of this strange, perverted, embittered stream of
nature; if you go to the lunatic asylums and question those who have
charge of them, and study their pathology, you will find an unbro-
ken line of evidence joining the strange unnatural flower of so-called
chastity with the ugly fungus of sexual lunacy. It is not that the Irish

---

[3] Reference to Canute (985–1035), the Viking king who set his throne by the sea and
(fruitlessly) ordered the waves not wet his robes. He is supposed to have then said
"Let all men know how empty and worthless is the power of kings, for there is none
worthy of the name, but He whom heaven, earth, and sea obey by eternal laws."

[4] Children born to unmarried parents, and thus without rights to maintenance or
inheritance.

are by nature what is called unchaste, and that this great moral policing has been necessary on social grounds. The very reverse is the case. Warm-hearted as they are, they are cool-blooded; and nowhere in the world is the family a more sacred institution than it is in Ireland. So far as statistics are concerned there might be little enough change if this ban of the Church upon free intercourse between the sexes were suddenly removed; but what an upspringing of life and happiness, of incentive and industry there would be!

Evidence for all these statements would make dreary and unsavoury reading, but I do not think they will be contradicted by any person whose knowledge of Ireland is sympathetic and unbiassed. I will give but one more ugly fact, and that is that in the lunatic asylums of Ireland you will find a numerical majority of physically healthy young women of a marriageable age. And even among those who do marry the evil still persists; for the priests, in their terror of what the Church describes as "mortal sin," rush the people into early marriages in which mutual choice, as often as not, plays little or no part. The large families produced by these early marriages contribute materially to the two leaks in Irish life; for where the means are so small and the families so large, proper feeding is impossible, and the tendency to lunacy frightfully increased among the weaklings; while those who do grow up and are strong have no means of support from the soil which produced them, and join, in their turn, the stream of emigration.

So here again the evidence of facts points out the Church as a chief offender. Anti-national and anti-social in all but a very narrow sense, it must stand to be judged by the state of the society over which it holds an undisputed sway. It is a society rotten at the heart, and consequently rotten throughout. It is enslaved, and therefore its activities are restricted; it is without social admixture, and therefore it is without gladness of heart; its intellect is dominated and therefore it produces little or nothing and cannot keep even what it produces. Such strong intellectual life as it does produce cannot exist in its environment, and therefore must seek another and more congenial atmosphere. The crowning indictment of the religious social system of Ireland is that a strong mind, a brave heart, a life that refuses to keep within the boundaries assigned to it by the iron and inhuman law, cannot exist there, cannot come to itself there, to be stimulated or regulated. And so the emigrant ships are filled, and so also is preserved that melancholy survival—the survival of the unfittest.

Composition, Publication, Early Reviews

ORDER OF COMPOSITION

Joyce began what would become *Dubliners* with three short stories in an agricultural magazine, the *Irish Homestead*, in 1904. The bitter ironies and urban settings of "The Sisters," "Eveline," and "After the Race" were uncomfortably out of place next to advertisements for dairy machinery and creamery supplies. The paper's fiction editor, having hoped for something "simple," "rural," and "live-making" that might appeal "to the common understanding," asked Joyce for no further contributions. Not discouraged, Joyce began to develop these early pieces into a larger collection in the summer and winter of 1905, completing eight of the fifteen stories as he struggled to set up his new life in Trieste. The final piece, "The Dead," was not completed until almost a year later, while a preliminary manuscript was being sent to potential publishers. The collection, Joyce told his brother Stanislaus, progressed through stories of childhood ("The Sisters," "An Encounter," and "Araby"), to adolescence ("The Boarding House," "After the Race," and "Eveline"), maturity ("Clay," "Counterparts," and "A Painful Case"), and then public life ("Ivy Day in the Committee Room," "A Mother," and "Grace"). Although Joyce continued to tinker with the titles and their order, his projected arc remains visible.

PUBLICATION AND RECEPTION

Joyce fought for nearly a decade to see *Dubliners* into print—a process that began, promisingly enough, in 1905 when Dublin publisher Grant Richards first offered him a contract. In February 1906, the printer refused to set "Two Gallants," fearing that its sexual innuendo might

Order of Composition

1904	July	"The Sisters" (revised June 1906)
	September	"Eveline"
	October	"After the Race"
1905	January	"Clay" (originally, "Hallow Eve"; lightly revised 1906)
	July	"The Boarding House"
		"Counterparts"
	August	"A Painful Case" (revised 1906)
		"Ivy Day in the Committee Room"
	September	"An Encounter"
		"A Mother"
	October	"Araby"
	November	"Grace"
1906	February	"Two Gallants"
	April	"A Little Cloud"
1907	September	"The Dead"

subject him to prosecution for obscenity. An argument between Richard and Joyce ensued, as the editor then raised objections to other stories, too, including "Counterparts" and "Grace." Joyce refused to make any substantive changes to his manuscript and in October, Richards finally canceled the contract. Over the next three years Joyce continued to work on the collection, adding "The Dead" and even contemplating a companion volume titled *Provincials*. Some dozen other publishers declined *Dubliners* as too risky, too local, or too dreary. By 1909, however, Joyce had new a contract with Maunsel and Co., only to have an editor demand changes to the crude language in "Ivy Day in the Committee Room." "A Curious History" recounts this ordeal, along with the cancellation of yet another contract. Finally, in 1914, Grant Richards reconsidered and brought out *Dubliners* without requiring any additional changes. In 1916, B. W. Huebsch published the first American edition, the basis of this Longman edition.

On the cusp or World War One, Joyce's first work of fiction received only slight notice. A brief, unsigned review in the *Times Literary Supplement* deemed it "admirably written," but suggested it would be of interest only to those with a taste for "the drab." Other reviews echoed the sentiment that good writing had been imperfectly mixed with dull subject matter. Poet and avant-garde impresario, Ezra Pound, however, admired *Dubliners* and became one of Joyce's life-long promoters and advocates. During Joyce's difficulties in securing a publisher, Pound placed "A Curious History" in the January 15, 1914 issue of the *Egoist*, an influential British magazine that published the new, often experimental writing we call modernism. Then, when *Dubliners* appeared, he reviewed it favorably—one of the only substantive notices the book received. Pound also helped arrange for *A Portrait of the Artist as a Young Man*, Joyce's first novel, to appear serially in the pages of the *Egoist*.

JAMES JOYCE, "A CURIOUS HISTORY"
From *Sinn Féin*.

Via della Barriera Vecchia 32 III.,
Trieste, Austria

SIR,

May I ask you to publish this letter, which throws some light on the present conditions of authorship in England and Ireland?

Nearly six years ago Mr. Grant Richards, publisher, of London, signed a contract with me for the publication of a book of stories written by me, entitled "Dubliners." Some ten months later he wrote asking me to omit one of the stories and passages in others which, as he said, his printer refused to set up. I declined to do either, and a correspondence began between Mr. Grant Richards and myself which lasted more than three months. I went to an international jurist in Rome (where I lived then) and was advised to omit. I declined to do so, and the MS.[1] was returned to me, the publisher refusing to publish, notwithstanding his pledged printed word, the contract remaining in my possession.

Six months afterwards a Mr. Hone wrote to me from Marseilles to ask me to submit the MS. to Messrs. Maunsel, publishers, of Dublin. I did so; and after about a year, in July, 1909, Messrs. Maunsel signed a contract with me for the publication of the book on or before 1ˢᵗ September, 1910. In December, 1909, Messrs. Maunsel's manager begged me to alter a passage in one of the stories, "Ivy Day in the Committee Room," wherein some reference was made to Edward VII. I agreed to do so, much against my will, and altered one or two phrases. Messrs. Maunsel continually postponed the date of publication and in the end

[1] Manuscript.

wrote, asking me to omit the passage or to change it radically. I declined to do either, pointing out that Mr. Grant Richards, of London, had raised no objection to the passage when Edward VII was alive, and that I could not see why an Irish publisher would raise an objection to it when Edward VII had passed into history. I suggested arbitration or a deletion of the passage with a prefatory note of explanation by me, but Messrs. Maunsel would agree to neither. As Mr. Hone (who had written to me in the first instance) disclaimed all responsibility in the matter and any connection with the firm I took the opinion of a solicitor in Dublin, who advised me to omit the passage, informing me that as I had no domicile in the United Kingdom I could not sue Messrs. Maunsel for breach of contract unless I paid £100 into court, and that even if I paid £100 into court and sued them, I should have no chance of getting a verdict in my favor from a Dublin jury if the passage in dispute could be taken as offensive in any way to the late King. I wrote then to the present king, George V, enclosing a printed proof of the story, with the passage therein marked, and begging him to inform me whether in his view the passage (certain allusions made by a person of the story in the idiom of his social class) should be withheld from publication as offensive to the memory of his father. His Majesty's private secretary sent me this reply:—

Buckingham Palace

The private secretary is commanded to acknowledge the receipt of Mr. James Joyce's letter of the 1ˢᵗ instant, and to inform him that it is inconsistent with rule for his Majesty to express his opinion in such cases. The enclosures are returned herewith.

11 August, 1911.

Here is the passage in dispute:

—But look here, John, said Mr O'Connor. Why should we welcome the King of England? Didn't Parnell himself ...

—Parnell, said Mr Henchy, is dead. Now, here's the way I look at it. Here's this chap come to the throne after his owl' mother keeping him out of it till the man was grey. He's a man of the world, and he means well by us. He's a jolly fine decent fellow, if y'ask me, and no damn nonsense about him. He just says to himself: *The owl' one never went to see these wild Irish. Be Christ, I'll go meself and see what they're like.* And are we going to insult the man when he comes over here on a friendly visit? Eh? Isn't that right, Crofton?

Mr Crofton nodded his head.

But after all now, said Mr Lyons argumentatively, King Edward's life, you know, is not the very ...

—Let bygones be bygones, said Mr Henchy. I admire the man personally. He's just an ordinary knockabout like you and me. He's fond of his glass of grog and he's a bit of a rake, perhaps, and he's a good sportsman. Damn it, can't we Irish play fair?

I wrote seven years ago and hold two contracts for its publication. I am not even allowed to explain my case in a prefatory note: wherefore, as I cannot see in any quarter a chance that my rights will be protected, I hereby give Messrs. Maunsel publicly permission to publish this story with what changes or deletions they may please to make, and shall hope that what they may publish may resemble that to the writing of which I gave thought and time. Their attitude as an Irish publishing firm may be judged by Irish public opinion. I, as a writer, protest against the systems (legal, social, and ceremonious) which have brought me to this pass.

Thanking you for your courtesy,
I am, Sir,
Your obedient servant,
James Joyce
18 August, 1911.

I waited nine months after the publication of this letter. Then I went to Ireland and entered into negotiations with Messrs. Maunsel. They asked me to omit from the collection the story, "An Encounter," passages in "Two Gallants," the "Boarding House," "A Painful Case," and to change everywhere through the book the names of restaurants, cake-shops, railway stations, public-houses, laundries, bars, and other places of business. After having argued against their point of view day after day for six weeks and after having laid the matter before two solicitors (who, while they informed me that the publishing firm had made a breach of contract, refused to take up my case or to allow their names to be associated with it in any way), I consented in despair to all these changes on condition that the book were brought out without delay and the original text were restored in future editions, if such were called for. Then Messrs. Maunsel asked me to pay into the bank as security £1,000 or to find two sureties of £500 each. I declined to do either; and they then wrote to me, informing me that they would not publish the book, altered or unaltered, and that if I did not make them an offer to cover their losses on printing it they would sue me to recover same. I offered to pay sixty per cent. of the cost of printing the first edition of one thousand copies if the edition were made over to my order. This offer was accepted, and I arranged with my brother in Dublin to publish and sell the book for me. On the morning when the draft and agreement were to be signed the publishers informed me that the matter was at an end because the printer refused to hand over the copies. I took legal advice upon this and was informed that the printer could not claim the money due to him by the publisher until he had handed over the copies. I then went to the printer. His foreman told me that the printer had decided to forego all claim to the money due to him. I asked whether the printer would hand over the complete edition to a London or Continental firm or to my brother or to me if he were fully indemnified. He said that the copies would never leave his printing-house, and added that the type had been broken up, and the entire edition of one thousand copies would be burnt the next day. I left Ireland the next day, bringing with me a printed copy of the book which I had obtained from the publisher.

James Joyce
Via Donato Bramante 4, II.,
Trieste,
30th November, 1913.

UNSIGNED REVIEW

From the *Times Literary Supplement*, June 18, 1914.

Dubliners is a collection of short stories, the scene of which is laid in Dublin. Too comprehensive for the theme, the title is nevertheless typical of a book which purports, we assume, to describe life as it is and yet regards it from one aspect only. The author, Mr. James Joyce, is not concerned with all Dubliners, but almost exclusively with those of them who would be submerged if the tide of material difficulties were to rise a little higher. It is not so much money they lack as the adaptability which attains some measure of success by accepting the world as it is. It is in so far as they are failures that his characters interest Mr. Joyce. One of them—a capable washerwoman—falls an easy prey to a rogue in a tramcar and is cozened out of the little present she was taking to her family. Another—a trusted cashier—has so ordered a blameless life that he drives to drink and suicide the only person in the world with whom he is in sympathy. A third—an amiable man of letters—learns at the moment he feels most drawn to his wife that her heart was given once and for all to a boy long dead.

Dubliners may be recommended to the large class of readers to whom the drab makes an appeal, for it is admirably written. Mr. Joyce avoids exaggeration. He leaves the conviction that his people are as he describes them. Shunning the emphatic, Mr. Joyce is less concerned with the episode than with the mood which it suggests. Perhaps for this reason he is more successful with his shorter stories. When he writes at greater length, the issue seems trivial, and the connecting thread becomes so tenuous as to be scarcely perceptible. The reader's difficulty will be enhanced if he is ignorant of Dublin customs; if he does not know, for instance, that a "curate" is a man who brings strong waters.

Ezra Pound, "*Dubliners* and Mr. James Joyce"

From the *Egoist*, July 15, 1914.

Freedom from sloppiness is so rare in contemporary English prose that one might well say simply, "Mr. Joyce's book of short stories is prose free from sloppiness," and leave the intelligent reader ready to run from his study, immediately to spend three and sixpence on the volume.

Unfortunately one's credit as a critic is insufficient to produce this result.

The readers of *The Egoist*, having had Mr. Joyce under their eyes for some months,[2] will scarcely need to have his qualities pointed out to them. Both they and the paper have been very fortunate in his collaboration.

Mr. Joyce writes a clear hard prose. He deals with subjective things, but he presents them with such clarity of outline that he might be dealing with locomotives or with builders' specifications. For that reason one can read Mr. Joyce without feeling that one is conferring a favour. I must put this thing my own way. I know about 168 authors. About once a year I read something contemporary without feeling that I am softening the path for poor Jones or poor Fulano de Tal.[3]

---

[2] *A Portrait of the Artist as a Young Man* was appearing serially in the magazine's pages.

[3] "Someone; the writer of the day" in Spanish.

I can lay down a good piece of French writing and pick up a piece of writing by Mr. Joyce without feeling as if my head were being stuffed through a cushion. There are still impressionists about and I dare say they claim Mr. Joyce. I admire impressionist writers. English prose writers who haven't got as far as impressionism (that is to say, 95 per cent. of English writers of prose and verse) are a bore.

Impressionism has, however, two meanings, or perhaps I had better say, the word "impressionism" gives two different "impressions."

There is a school of prose writers, and of verse writers for that matter, whose forerunner was Stendhal and whose founder was Flaubert. The followers of Flaubert deal in exact presentation. They are often so intent on exact presentation that they neglect intensity, selection, and concentration. They are perhaps the most clarifying and they have been perhaps the most beneficial force in modern writing.

There is another set, mostly of verse writers, who founded themselves not upon anybody's writing but upon the pictures of Monet. Every movement in painting picks up a few writers who try to imitate in words what someone has done in paint. Thus one writer saw a picture by Monet and talked of "pink pigs blossoming on a hillside," and a later writer talked of "slate-blue" hair and "raspberry-coloured flanks."

These "impressionists" who write in imitation of Monet's softness instead of writing in imitation of Flaubert's definiteness, are a bore, a grimy, or perhaps I should say, a rosy, floribund bore.

The spirit of a decade strikes properly upon all of the arts. There are "parallel movements." Their causes and their effects may not seem, superficially, similar.

This mimicking of painting ten or twenty years late is not in the least the same as the "literary movement" parallel to the painting movement imitated.

The force that leads a poet to leave out a moral reflection may lead a painter to leave out representation. The resultant poem may not suggest the resultant painting.

Mr. Joyce's merit, I will not say his chief merit but his most engaging merit, is that he carefully avoids telling you a lot that you don't want to know. He presents his people swiftly and vividly, he does not sentimentalise over them, he does not weave convolutions. He is a realist. He does not believe "life" would be all right if we stopped vivisection or if we instituted a new sort of "economics." He gives the thing as it is. He is not bound by the tiresome convention that any part of life, to be interesting, must be shaped into the conventional form of a "story." Since De Maupassant we have had so many people trying to write "stories" and so few people presenting life. Life for the most part does not happen in neat little diagrams and nothing is more tiresome than the continual pretence that it does.

Mr. Joyce's "Araby," for instance, is much better than a "story," it is a vivid waiting.

It is surprising that Mr. Joyce is Irish. One is so tired of the Irish or "Celtic" imagination (or "phantasy" as I think they now call it) flopping about.[4] Mr. Joyce does not flop about. He defines. He is not an institution for the promotion of Irish peasant industries. He accepts an international standard of prose writing and lives up to it.

He gives us Dublin as it presumably is. He does not descend to farce. He does not rely upon Dickensian caricature. He gives us things as they are, not only for Dublin, but for every city. Erase the local names and a few specifically local allusions, and a few historic events of the past, and substitute a few different local names, allusions and events, and these stories could be retold of any town.

That is to say, the author is quite capable of dealing with things about him, and dealing directly, yet these details do not engross him, he is capable of getting at the universal element beneath them.

The main situations of "Madame Bovary" or of "Dona Perfecta"[5] do not depend on local colour or upon local detail; that is their strength. Good writing, good presentation can be specifically local, but it must not depend on locality. Mr. Joyce does not present "types" but individuals. I mean he deals with common emotions which run through all races. He does not bank on "Irish character." Roughly speaking, Irish literature has gone through three phases in our time, the shamrock period, the dove-grey period, and the Kiltartan period. I think there is a new phase in the works of Mr. Joyce. He writes as a contemporary of continental writers. I do not mean that he writes as a faddist, mad for the last note, he does not imitate Strindberg, for instance, or Bang.[6] He is not ploughing the underworld for horror. He is not presenting a macabre subjectivity. He is classic in that he deals with normal things and with

[4] A reference to the Revival. See p. xxx.

[5] The first is a meticulously realist novel by Gustav Flaubert (1821–1880); the second is an equally intense realist work by Benito Pérez Galdós (1843–1920).

[6] Johan August Strindberg (1849–1912) was a widely influential Swedish playwright known for his penetrating realism; Herman Bang (1857–1912) was Danish writer and critic who became a leading figure in the impressionist movement.

normal people. A committee room, Little Chandler, a nonentity, a boarding house full of clerks—these are his subjects and he treats them all in such a manner that they are worthy subjects of art.

Francis Jammes, Charles Vildrac and D. H. Lawrence[7] have written short narratives in verse, trying, it would seem, to present situations as clearly as prose writers have done, yet more briefly. Mr. Joyce is engaged in a similar condensation. He has kept to prose not needing the privilege supposedly accorded to verse to justify his method.

I think that he excels most of the impressionist writers because of his more rigorous selection, because of his exclusion of all unnecessary detail.

There is a very clear demarcation between unnecessary detail and irrelevant detail. An impressionist friend of mine talks to me a good deal about "preparing effects," and on that score he justifies much unnecessary detail, which is not "irrelevant," but which ends by being wearisome and by putting one out of conceit with his narrative.

Mr. Joyce's more rigorous selection of the presented detail marks him, I think, as belonging to my own generation, that is, to the "nineteen-tens," not to the decade between "the 'nineties" and to-day.

At any rate these stories and the novel now appearing in serial form are such as to win for Mr. Joyce a very definite place among English contemporary prose writers, not merely a place in the "Novels of the Week" column, and our writers of good clear prose are so few that we cannot afford to confuse or to overlook them.

---

[7] Francis Jammes (1868–1938) and Charles Vildrac (1882–1971) were French prose poets; D.H. Lawrence (1885–1930) was an innovative English novelist and poet.

The Stories in Context

THE SISTERS

This story was first published on August 13, 1904, in the Irish Home-stead *under the pseudonym Stephen Daedalus, a name Joyce later used (in a modified form) for the protagonist of* A Portrait of the Artist as a Young Man *(1916). When he revised this story, Joyce added the key term "paralysis," introducing a theme that runs throughout Dubliners. This medical condition was only vaguely understood and as the excerpt from the 1844 Report of the Metropolitan Commissioners in Lunacy suggests, it was linked to a range of illnesses including insanity, syphilis, and alcoholism.*

Our Weekly Story

The Sisters

By Stephen Daedalus

Three nights in succession I had found myself in Great Britain-street at that hour, as if by Providence. Three nights also I had raised my eyes to that lighted square of window and speculated. I seemed to understand that it would occur at night. But in spite of the Providence that had led my feet, and in spite of the reverent curiosity of my eyes, I had discovered nothing. Each night the square was lighted in the same way, faintly and evenly. It was not the light of candles, so far as I could see. Therefore, it had not yet occurred.

On the fourth night at that hour I was in another part of the city. It may have been the same Providence that led me there—a whimsical kind of Providence to take me at a disadvantage. As I went home I wondered was that square of window lighted as before, or did it reveal the ceremonious candles in whose light the Christian must take his last sleep. I was not surprised, then, when at supper I found myself a prophet. Old Cotter and my uncle were talking at the fire, smoking. Old Cotter is the old distiller who owns the batch of prize setters. He used to be very interesting when I knew him first, talking about "faints" and "worms." Now I find him tedious.

While I was eating my stirabout I heard him saying to my uncle:

"Without a doubt. Upper storey—(he tapped an unnecessary hand at his forehead)—gone."

"So they said. I never could see much of it. I thought he was sane enough."

"So he was, at times," said old Cotter.

I sniffed the "was" apprehensively, and gulped down some stirabout.

"Is he better, Uncle John?"

"He's dead."

"O ... he's dead?"

"Died a few hours ago."

"Who told you?"

"Mr. Cotter here brought us the news. He was passing there."

"Yes, I just happened to be passing, and I noticed the window ... you know."

"Do you think they will bring him to the chapel?" asked my aunt.

"Oh, no, ma'am. I wouldn't say so."

"Very unlikely," my uncle agreed.

So old Cotter had got the better of me for all my vigilance of three nights. It is often annoying the way people will blunder on what you have elaborately planned for. I was sure he would die at night.

The following morning after breakfast I went down to look at the little house in Great Britain-street. It was an unassuming shop registered under the vague name of "Drapery." The drapery was principally children's boots and umbrellas, and on ordinary days there used to be a notice hanging in the window, which said "Umbrellas recovered." There was no notice visible now, for the shop blinds were drawn down and a crape bouquet was tied to the knocker with white ribbons. Three women of the people and a telegram boy were reading the card pinned on the crape. I also went over and read:—"July 2nd, 189—The Rev. James Flynn (formerly of St. Ita's Church), aged 65 years. R.I.P."

Only sixty-five! He looked much older than that. I often saw him sitting at the fire in the close dark room behind the shop, nearly smothered in his great coat. He seemed to have almost stupefied himself with heat, and the gesture of his large trembling hand to his nostrils had grown automatic. My aunt, who is what they call good-hearted, never went into the shop without bringing him some High Toast, and he used to take the packet of snuff from her hands, gravely inclining his head for sign of thanks. He used to sit in that stuffy room for the greater part of the day from early morning while Nannie (who is almost stone deaf) read out the newspaper to him. His other sister, Eliza, used to mind the shop. These two old women used to look after him, feed him, and clothe him. The clothing was not difficult, for his ancient, priestly clothes were quite green with age, and his dogskin slippers were everlasting. When he was tired of hearing the news be used to rattle his snuff-box on the arm of his chair to avoid shouting at her, and then he used to make believe to read his Prayer Book. Make believe, because, when Eliza brought his a cup of soup from the kitchen, she had always to waken him.

As I stood looking up at the crape and the card that bore his name I could not realise that he was dead. He seemed like one who could go on living for ever if he only wanted to; his life was so methodical and uneventful. I think he said more to me than to any-one else. He had an egoistic contempt for all women-folk, and suf-fered all their services to him in polite silence. Of course, neither of his sisters were very intelligent. Nannie, for instance, had been read-ing out the newspaper to him every day for years, and could read tol-erably well, and yet she always spoke of it as the *Freeman's General*. Perhaps he found me more intelligent, and honoured me with words for that reason. Nothing, practically nothing, ever occurred to remind him of his former life (I mean friends or visitors), and still he could remember every detail of it in his own fashion. He had studied at the college in Rome, and he taught me to speak Latin in the Italian way. He often put me through the responses of the Mass, he smiling often and pushing huge pinches of snuff up each nostril alternately. When he smiled he used to uncover his big, discoloured teeth, and let his tongue lie on his lower lip. At first this habit of his used to make me feel uneasy. Then I grew used to it.

That evening my aunt visited the house of mourning and took me with her. It was an oppressive summer evening of faded gold. Nannie received us in the hall, and, as it was no use saying anything to her, my aunt shook hands with her for all. We followed the old woman upstairs and into the dead-room. The room, through the lace end of the blind, was suffused with dusky golden light, amid which the candles looked like pale, thin flames. He had been coffined. Nannie gave the lead, and we three knelt down at the foot of the bed. There was no sound in the room for some minutes except the sound of Nannie's mutterings—for she prays noisily. The fancy came to me that the old priest was smiling as he lay there in his coffin.

But, no. When we rose and went up to the head of the bed I saw that he was not smiling. There he lay solemn and copious in his brown habit, his large hands loosely retaining his rosary. His face was very grey and massive, with distended nostrils and circled with scanty white fur. There was a heavy odour in the room—the flowers.

We sat downstairs in the little room behind the shop, my aunt and I and the two sisters. Nannie sat in a corner and said nothing, but her lips moved from speaker to speaker with a painfully intelligent motion. I said nothing either, being too young, but my aunt spoke a good deal, for she is a bit of a gossip—harmless.

"Ah, well, he's gone!"

"To enjoy his eternal reward, Miss Flynn, I'm sure. He was a good and holy man."

"He was a good man, but, you see … he was a disappointed man … You see, his life was, you might say, crossed."

"Ah, yes! I know what you mean."

"Not that he was anyway mad, as you know yourself, but he was always a little queer. Even when we were all growing up together he was queer. One time he didn't speak hardly for a month. You know, he was that kind always."

"Perhaps he read too much, Miss Flynn?"

"O, he read a good deal, but not latterly. But it was his scrupulousness, I think, affected his mind. The duties of the priesthood were too much For him."

"Did he … peacefully?"

"O, quite peacefully, ma'am. You couldn't tell when the breath went out of him. He had a beautiful death, God be praised."

"And everything … ?"

"Father O'Rourke was in with him yesterday and gave him the Last Sacrament."

"He knew then?"

"Yes; he was quite resigned."

Nannie gave a sleepy nod and looked ashamed.

"Poor Nannie," said her sister, "she's worn out. All the work we had, getting in a woman, and laying him out; and then the coffin and arranging about the funeral. God knows we did all we could, as poor as we are. We wouldn't see him want anything at the last."

"Indeed you were both very kind to him while he lived."

"Ah, poor James; he was no great trouble to us. You wouldn't hear him in the house no more than now. Still I know he's gone and all that.... I won't be bringing him in his soup any more, nor Nannie reading him the paper, nor you, ma'am, bringing him his snuff. How he liked that snuff! Poor James!"

"O, yes, you'll miss him in a day or two more than you do now."

Silence invaded the room until memory reawakened it, Eliza speaking slowly—

"It was that chalice he broke.... Of course, it was all right. I mean it contained nothing. But still ... They say it was the boy's fault. But poor James was so nervous, God be merciful to him."

"Yes, Miss Flynn, I heard that ... about the chalice ... He ... his mind was a bit affected by that."

"He began to mope by himself, talking to no one, and wandering about. Often he couldn't be found. One night he was wanted, and they looked high up and low down and couldn't find him. Then the clerk suggested the chapel. So they opened the chapel (it was late at night), and brought in a light to look for him ... And there, sure enough, he was, sitting in his confession-box in the dark, wide awake, and laughing like softly to himself. Then they knew something was wrong."

"God rest his soul!"

From *Report of the Metropolitan Commissioners in Lunacy* (London, 1844)

Paralysis is not unfrequently complicated with Insanity, and is almost an invariable indication that the case is incurable and hopeless, marking the existence of organic disease in the brain.

In some instances, Insanity is the consequence of an attack of apoplexy,[1] or of hemiplegia.[2] This happens more especially in aged persons. In others, apoplexy or paralysis supervenes on protracted mania or dementia.

The most strongly marked case of the complication of paralytic symptoms with those of mental disorder, is the disease termed General Paralysis of the Insane. This is more properly to be considered as an affliction distinct both from ordinary paralysis and from insanity. The paralytic symptoms in this affliction are sometimes observed to precede those of mental disturbance; and others they follow. General Paralysis of the Insane seldom occurs in females, but mostly in men,

[1] A now outdated term that here refers to bleeding in the brain and other internal organs.

[2] Stroke. Joyce referred to Dublin itself as "the soul of...hemiplegia or paralysis" in a letter written to his publisher about the book.

Cover from *Pluck*.

and is the result almost uniformly of a debauched and intemperate life. Its duration is scarcely ever longer than two or at most three years, when it generally brings its victim to the grave. The onset of the disease is distinguished by an impediment in the articulation, an effort is required in speaking and the words are uttered with a sort of

mumbling, and stammering. At this period, there is no other perceptible sign of paralysis, and the mobility of the limbs is not at all
impaired. In a second stage, the patient is observed to have a tottering
gait: the limbs are weaker than in health, especially the lower extrem-
ities, while the functions of the organs of sense are likewise enfeebled.
In the progress of time, a third stage appears, during which the victim
of the malady loses not only the power of locomotion, but can neither
feed himself nor answer the calls of nature. He becomes more and
more weak and emaciated, but generally perishes under some second-
ary disease, such as gangrene, sloughing of the surface of the body, or
diarrhoea, unless he be cut off at an earlier period by an apoplectic or
epileptic attack, to which these patients are very liable. The disorder
of the mind is peculiar in this affection. It is generally a species of
monomania, in which the individual affected fancies himself possessed of vast riches, and power.

An Encounter

*Tales of excitement, battle, and intrigue abided not only in school
texts, such as Caesar's* Gallic Wars, *but also beckoned from such popular pulp magazines as* Pluck *and the* Halfpenny Marvel *(precursors to
comic books), featuring the "daring deeds" of sailors, soldiers, detec-
tives, cowboys, and firemen.*

Araby

*Joyce's inspiration, a bazaar in Dublin, carried this advertisement in
its catalog.*

Araby Catalog (1894)

"Araby" 1894
Magnificent Representation
of
An Oriental City
CAIRO DONKEYS AND DONKEY BOYS
AN ARAB ENCAMPMENT.
INTERNATIONAL TUG-OF-WAR
Dances by 250 Trained Children.
Eastern Magic from the Egyptian Hall, London.

•

CAFÉ CHANTANT WITH ALL THE LATEST PARISIAN SUCCESSES.

SKIRT DANCING up to Date.

Tableaux. Theatricals. Christy Minstrels.

Grand Theatre of Varieties.

"THE ALHAMBRA," An Orchestra of 50 Performers.

Switchback Railways and Roundabouts.

"MENOTTI," *The King of the Air.*

The Great Stockholm Wonder.

Bicycle Polo. Rifle & Clay Pigeon Shooting.

Dancing.

The Euterpean Ladies' Orchestra.

Eight Military Bands.

Magnificent Displays of Fireworks.

By Brock, of the Crystal Palace, London.

ADMISSION . . ONE SHILLING

Popular lore cast the Irish as distant descendants of the ancient Phoenicians and thus a Near Eastern rather than European people. Irish poet Thomas Moore (1779–1852) drew on this mythical history for his immensely popular long poem Lalla Rookh, *which in turn inspired such songs and poems as "I'll Sing Thee Songs of Araby" and Caroline Norton's "An Arab's Farewell to his Steed." For Web sites and other resources providing recordings of the music Joyce uses in this and other stories, see p. xxx.*

Thomas Moore, "Araby's Daughter"

From *Lalla Rookh.*

Farewell—farewell to thee. Araby's daughter!
(Thus warbled a PERI[3] beneath the dark sea.)
No pearl ever lay under Oman's[4] green water
More pure in its shell than thy Spirit in thee.
Oh! fair as the sea-flower close to thee growing.
How light was thy heart till Love's witchery came.

---

[3] In Persian mythology, a fallen angel who must do penance on Earth.
[4] Ancient Middle-Eastern nation.

Like the wind of the south[5] o'er a summer lute blowing,
And husht all its music and withered its frame!
But long upon Araby's green sunny highlands
Shall maids and their lovers remember the doom
Of her who lies sleeping among the Pearl Islands
With naught but the sea-star[6] to light up her tomb.
And still when the merry date-season° is burning   *harvest*
And calls to the palm-groves the young and the old.[7]
The happiest there from their pastime returning
At sunset will weep when thy story is told.
The young village-maid when with flowers she dresses
Her dark flowing hair for some festival day
Will think of thy fate till neglecting her tresses
She mournfully turns from the mirror away.
Nor shall Iran, beloved of her Hero! forget thee—
Tho' tyrants watch over her tears as they start,
Close, close by the side of that Hero she'll set thee,
Embalmed in the innermost shrine of her heart.
Farewell—be it ours to embellish thy pillow
With everything beauteous that grows in the deep;
Each flower of the rock and each gem of the billow
Shall sweeten thy bed and illumine thy sleep.
Around thee shall glisten the loveliest amber
That ever the sorrowing sea-bird has wept;[8]
With many a shell in whose hollow-wreathed chamber
We Peris of Ocean by moonlight have slept.
We'll dive where the gardens of coral lie darkling
And plant all the rosiest stems at thy head;
We'll seek where the sands of the Caspian[9] are sparkling

---

[5] "This wind (the Samoor) so softens the strings of lutes, that they can never be tuned while it lasts."—*Stephen's Persia*. [Thomas Moore]

[6] "One of the greatest curiosities found in the Persian Gulf is a fish which the English call Star-fish. It is circular, and at night very luminous, resembling the full moon surrounded by rays."—Mina Abu Taleb. [Thomas Moore]

[7] For a description of the merriment of the date-time, of their work, their dances, and their return home from the palm-groves at the end of autumn with the fruits, see *v. Kempfer, Amoenitat. Exot.* [Thomas Moore]

[8] Some naturalists have imaged that amber is a concretion of the tears of birds—*v. Trevoux, Chambers.* [Thomas Moore]

[9] Inland sea on the border of Asia and the Middle East.

And gather their gold to strew over thy bed.
Farewell—farewell!—Until Pity's sweet fountain
Is lost in the hearts of the fair and the brave,
They'll weep for the Chieftain who died on that mountain,
They'll weep for the Maiden who sleeps in this wave.

"I'll Sing Thee Songs of Araby"

Words by W. G. Wills and music by Frederick Clay.

I'll sing thee songs of Araby
And tales of fair Cashmere.[1]
Wild tales to cheat thee of a sigh
Or charm thee to a tear.
And dreams of delight shall on thee break
And rainbow visions rise,
And all my soul shall strive to wake
Sweet wonder in thine eyes …
And all my soul shall strive to wake
Sweet wonder in thine eyes.

Through those twin lakes where wonder wakes
My raptured song shall sink
And, as the diver dives for pearls,
Bring tears, bright tears, to their brink.
And dreams of delight shall on thee break
And rainbow visions rise,
And all my soul shall strive to wake
Sweet wonder in thine eyes …
And all my soul shall strive to wake
Sweet wonder in thine eyes.

Caroline Norton, "An Arab's Farewell to his Steed" (1869)

My beautiful! my beautiful! that standest meekly by,
With thy proudly arch'd and glossy neck, and dark and fiery eye,
Fret not to roam the desert now with all they winged speed;
I may not mount on thee again—thou art sold, my Arab steed.
Fret not with that impatient hoof, snuff not the breezy wind,
The further that thou fliest now, so far am I behind,
The stranger hath thy bridle rein—thy master hath his gold—

[1] Mountainous and romantic region in the north of present-day India.

Fleet-limbed and beautiful, farewell, thou'rt sold, my steed, thou'rt sold.
Farewell, those free, untired limbs full many a mile must roam,
To reach the chill and wintry sky which clouds the stranger's home.
Some other hand, less fond, must now thy corn and bed prepare—
The silky mane I braided once must be another's care.
The morning sun shall dawn again, but never more with thee
Shall I gallop o'er the desert paths, where we were wont to be;
Evening shall darken on the earth, and o'er the sandy plain,
Some other steed, with slower step, shall bear me home again.
Yes, thou must go, the wild free breeze, the brilliant sun and sky,
Thy master's home, from all of these my exiled one must fly.
Thy proud dark eye will grow less proud, thy step become less fleet,
And vainly shalt thou arch thy neck thy master's hand to meet.
Only in sleep shall I behold that dark eye glancing bright;
Only in sleep shall hear again that step so firm and light;
And when I raise my dreaming arm to check or cheer thy speed,
Then must I starting wake to feel thou'rt sold, my Arab steed.
Ah! rudely then, unseen by me, some cruel hand may chide,
Till foam-wreaths lie, like crested waves, along thy panting side,
And the rich blood that is in thee swell in thy indignant pain,
Till careless eyes, which rest on thee, may count each started vein.
Will they ill-use thee? If I thought—but no, it cannot be—
Thou art so swift, yet easy curbed; so gentle yet so free.
And yet, if haply, when thou'rt gone, my lonely heart should yearn,
Can the hand which casts thee from it now command thee to return?
Return, alas! my Arab steed, what shall thy master do,
When thou, who wert his all of joy, has vanished from his view;
When the dim distance cheats mine eye, and, through the gathering tears,
Thy bright form, for a moment, like the false mirage appears?
Slow and unmounted will I roam, with weary foot alone,
Where with fleet step and joyous bound thou oft hast borne me on.
And sitting down by that green well, I'll pause and sadly think,
It was here he bowed his glossy neck when last I saw him drink.
When last I saw thee drink? Away! the fevered dream is o'er,
I could not live a day and know that we should meet no more.
They tempted me, my beautiful! for hunger's power is strong,
They tempted me, my beautiful! but I have loved too long.
Who said that I'd giv'n thee up? who said that thou wert sold?
'Tis false, 'tis false, my Arab steed, I fling them back their gold!
Thus, thus, I leap upon thy back, and scour the distant plains,
Away! who overtakes us now shall claim thee for his pains.

EVELINE

This was the second story to appear in the Irish Homestead, *and scraps of religious texts as well as popular songs play across Eveline's troubled mind. On the wall of her house is a color print of the* Sacred Heart of Jesus *along with the twelve promises revealed to Margaret Mary Alacoque, a seventeenth-century French nun, guaranteeing the pious a peaceful and blessed home life. Also in the air are some popular songs: "Come with the Gypsy Bride" (from the operetta,* The Bohemian Girl) *and "The Lass That Loves a Sailor." Equally important is the vague fear that Frank may be a "white slaver" who intends to lure Eveline into a life of prostitution—a threat made explicit in advertising campaigns and works like Clifford G. Roe's 1911* The Horrors of the White Slave Trade: The Mighty Crusade to Protect the Purity of Our Homes.

The Twelve Promises of the Sacred Heart of Jesus as Given to Blessed Margaret Mary Alacoque

1. I will give them all the graces necessary for their state of life.
2. I will give peace in their families.
3. I will console them in all their troubles.
4. They shall find in My Heart an assured refuge during life and especially at the hour of death.
5. I will pour abundant blessings on all their undertakings.
6. Sinners shall find in My Heart the source and infinite ocean of mercy.
7. Tepid souls shall become fervent.
8. Fervent souls shall speedily rise to great perfection.
9. I will bless the homes in which the image of My Heart shall be exposed and honored.
10. I will give to priests the power to touch the most hardened hearts.
11. Those who propagate this devotion shall have their name written in My Heart, and it shall never be effaced.
12. The all-powerful love of My Heart will grant to all those who shall receive Communion on the First Friday of nine consecutive months the grace of final repentance;[1] they shall not die under My displeasure, nor without receiving their Sacraments; My Heart shall be their assured refuge at the last hour.

[1] The assurance of heaven.

"Come with the Gypsy Bride"

From *The Bohemian Girl* by Michael Balfe and
Alfred Bunn, 1843.

Come with the Gipsy bride,
Where souls as light preside!
Life can give nothing beyond
One heart you know to be fond.
Wealth with its hoards cannot buy
The peace content can supply.
Wealth with its hoards cannot buy
The peace content can supply.
And rank in its halls cannot find
The calm of a happy mind.
And rank in its halls cannot find
The calm of a happy mind.
Come with the Gipsy bride,
And repair to the fair,
Where the mazy dance
Will the hours entrance!

Charles Dibdin, "The Lass that Loves a Sailor"

The moon on the ocean was dimmed by a ripple
Affording a chequered delight:
The gay jolly tars° passed a word for the tipple.°   *sailors / drink*
And the toast—for 'twas Saturday night:
Some sweetheart or wife he loved as his life
Each drank, and wished he could hail her:
    But the standing toast that pleased the most
    Was "The wind that blows,
    The ship that goes,
    And the lass that loves a sailor!"

Some drank "The Queen," and some her brave ships,
And some "The Constitution":
Some "May our foes, and all such rips,
Yield to English resolution!"

That fate might bless some Poll° or Bess,   *Polly*
And that they soon might hail her:
> *But the standing toast that pleased the most*
> *Was "The wind that blows,*
> *The ship that goes,*
> *And the lass that loves a sailor!"*

Some drank "The Prince," and some "Our Land,"
This glorious land of freedom!
Some "That our tars may never want
For heroes brave to lead them!"
"That she who's in distress may find,
Such friends as ne'er will fail her."
> *But the standing toast that pleased the most*
> *Was "The wind that blows,*
> *The ship that goes,*
> *And the lass that loves a sailor!"*

THE SECOND MEETING—SHE KNOWS NOT THE DANGEROUS TRAP BEING SET FOR HER.
The smooth tongued villain tells of his affection and undying love for her. He paints a beautiful picture of how happy they will be. She is enraptured and promises to meet him and go to dinner with him.

"The Second Meeting," from Clifford G. Roe, *The Horrors of the White Slave Trade: The Mighty Crusade to Protect the Purity of Our Homes* (1912).

AFTER THE RACE

Joyce published a version of this story in the Irish Homestead *on December 17, 1904 (the last of the* Dubliners *stories to appear in this paper). He drew on the 1903 Gordon Bennett Cup, an international auto race staged in Ireland and recounted in the* Leinster Leader. *While in Paris that year struggling to begin his career, Joyce interviewed famous French racecar driver Henri Fournier (who wound up not participating in the Bennett Cup race), and took his title for the story from a line in this conversation, which was later published anonymously in the* Irish Times.

"Motor Race"

From the *Leicester Leader*, July 4, 1903.

MOTOR RACE.
GERMANY WINS.
INCIDENTS AND ACCIDENTS.
ENGLISH AND AMERICAN ILL-LUCK.
CARS WRECKED AND DISABLED.

The "Motor Fortnight," from the standpoint of local popular interest, opened on Sunday last, when—in the pleasant and sunny weather succeeding the rough, stormy and wintrish experience of the preceding days—considerable numbers from Naas, Athy, Newbridge, Kildare and other districts made pilgrimage to Ballyshannon Cross Roads on car and cycle. The roads were lively with motors and both wheel-men and car-drivers had to exercise care and caution, more especially at the Grand Stand, where a narrow passage of roadway, encroached upon by the supports of the structure and pulverised for some depth on the surface by the passage of traction engines, had to be negotiated, amidst a crush of vehicles, automobile and otherwise. Though the course and its approaches were the scene of such brisk traffic, no accident occurred worth recording. The various private stands abundantly in evidence were inspected with interest, their strength and points of advantage being discussed. A staff of workmen were busily engaged completing the Grand Stand, whose capacity to bear its probable load was the subject of more than one sceptical conjecture. However, the assurance that all defects had by this time been remedied and the Stand certified as absolutely safe, robbed these suppositions of the element of sensation that they might have possessed. There was not much otherwise to engage the visitors' attention. A series of very unpicturesque eye-sores such as the stands really were—an odd tent—an atmosphere flavoured with petrol from the passing and re-passing cars—momentary glimpses of veiled heads, "goggled" eyes, and their dust-ful owners—such was the complete picture and impression that Sunday at Ballyshannon provided. There was little to suggest the threshold of a great International event, and nothing but the occasional fleeting glimpse of a foreign car to give the expected cosmopolitan touch to the scene of a great world-gathering.

[James Joyce] THE MOTOR DERBY
Interview with a French Champion
(from a Correspondent, the *Irish Times*, April 7, 1903)

Paris, Sunday.
In the Rue d'Anjou, not far from the Church of the Madeleine, is M. Henri Fournier's place of business. 'Paris-Automobile'—a company of which M. Fournier is the manager—has its headquarters there. Inside the gateway is a big square court, roofed over, and on the floor of the court and on great shelves extending from the floor to the roof are ranged motor-cars of all sizes, shapes, and colours. In the afternoon this court is full of noises—the voices of workmen, the voices of buyers talking in half-a-dozen languages, the ringing of telephone bells, the horns sounded by the 'chauffeurs' as the cars come in and go out—and it is almost impossible to see M. Fournier unless one is prepared to wait two or three hours for one's turn. But the buyers of 'autos' are, in one sense, people of leisure. The morning, however, is more favourabie, and yesterday morning, after two failures, I succeeded in seeing M. Fournier.

M. Fournier is a slim, active-looking young man, with dark reddish hair. Early as the hour was our interview was now and again broken in upon by the importunate telephone.

'You are one of the competitors for the Gordon-Bennett Cup, M. Fournier?'

'Yes, I am one of the three selected to represent France.'

'And you are also a competitor, are you not, for the Madrid prize.'

'Yes.'

'Which of the races comes first—the Irish race or the Madrid race?'

'The Madrid race. It takes place early in May, while the race for the International Cup does not take place till July.'

'I suppose that you are preparing actively for your races?'

'Well, I have just returned from a tour to Monte Carlo and Nice.'

'On your racing machine?'

'No, on a machine of smaller power.

'Have you determined what machine you will ride in the Irish race?'

'Practically.'

'May I ask the name of it—is it a Mercedes?'

'No, a Mors.'

'And its horse-power?'

'Eighty.'

'And on this machine you can travel at a rate of—?'

'You mean its highest speed?'

'Yes.'

'Its highest speed would be a hundred and forty kilometres an hour.'

'But you will not go at that rate all the time during the race?'

'Oh, no. Of course its average speed for the race would be lower than that.'

'An average speed of how much?'

'Its average speed would be a hundred kilometres an hour, perhaps a little more than that, something between a hundred and a hundred and ten kilometres an hour.'

'A kilometre is about a half-mile, is it not?'

'More than that, I should think. There are how many yards in your mile?'

'Seventeen hundred and sixty, if I am right.'

'Then your half-mile has eight hundred and eighty yards. Our kilometre is just equal to eleven hundred yards.'

'Let me see. Then your top speed is nearly eighty-six miles an hour, and your average speed is sixty-one miles an hour?'

'I suppose so, if we calculate properly.'

'It is an appalling pace! It is enough to burn our roads. I suppose you have seen the roads you are to travel?'

'No.'

'No? You don't know the course, then?'

'I know it slightly. I know it, that is, from some sketches that were given of it in the Paris newspapers.'

'But, surely, you will want a better knowledge than that?'

'Oh, certainly. In fact, before the month is over, I intend to go to Ireland to inspect the course. Perhaps I shall go in three weeks' time.'

'Will you remain any time in Ireland?'

'After the race?'

'Yes.'

'I am afraid not. I should like to, but I don't think I can.'

'I suppose you would not like to be asked your opinion of the result?'

'Hardly.'

'Yet, which nation do you fear most?'

'I fear them all—Germans, Americans, and English. They are all to be feared.'

'And how about Mr Edge?'

No answer.

'He won the prize the last time, did he not?'

'O, yes.'

'Then he should be your most formidable opponent?'

'O, yes ... But you see, Mr Edge won, of course, but ... a man who was last of all, and had no chance of winning might win if the other machines broke.'

Whatever way one looks at this statement it appears difficult to challenge its truth.

THE BOARDING HOUSE

Boarding houses and unlicensed rented rooms were common in Dublin, extending beyond the overcrowded tenements and into more respectable districts. With sexes mixing under little supervision, such establishments focused concerns about sexual license and public morality—evident in one of Joyce's probable references, "A Dublin Boarding House," by Sir Jonah Barrington (1827). The song with which Polly Mooney entertains the boarders is a rollicking tune from the musical comedy, A Greek Slave, a two-act show that initially ran in London from 1898 to 1899 as one of Daley's Musicals, a popular series produced by George Edwardes at Daly's Theatre.

Jonah Barrington, *Personal Sketches and Recollections of His Own Times*, (1827)

A Dublin Boarding-House

On my return to Dublin from London, before I could suit myself with a residence to my satisfaction, I lodged at the house of Mr. Kyle, in Frederick Street, uncle to the present provost of Dublin University. Mrs. Kyle was a remarkably plain woman, of the most curious figure, being round as a ball; but she was as good as she was ordinary. This worthy creature, who was a gentlewoman by birth, had married Kyle, who, though of good family, had been a trooper. She had lived many years, as companion, with my grandmother, and in fact regarded me as if I had been her own child.

In her abode so many human curiosities were collected, and so many anecdotes occurred, that, even at this distance of time, the recollection of it amuses me. Those who lodged in the house dined in company: the table was most plentifully served, and the party generally comprised from eight to ten select persons. I will endeavour to sketch the leading members of the society there at the period of which I speak. [...]

Lady Barry's only daughter, afterwards the unfortunate Mrs. Baldwin, was also of the party. Though this young female had not a beautiful face, it was yet peculiarly pleasing, and she certainly possessed one of the finest figures—tall, slender in its proportions, and exquisitely graceful—I had ever seen. Her father, Sir Nathaniel Barry, many years the principal physician of Dublin, adored his daughter, and had spared no pains or expense on her education. She profited by all the instruction she received, and was one of the most accomplished young women of her day.

But unfortunately he had introduced her to the practice of one very objectionable accomplishment, calculated rather to give unbounded latitude to, than check, the light and dangerous particles of a volatile and thoughtless disposition. He was himself enthusiastically fond of *theatricals*, and had fitted up a theatre in the upper storey of his own house. There the youthful mind of his daughter was initiated into all the schemes and deceptions of lovers and of libertines! At sixteen, with all the warmth of a sensitive constitution, she was taught to personify the vices, affect the passions, and assume the frivolities, of her giddy sex!

Thus, through the folly or vanity of her father, she was led to represent by turns the flirt, the jilt, the silly wife, the capricious mistress, and the frail maiden, before her understanding had arrived at sufficient maturity, or his more serious instructions had made sufficient impression, to enable her to resist evil temptation. She saw the world's pleasures dancing gaily before her, and pursued the vision— until her mimicry, at length, became nature, and her personification identity. After two or three years, during which this mistaken course was pursued, Sir Nathaniel died, leaving his daughter in possession of all the powers of attraction without the guard of prudence.

The misfortunes which ensued should therefore be attributed rather to the folly of the parent than to the propensities of the child.

Her heart once sunk into the vortex of thoughtless variety and folly, her mother was unable to restrain its downward progress; and as to her weak dissipated brother, Sir Edward, I have myself seen him, late at night, require her to come from her chamber to sing, or play, or spout, for the amusement of his inebriated companions; conduct which the mother had not sufficient sense or resolution to control. However, good fortune still gave Miss Barry a fair chance of rescuing herself, and securing complete comfort and high respectability. She married well, being united to Colonel Baldwin, a gentleman of character and fortune; but alas! that delicacy of mind which is the best guardian of female conduct had been irrecoverably lost by her pernicious education, and in a few years she sank beyond the possibility of regaining her station in society. [...]

I have related these events, as I confess myself to be an avowed enemy to a dramatic education. That sexual familiarity which is indispensable upon the stage, undermines, and is, in my opinion, utterly inconsistent with, the delicacy of sentiment, the refinement of thought, and reserve of action, which constitute at once the surest guards and the most precious ornaments of female character. Strong minds and discriminating understandings may occasionally escape; but, what a vast majority of Thalia's[1] daughters fall victims to the practices of their own calling!

"I'm a Naughty Girl"

From *A Greek Slave* by Owen Hall, Harry Greenbank, Adrian Ross, Lionel Monckton, and Sydney Jones, 1898.

> *Iris:* I'm an imp on mischief bent.
> Only feeling quite content
> When doing wrong!
> > *Chorus:* When doing wrong!
> *Iris:* Sometimes when I've had the fun —
> I repent of what I've done
> But not for long!
> > *Chorus:* But not for long!

---

[1] One of the Greek Muses—goddess of poetry and comedy.

Iris: On my mistress tricks I play,
       Telling her what love should say,
       Whispering what love should do:
       She believes and does it too!
       I'm a naughty girl!
       You needn't sham:
       You know I am!
       Rome is in a whirl,
       Because they're all afraid
       Of this naughty little maid!
           Chorus: She's a naughty girl!
                   We know it well
                   And mean to tell!
                   She's a bad one
                   If we ever had one:
                   Oh, she's a very, very naughty little girl!

Iris: At the Roman Clubs, no doubt,
       Funny tales you hear about
       My goings on!
           Chorus: Your goings on!

Iris: If I like to sit and chat,
       What can be the harm in that—
       Though daylight's gone?
           Chorus: Though daylight's gone?

Iris: If some youth with manners free,
       Dares to snatch a kiss from me,
       Do I ask him to explain?
       No—I kiss him back again!
       I'm a naughty girl!
       You needn't sham:
       You know I am!
       Rome is in a whirl,
       Because they're all afraid
       Of this naughty little maid!
           Chorus: She's a naughty girl!
                   We know it well
                   And mean to tell!
                   She's a bad one
                   If we ever had one:
                   Oh, she's a very, very naughty little girl!

A LITTLE CLOUD

Home after his visit with Gallaher, Little Chandler reads one of Byron's teenage poems, an elegy on the death of his cousin.

Lord Byron, "On the Death of a Young Lady, Cousin to the Author and Very Dear to Him" (1802; published 1807)

1.
Hush'd are the winds, and still the evening gloom,
    Not e'en a zephyr° wanders through the grove,   *spring breeze*
Whilst I return to view my Margaret's tomb,
    And scatter flowers on the dust I love.

2.
Within this narrow cell reclines her clay,
    That clay, where once such animation beam'd;
The king of terrors seiz'd her as his prey;
    Not worth, nor beauty, have her life redeem'd.

3.
Oh! could that king of terrors pity feel,
    Or Heaven reverse the dread decree of fate!
Not here the mourner would his grief reveal,
    Not here the Muse her virtues would relate.

4.
But wherefore weep! her matchless spirit soars
    Beyond where splendid shines the orb of day;
And weeping angels lead her to those bowers,
    Where endless pleasures virtuous deeds repay.

5.
And shall presumptuous mortals Heaven arraign!
    And, madly, Godlike Providence accuse!
Ah! no, far fly from me attempts so vain;—
    I'll ne'er submission to my God refuse.

6.
Yet is remembrance of those virtues dear,
    Yet fresh the memory of that beauteous face;
Still they call forth my warm affection's tear,
    Still in my heart retain their wonted° place.   *Accustomed*

CLAY

> *When Maria performs a song from* The Bohemian Girl *(the popular operetta that Eveline attended), instead of the second verse, she repeats the first. Everyone recognizes this and Joe is moved to tears; Joyce ends his tale leaving it to us to ponder the mistake's significance.*

"I Dreamt I Dwelt in Marble Halls"

From *The Bohemian Girl* by Michael Balfe and
Alfred Bunn (1843).

> I dreamt that I dwelt in marble halls,
>   With vassals and serfs at my side,
> And of all who assembled within those walls,
>   That I was the hope and the pride.
> I had riches too great to count, could boast
>   Of a high ancestral name;
> But I also dreamt, which pleased me most,
>   That you lov'd me still the same ...
>
> *That you lov'd me, you lov'd me still the same,*
> *That you lov'd me, you lov'd me still the same.*
>
> I dreamt that suitors sought my hand;
>   That knights upon bended knee,
> And with vows no maiden heart could withstand,
>   They pledg'd their faith to me;
> And I dreamt that one of that noble host
>   Came forth my hand to claim.
> But I also dreamt, which charmed me most,
>   That you lov'd me still the same ...
>
> *That you lov'd me, you lov'd me still the same,*
> *That you lov'd me, you lov'd me still the same.*

A PAINFUL CASE

> *Mr. Duffy's cold and snobbish egoism is reflected in the few items in his spartan rooms, among these* Thus Spake Zarathustra *by the radical German philosopher Friedrich Nietzsche. The opening pages of this book give a sense of the writer's elliptical style while touching on key themes such as the* Übermensch *(here translated as "the beyond-man"),*

the death of God, and the "will to power," all of which resonate with
potent irony throughout Joyce's story.

Friedrich Nietzsche, *Thus Spake Zarathustra: A Book for All and None* (trans. Alexander Tille, 1896)

1.

Having attained the age of thirty Zarathustra left his home and the lake of his home and went into the mountains. There he rejoiced in his spirit and his loneliness and, for ten years, did not grow weary of it. But at last his heart turned,—one morning he got up with the dawn, stepped into the presence of the Sun and thus spake unto him:

"Thou great star! What would be thy happiness, were it not for those for whom thou shinest.

For ten years thou hast come up here to my cave. Thou wouldst have got sick of thy light and thy journey but for me, mine eagle, and my serpent.

But we waited for thee every morning and, receiving from thee thine abundance, blessed thee for it.

Lo! I am weary of my wisdom, like the bee that hath collected too much honey; I need hands reaching out for it.

I would fain grant and distribute until the wise among men could once more enjoy their folly, and the poor once more their riches.

For that end I must descend to the depth: as thou dost at even, when, sinking behind the sea, thou givest light to the lower regions, thou resplendent star!

I must, like thee, go down, as men say—men to whom I would descend.

Then bless me, thou impassive eye that canst look without envy even upon over-much happiness!

Bless the cup which is about to overflow so that the water golden-flowing out of it may carry everywhere the reflection of thy rapture.

Lo! this cup is about to empty itself again, and Zarathustra will once more become a man."

—Thus Zarathustra's going down began.

[…]

3.

Arriving at the next town which lieth nigh the forests Zarathustra found there many folk gathered in the market; for a performance had been promised by a rope-dancer. And Zarathustra thus spake unto the folk:

"*I teach you beyond-man.* Man is a something that shall be surpassed. What have ye done to surpass him?

All beings hitherto have created something beyond themselves: and are ye going to be the ebb of this great tide and rather revert to the animal than surpass man?

What with man is the ape? A joke or a sore shame. Man shall be the same for beyond-man, a joke or a sore shame.

Ye have made your way from worm to man, and much within you is still worm. Once ye were apes, even now man is ape in a higher degree than any ape.

He who is the wisest among you is but a discord and hybrid of plant and ghost. But do I order you to become ghosts or plants?

Behold, I teach you beyond-man! Beyond-man is the significance of earth. Your will shall say: beyond-man shall be the significance of earth.

I conjure you, my brethren, *remain faithful to earth* and do not believe those who speak unto you of superterrestrial hopes! Poisoners they are whether they know it or not.

Despisers of life they are, decaying and themselves poisoned, of whom earth is weary: begone with them!

Once the offence against God was the greatest offence, but God died, so that these offenders died also. Now the most terrible of things is to offend earth and rate the intestines of the inscrutable one higher than the significance of earth!

Once soul looked contemptuously upon body; that contempt then being the highest ideal:—soul wished the body meagre, hideous, starved. Thus soul thought it could escape body and earth.

Oh! that soul was itself meagre, hideous, starved: cruelty was the lust of that soul!

But ye also, my brethren, speak: what telleth your body of your soul? Is your soul not poverty and dirt and a miserable ease?

Verily, a muddy stream is man. One must be a sea to be able to receive a muddy stream without becoming unclean.

Behold, I teach you beyond-man: he is that sea, in him your great contempt can sink.

What is the greatest thing ye can experience? That is the hour of great contempt. The hour in which not only your happiness, but your reason and virtue as well turn loathsome.

The hour in which ye say: 'What is my happiness worth! It is poverty and dirt and a miserable ease. But my happiness should itself justify existence!'

The hour in which ye say: 'What is my reason worth! Longeth it for knowledge as a lion for its food? It is poverty and dirt and a miserable ease.'

The hour in which ye say: 'What is my virtue worth! It hath not yet lashed me into rage. How tired I am of my good and mine evil! All that is poverty and dirt and a miserable ease!'

The hour in which ye say: 'What is my justice worth! I do not see that I am flame and fuel. But the just one is flame and fuel! '

The hour in which ye say: 'What is my pity worth! Is pity not the cross to which he is being nailed who loveth men? But my pity is no crucifixion.'

Spake ye ever like that? Cried ye ever like that? Alas! would that I had heard you cry like that!

Not your sin, your moderation crieth unto heaven, your miserliness in sin even crieth unto heaven!

Where is the lightning to lick you with its tongue? Where is that insanity with which ye ought to be inoculated?

Behold! I teach you beyond-man: he is that lightning, he is that insanity!" Zarathustra having spoken thus one of the folk shouted: "We have heard enough of the rope-dancer; let us see him now!" And all the folk laughed at Zarathustra. The rope-dancer, however, who thought he was meant by that word started with his performance.

Ivy Day in the Committee Room

For more on Parnell and the politics of turn-of-the-century Dublin, see Ireland: Home Rule and Empire, p.xxx.

A Mother

The musical performance at the core of this story attempts to exploit the Irish Revival: See The Irish Revival: Culture, Politics, and Identity p. xxx.

Grace

Joyce told his brother that he structured this story's subtle ironies on the tripartite scheme of Dante's epic, The Divine Comedy: *a descent into hell (Mr. Kernan's fall down the steps), a term in purgatory (the scene in the bedroom), and a final ascent into heavenly "grace" (at the church). A section here from Dante's* Inferno *describes the entrance to hell. It is followed by a passage on divine grace from* The Deharbe Catechism *(a book of religious instruction Joyce would have known*

*well) and Jesus's "Parable of the Unjust Steward," Father Purdon's
text for the retreat.*

Dante Alighieri, *The Inferno, Canto III* (trans. Ichabod Charles Wright, 1833), lines 1–18

"Through me ye enter the abode of woe:
Through me to endless sorrow are convey'd:
Through me amid the souls accurst ye go.
Justice did first my lofty Maker move:
By Power Almighty was my fabric made.
By highest Wisdom. and by primal Love.
Ere I was form'd. no things created were.
Save those eternal—I eternal last:
All hope abandon—ye who enter here."
These words. inscribed in colour dark. I saw
High on the summit of a portal vast:
Whereat I cried: "O master! with deep awe
Their sense I mark." Like one prepared he said:
"Here from thy soul must doubt be cast away:
Here must each thought of cowardice be dead.
Now to that place I told thee of. arrived.
The melancholy shades shalt thou survey,
Of God—the mind's supremest good—deprived."

The Deharbe Catechism

—What fatal consequences have, with original sin, passed to all mankind?

—1, The privation of sanctifying grace, of the dignity of God's children, and of the right of inheriting the kingdom of Heaven; 2, ignorance, corncupiscence[2] and proneness to evil; 3, all sorts of hardships, pains, calamities, and, lastly, death.

"Parable of the Unjust Steward," Luke 16: 1–10

From Douhay-Rheims translation.

And he said also to his disciples: "There was a certain rich man who had a steward: and the same was accused unto him, that he had

[2] Sexual desire; lust.

wasted his goods. And he called him, and said to him: 'How is it that I hear this of thee? give an account of thy stewardship: for now thou canst be steward no longer.'

And the steward said within himself: 'What shall I do, because my lord taketh away from me the stewardship? To dig I am not able; to beg I am ashamed. I know what I will do, that when I shall be removed from the stewardship, they may receive me into their houses.' Therefore calling together every one of his lord's debtors, he said to the first: 'How much dost thou owe my lord?' But he said: 'An hundred barrels of oil.' And he said to him: 'Take thy bill and sit down quickly, and write fifty.' Then he said to another: 'And how much dost thou owe?' Who said: 'An hundred quarters of wheat.' He said to him: 'Take thy bill, and write eighty.'

And the lord commended the unjust steward, forasmuch as he had done wisely: for the children of this world are wiser in their generation than the children of light. And I say to you: Make unto you friends of the mammon of iniquity; that when you shall fail, they may receive you into everlasting dwellings. He that is faithful in that which is least, is faithful also in that which is greater: and he that is unjust in that which is little, is unjust also in that which is greater."

The Dead

More than any other story, this one is saturated with musical references to death and mourning—even "Arrayed for the Bridal," when performed by Gabriel's elderly aunt, feels like a dirge. Later, as the snow falls outside the Gresham hotel where the electric lights have failed, Gretta is haunted by "The Lass of Aughrim"—a west-Ireland folk ballad in which a young woman, babe in arms on a stormy night, begs for admission to her skeptical, unpitying seducer's manor. Joyce may have derived the title for his story from Thomas Moore's "O Ye Dead," a poem in Irish Melodies, *often adapted for song, in which the living and the dead each envy the other's happiness.*

"Arrayed for the Bridal"

Adapted by George Linley from Bellini's opera,
I Puritani di Scozia (1835).

> Arrayed for the bridal, in beauty behold her
> A white wreath entwineth a forehead more fair
> I envy the zephyrs that softly enfold her
> > enfold her

And play with the locks of her beautiful hair
May life to her prove full of sunshine and love
                                    full of love yes! yes! yes!
Who would not love her?
Sweet star of the morning![1] shining so bright!
Earth's circle adorning, fair creature of light
                                    fair creature of light.

"The Lass of Aughrim"

"Oh if you be the lass of Aughrim,
As I suppose you not to be,
Come tell me the last token
Between you and me."
     Refrain   "The dew wets my yellow locks,
             The rain wets my skin,
             The babe's cold in my arms.
             Oh Gregory, let me in!"
"Oh Gregory, don't you remember
One night on the hill,
When we swapped rings off each other's hands,
Sorely against my will?
Mine was of the beaten gold.
Yours was but black tin."
     Refrain: The dew wets, etc.
"Oh if you be the lass of Aughrim,
As I suppose you not to be,
Come tell me the last token
Between you and me."
     Refrain: The dew wets, etc.
"Oh Gregory don't you remember
One night on the hill,
When we swapped smocks off each other's backs,
Sorely against my will?
Mine was of the holland fine,
Yours was but Scotch cloth."
     Refrain: The dew wets, etc.

---

[1] Venus: the "morning star" and the Greek goddess of love.

"Oh if you be the lass of Aughrim,
As I suppose you not to be,
Come tell me the last token
Between you and me."

    Refrain: The dew wets, etc.

"Oh Gregory, don't you remember,
In my father's hall,
When you had your will of me?
And that was worse than all."

    Refrain: The dew wets, etc.

Thomas Moore, "O Ye Dead"

From *Irish Melodies*.

1.

Oh, ye Dead! oh, ye Dead! whom we know by the light you give
From your cold gleaming eyes, though you move like men who live,
Why leave you thus your graves,
In far off fields and waves,
Where the worm and the sea-bird only know your bed,
To haunt this spot where all
Those eyes that wept your fall,
And the hearts that wail'd you, like your own, lie dead?

2.

It is true, it is true, we are shadows cold and wan;
And the fair and the brave whom we loved on earth are gone;
But still thus even in death,
So sweet the living breath
Of the fields and the flowers in our youth we wander'd o'er,
That ere, condemn'd, we go
To freeze 'mid Hecla's[1] snow,
We would taste it a while, and think we live once more!

---

[1] Volcano in Iceland once known as "The Gateway to Hell."

Further Reading, Viewing, Listening

[*JJQ: James Joyce Quarterly*   P: Press/Publishers   U: University]

Biography

Curran, C. P. *James Joyce Remembered*. Oxford UP, 1968.

Ellmann, Richard. *James Joyce. New and Revised Edition*. Oxford UP, 1982.

Gibson, Andrew. *James Joyce*. Reaktion Books, 2006.

Jackson, John Wyse and Peter Costello. *John Stanislaus Joyce: The Voluminous Life and Genius of James Joyce's Father*. St. Martins, 1998.

Joyce, James. *Letters of James Joyce*. 3 vols., ed. Stuart Gilbert and Richard Ellmann. Viking, 1966; *Selected Letters*, ed. Richard Ellmann. Viking, 1975.

Joyce, Stanislaus. *The Complete Dublin Diary of Stanislaus Joyce*. Cornell UP, 1971; *My Brother's Keeper: James Joyce's Early Years*, ed. Richard Ellmann. Viking, 1969.

Maddox, Brenda. *Nora: A Biography of Nora Joyce*. H. Hamilton, 1988.

McCourt, John. *The Years of Bloom: Joyce in Trieste 1904–1920*. Lilliput P, 2000.

Norburn, Roger. *A James Joyce Chronology*. Palgrave, 2004.

Textual History and Editions

Joyce, James. *Dubliners: An Annotated Edition*, eds. John Wyse Jackson and Bernard McGinley. Sinclair-Stevenson, 1993.

Joyce, James. *Dubliners: A Facsimile of Proofs for the 1914 Edition*, and *Dubliners: A Facsimile of Proofs for the 1910 Edition*, and *Dubliners: Drafts and Fragments*. Garland P, 1977.

Joyce, James and Hans Walter Gabler. *Dubliners: A Facsimile of Drafts & Manuscripts*. Garland P, 1978.

—. *The James Joyce Archive*. 63 vols. Ed. Michael Groden. (v. 1–4: materials related to *Dubliners*); Garland P, 1980.

—. *The Workshop of Daedelus: James Joyce and the Raw Materials for "A Portrait of the Artist as a Young Man,"* eds. Robert Scholes and Richard M. Kain. U Illinois P, 1965.

Spoo, Robert. "Injuries, Remedies, Moral Rights, and the Public Domain." *JJQ* 37 (2000): 333–51.

General Criticism

Attridge, Derek, ed. *The Cambridge Companion to James Joyce*. Cambridge UP, 2004.

Attridge, Derek. *Joyce Effects: On Language, Theory, and History*. Cambridge UP, 2000.

Attridge, Derek and Marjorie Howes, ed. *Semi-Colonial Joyce*. Cambridge UP, 2000.

Cheng, V. *Joyce, Race, and Empire*. Cambridge UP, 1995.

Dettmar, Kevin. *The Illicit Joyce of Postmodernism: Reading Against the Grain*. U Wisconsin P, 1996.

Gibson, Andrew and Len Platt eds. *Joyce, Ireland, Britain*. UP Florida, 2006.

Henke, Suzette A. *James Joyce and the Politics of Desire*. Routledge, 1990.

Kelly, Joseph. *Our Joyce: From Outcast to Icon*. U Texas P, 1998.

Kenner, Hugh. *Dublin's Joyce*. Columbia UP, 1987.

Kershner, R. B. *Joyce, Bakhtin, and Popular Literature: Chronicles of Disorder*. U North Carolina P, 1989.

Latham, Sean, ed. *James Joyce*. Irish Academic Press, 2010.

Leonard, Garry. *Advertising and Commodity Culture in Joyce*. UP of Florida, 1998.

Leonard, Garry and Jennifer Wicke, eds. "Joyce and Advertising." Special issue, *JJQ* 30:4 /31:1 (Summer/Fall 1993).

Mahaffey, Vicki. *States of Desire: Wilde, Yeats, Joyce, and the Irish Experiment*. Oxford UP, 1998.

McCourt, John, ed. *James Joyce in Context*. Cambridge UP, 2009.

Mullin, Katy. *James Joyce, Sexuality and Social Purity*. Cambridge UP, 2003.

Nolan, Emer. *James Joyce and Nationalism*. London: Routledge, 1999.

Pierce, David. *James Joyce's Ireland*. New Haven and London: Yale UP, 1992.

Potts, Willard. *Joyce and the Two Irelands.* U Texas P, 2000.

Riquelme, John-Paul. *Teller and Tale in Joyce's Fiction: Oscillating Perspectives.* Johns Hopkins UP, 1983.

Scholes, Robert. *In Search of James Joyce.* U Illinois P, 1992.

Scott, Bonnie Kime. *Joyce and Feminism.* Indiana UP, 1984.

Valente, Joe, ed. *Quare Joyce.* U Michigan P, 1998.

Dubliners

Dublin and the Dubliners. JJQ 37.1/2 (1999–2000).

Baker, James R. and Thomas F. Staley. *James Joyce's Dubliners: A Critical Handbook.* Wadsworth P, 1969.

Beck, Warren. *Joyce's Dubliners: Substance, Vision, and Art.* Duke UP, 1969.

Beja, Morris. *James Joyce: Dubliners and A Portrait of the Artist as a Young Man: A Casebook.* Macmillan, 1973.

Benstock, Bernard. *Narrative Con/Texts in Dubliners.* U Illinois P, 1994.

Bidwell, Bruce. *The Joycean Way: A Topographic Guide To "Dubliners" & "A Portrait of the Artist as a Young Man."* Wolfhound, 1981.

Bosinelli Bollettieri, Rosa Maria and Harold Frederick Mosher. *Rejoycing: New Readings of Dubliners.* UP Kentucky, 1998.

Brandabur, Edward. *A Scrupulous Meanness: A Study of Joyce's Early Work.* U Illinois P, 1971.

Brown, Terrence. "Joyce's Magic Lantern." *JJQ* 28.4 (1991): 791–98.

Buzard, James. "'Culture' and the Critics of *Dubliners.*" *JJQ* 37.1/2 (1999–2000): 43–61.

Doherty, Gerald. *Dubliners' Dozen: The Games Narrators Play.* Fairleigh Dickinson UP, 2004.

Ehrlich, Heyward. "'Araby' in Context: The Splendid Bazaar, Irish Orientalism, and James Clarence Mangan." *JJQ* 35.2/3 (1998): 309–31.

Fairhall, James. "Big-Power Politics and Colonial Economics: The Gordon Bennett Cup Race and 'After the Race.'" *JJQ* 28.2 (1991): 387–97.

Frawley, Oona. *A New & Complex Sensation: Essays on Joyce's Dubliners.* Lilliput, 2004.

Gifford, Don. *Joyce Annotated: Notes for Dubliners and A Portrait of the Artist as a Young Man.* 2nd ed. U California P, 1982.

Hart, Clive. *James Joyce's Dubliners: Critical Essays.* Viking P, 1969; *Joyce, Huston and the Making of 'The Dead.'* Smythe, 1988.

Heller, Vivian. *Joyce, Decadence, and Emancipation.* U Illinois P, 1995.

Ingersoll, Earl G. *Engendered Trope in Joyce's Dubliners.* Southern Illinois UP, 1996.

Jackson, Roberta. "The Open Closet in *Dubliners*: James Duffy's Painful Case." *JJQ* 37.1/2 (1999–2000): 83–97.

James Joyce Centre (Dublin Ireland). *So This Is Dyoublong?: A Guide to the City of Dubliners, Stephen Hero, A Portrait of the Artist as a Young Man, Ulysses, and Finnegans Wake.* Guinness: James Joyce Center.

Leonard, Garry Martin. *Reading Dubliners Again: A Lacanian Perspective.* 1st ed. Syracuse UP, 1993.

Magalaner, Marvin. "Joyce, Nietzsche and Hauptmann in Joyce's 'The Dead.'" *PMLA* 68 (1953): 95–102; *Time of Apprenticeship: The Fiction of Young James Joyce.* Abelard-Schuman, 1959.

Norris, Margot. *Suspicious Readings of Joyce's Dubliners.* U Pennsylvania P, 2003.

Owens, Colílin. *James Joyce's Painful Case.* UP of Florida, 2008.

Percora, Vincent. " 'The Dead' and the Generosity of the Word." *PMLA* 101 (1986): 206–15.

Power, Mary and Ulrich Schneider, eds. *European Joyce Studies 7: New Perspectives on "Dubliners."* Rodopi, 1997.

Scholes, Robert. "Semiotics Approaches to a Fictional Text: Joyce's 'Eveline.'" *JJQ* 16.1/2 (1978–79): 65–80.

Schwartz, Daniel R., ed. *James Joyce's "The Dead": Case Studies in Contemporary Criticism.* Bedford, 1994.

Senn, Fritz. " 'The Boarding House' Seen as a Tale of Misdirection." *JJQ* 23.4 (1996): 405–13.

Spoo, Robert. " 'Una Piccola Nuvoletta': Ferrero's *Young Europe* and Joyce's Mature *Dubliners* Stories. *JJQ* 24.4 (1987): 401–10; "Uncanny Returns in 'The Dead': Ibsenian Intertexts and the Estranged Infant," in *Joyce: The Return of the Repressed*, ed. Susan Stanford Friedman. Cornell UP, 1993. 89–113.

Thacker, Andrew. *Dubliners: A Casebook.* Palgrave Macmillan, 2006.

Torchiana, Donald T. *Backgrounds for Joyce's Dubliners.* Allen & Unwin, 1986.

Ulin, Julieann Veronica. "Fluid Borders and Naughty Girls: Music, Domesticity, and Nation in Joyce's Boarding Houses." *JJQ* 44.2 (2007): 263–90.

Valente, Joseph. "Joyce's Sexual Differend: An Example from *Dubliners*." *JJQ* 28.2 (1991): 427–443.

Vesala-Varttala, Tanja. *Sympathy and Joyce's Dubliners: Ethical Probing of Reading, Narrative, and Textuality*. Tampere UP, 1999.

Walzl, Florence. "*Dubliners*: Women in Irish Society." *Women in Joyce*, eds. Suzette Henke and Elaine Unkeless. U Illinois P, 1982. 30–56.

Wright, David. "Dots Mark the Spot: Textual Gaps in *Dubliners*." *JJQ* 41.1/2 (2003–4): 151–60; "Interactive Stories in *Dubliners*." *Studies in Short Fiction* 32 (1995): 285–93; "The Secret Life of Leopold Bloom and Emily Sinico." *JJQ* 37.1/2 (1999–2000): 99–112.

Other Media

Araby. Directed by Dennis Courtney, 1999.

The Dead. Directed by John Huston. Liffey Films, 1987.

The Dead. Directed by Prince Bagdasarian. PIB Productions, 2004.

McDermott, Kevin and Ralph Rickey. *Music from the Work of James Joyce*. CD. Sunphone Records, 2004.

—. *More Music from the Work of James Joyce*. CD. Sunphone Records, 2007.

On the World Wide Web

The Brazen Head.	<http://www.themodernword.com/joyce/>
Dubliners Concordance.	<http://www.doc.ic.ac.uk/~rac101/concord/texts/dubliners/>
James Joyce Music.	<http://www.james-joyce-music.com/Dubliners.html
Joyce Images.	<http://www.joyceimages.com/>
"The Sisters."	<http://www.pafaculty.net/joyce/>
Web Resources for *Dubliners*.	<http://www.robotwisdom.com/jaj/dubliners/index.html>
World Wide Dubliners.	<http://www.mendele.com/WWD/>

Credits